The Great War, 1914–18

The Great War
1914–18

Spencer C. Tucker
Virginia Military Institute

Indiana University Press
Bloomington and Indianapolis

First published in North America in 1998 by

Indiana University Press
601 North Morton Street
Bloomington, Indiana 47404

Manufactured in Great Britain

Library of Congress Cataloging-in-Publication Data
Tucker, Spencer, date
    The great war, 1914–1918 / Spencer Tucker.
      p.   cm.
    Includes bibliographical references and index.
    ISBN 0-253-33372-5 (alk. paper). — ISBN 0-253-21171-9 (pbk. :
alk. paper)
      1. World War, 1914–18. I. Title.
D521.T83   1998
940.3—dc21   97-31430

2 3 4 5 6 04 03 02 01 99

Contents

Maps

1. Europe, 1914

2. *Schlieffen Plan as executed, 1914*

Donald S. Frazier

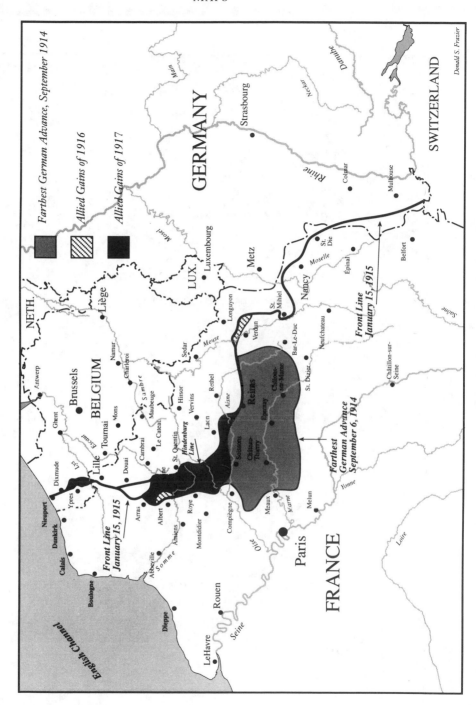

3. *Western Front, 1914–17*

Farthest German Advance, September 1914

Allied Gains of 1916

Allied Gains of 1917

Donald S. Frazier

4. Eastern Front, 1914–18

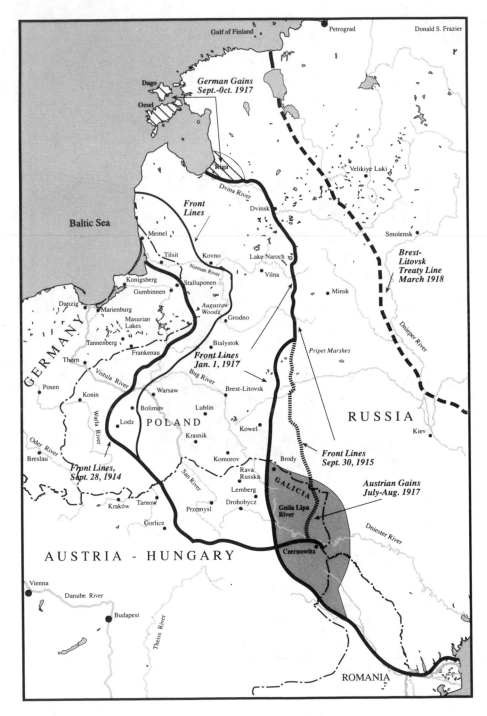

Donald S. Frazier

Gulf of Finland

Petrograd

Dago

**German Gains
Sept.-Oct. 1917**

Oesel

Velikiye Luki

Riga

Dvina River

**Front
Lines**

Dvinsk

Baltic Sea

Smolensk

Memel

Kovno

Lake Naroch

**Brest-
Litovsk
Treaty Line
March 1918**

Tilsit

Nieman River

Vilna

Konigsberg

Stalluponen

Gumbinnen

Minsk

Danzig

Augustow
Woods

Marienburg

Masurian
Lakes

Grodno

Dnieper River

Tannenberg

Bialystok

*Front Lines
Jan. 1, 1917*

Pripet Marshes

Frankenau

Thorn

Bug River

Vistula River

Warsaw

Brest-Litovsk

RUSSIA

Posen

Konin

Bolimov

Lublin

Lodz

POLAND

Kowel

Kiev

Warta River

Krasnik

Oder River

Komorov

Brody

**Front Lines
Sept. 30, 1915**

Breslau

**Front Lines,
Sept. 28, 1914**

Rava
Russka

San River

Lemberg

GALICIA

**Austrian Gains
July-Aug. 1917**

Kraków

Tarnow

Przemysl

Drohobycz

**Gnila Lipa
River**

Gorlice

Dniester River

AUSTRIA - HUNGARY

Czernowitz

Vienna

Danube River

Budapest

Theiss River

ROMANIA

5. Ypres, 1914–18

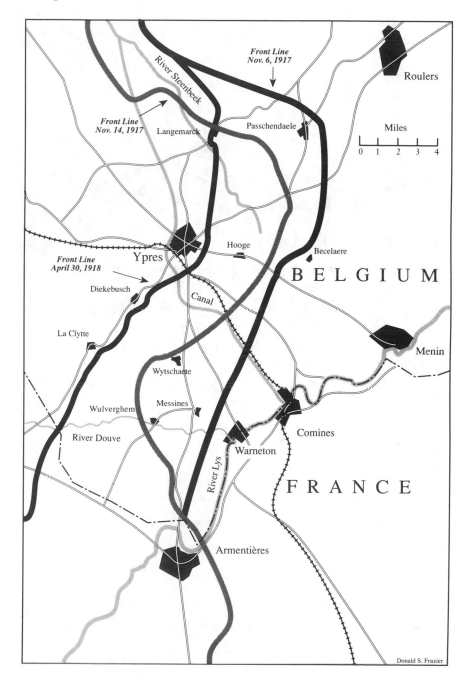

Donald S. Frazier

AUSTRIA–HUNGARY

Front Line
November 4, 1918

Italian Gains
June 1915 -
September 1917

Isonzo River

Gorizia

Trieste

Front Line
May 1916

Pontebba

Tolmezzo

Caporetto

Udine

Maniago

Front Line
Oct. 30,
1917

Front Line
Nov. 5,
1917

Adriatic Sea

Gulf of Venice

Vittorio
Veneto

Front Line
January 1918

Pieve

Belluno

Piave River

Venice

Brixen

Feltre

Bassano

Castelfranco

Treviso

Padua

ALPS

Meron

Bolzano

Asiago

Vicenza

Front Line
November 4, 1918

Austrian Gains
May-June 1916

Tonale Pass

Trent

Ala

Verona

Adige River

Po River

Mantua

Brescia

ITALY

SWITZERLAND

6. Italian Front, 1915–18

7. *The Somme, 1916–18*

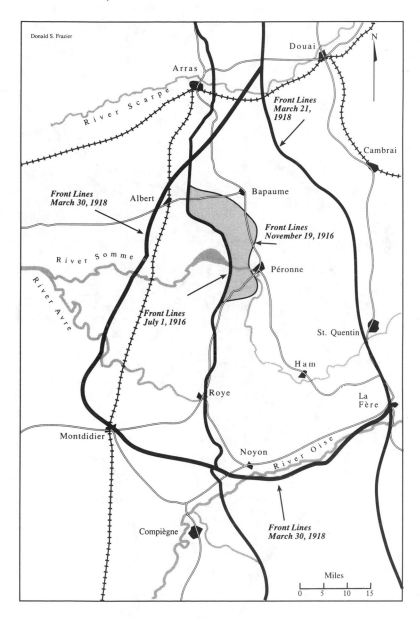

Donald S. Frazier

Douai

Arras

River Scarpe

**Front Lines
March 21,
1918**

Cambrai

**Front Lines
March 30, 1918**   Albert

Bapaume

**Front Lines
November 19, 1916**

River Somme

Péronne

River Avre

**Front Lines
July 1, 1916**

St. Quentin

H a m

Roye

La
Fère

Montdidier

Noyon   River Oise

**Front Lines
March 30, 1918**

Compiègne

Miles

0   5   10   15

N

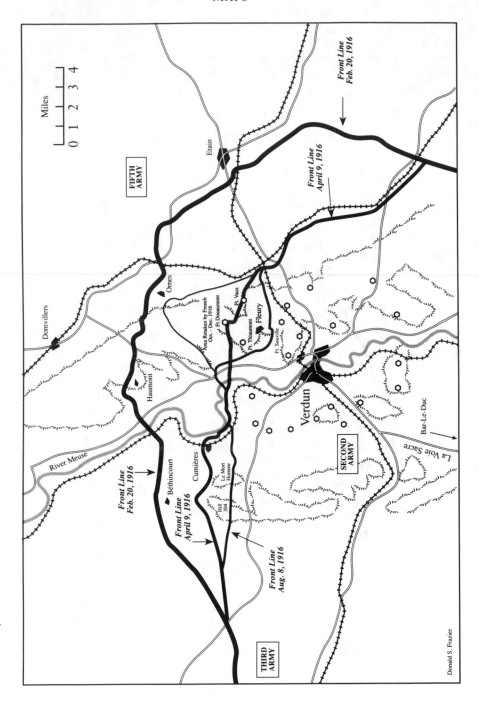

8. *Verdun, 1916*

Miles

0 1 2 3 4

FIFTH ARMY

Front Line
Feb. 20, 1916

Front Line
April 9, 1916

Etain

Domvillers

Ornes

Ft. Vaux
Fleury
Area Retaken by French
Oct. - Dec. 1916
Ft. Douaumont
Ft. Thiaumont
Ft. Souville

Haumont

Verdun

River Meuse

Béthincourt

Front Line
Feb. 20, 1916

Front Line
April 9, 1916

Cumières

Le Mort
Homme

Hill
304

SECOND ARMY

La Voie Sacré

Bar-Le-Duc

Front Line
April 9, 1916

Front Line
Aug. 8, 1916

THIRD ARMY

Donald S. Frazier

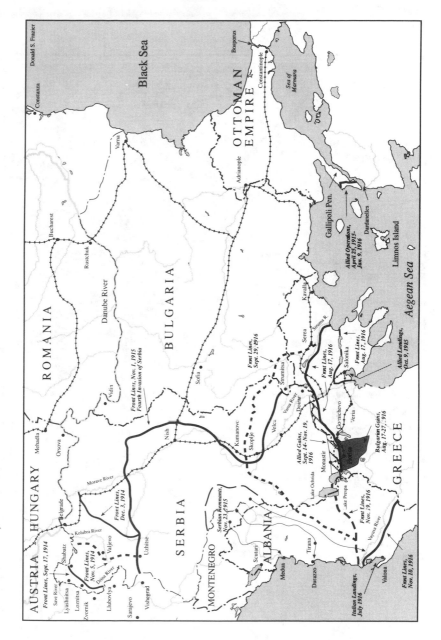

9. The Balkans, 1914–18

XV

10. The Turkish Front, 1915–18

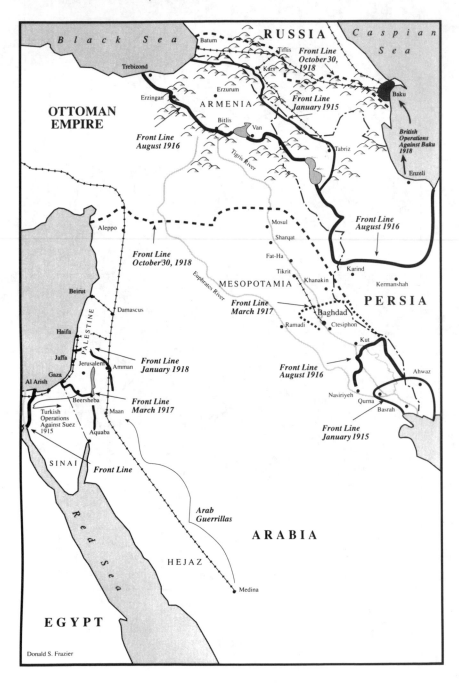

Donald S. Frazier

11. *The Ludendorff Offensives, 1918*

Somme Offensive, March 21 - April 4

Lys Offensive, April 9 - 29

Aisne Offensive, May 27 - June 4

Noyon - Montdidier Offensive, June 8 - 12

Champagne - Marne Offensive, June 15 - 17

Donald S. Frazier

GERMANY

SWITZERLAND

NETH.

BELGIUM

LUX.

FRANCE

English Channel

Front Line January 1, 1918

Front Line November 11, 1918

Front Line January 1, 1918

Strasbourg

Metz

Nancy

Luxembourg

Liège

Brussels

Antwerp

Namur

Charleroi

Sedan

Verdun

St. Mihiel

Longuyon

Neufchateau

Châtillon-sur-Seine

Bar-Le-Duc

St. Dizier

Châlons-sur-Marne

Epernay

Reims

Laon

Vervins

Hirson

Rethel

Maubeuge

Le Cateau

St. Quentin

Cambrai

Douai

Lille

Tournai

Mons

Ghent

Dixmude

Ypres

Nieuport

Dunkirk

Calais

Boulogne

Dieppe

LeHavre

Rouen

Abbeville

Amiens

Albert

Arras

Péronne

Roye

Montdidier

Compiègne

Meaux

Melun

Paris

Epinal

St. Die

Belfort

Colmar

Mulhouse

Rhine

Neckar

Danube

Moselle

Meuse

Aisne

Sambre

Escaut

Lys

Somme

Oise

Marne

Seine

Yonne

Saône

12. Europe, 1924

Preface

When Professor Jeremy Black told me of the series he is editing on warfare, I welcomed the opportunity to write the volume on the First World War. It was an event of unprecedented violence and we must remember why it was fought and its terrible cost.

The Great War is one of the turning points in history. The "short" war begun by Austria-Hungary to get rid of Serbia became a protracted struggle that swept up most of Europe and the rest of the world in its train. The conflict mobilized 65 million soldiers of whom nine million died and another 23 million were wounded. In the French and Russian armies three-quarters of the men were casualties. The war was hard on civilians as well; some 750,000 Germans died as a result of the British naval blockade. Beyond the immense human suffering the war had far-reaching consequences. It toppled the German, Austro-Hungarian, Ottoman, and Russian empires; it swept the Bolsheviks to power in Russia; it marked the beginning of the end of European empire overseas; it used up centuries of accumulated capital, transforming European states into debtors and the United States into financial leadership; and the profound disillusionment following the war sowed the seeds of fascism in Italy and Germany. The conflagration of 1939–45 cannot be understood without examining that of 1914–18. The Great War truly cast a long shadow. It is especially worth remembering in the 1990s that it originated in a city in the Balkans by the name of Sarajevo.

I am grateful to Professor Black and Steven Gerrard for the chance to write this book. Within the confines of a short book I can hardly achieve a complete history. I have tried to present a clearly written narrative for the general reader that concentrates on the military campaigns and dramatic turning points. I address the dilemmas posed by new technologies and the impact of military leadership and command decisions. I have also sought to analyze the coming of the war and to evaluate its impact on the home fronts and the significance of the war and its flawed peace settlement for Europe and the world.

Statistics for the First World War battles vary dramatically. I have, unless otherwise noted, used those in Randal Gray and Christopher Argyle, *Chronicle of the first world war* (2 vols; Oxford and New York: Facts on File, 1991).

I am grateful to a number of my graduate students and colleagues who read the manuscript and made helpful suggestions: Camille Dean, Jack McCallum, Ed Page, Jay Menzoff, Mike Nichols, Gary Shanafelt, Laura Wood, and David Zabecki. I am especially grateful to Gary Shanafelt for many helpful suggestions and to my colleague Don Worcester for his keen eye and awesome editing skills. History Department Office Manager Barbara Pierce was of great assistance. The Imperial War Museum graciously allowed use of the photographs. Don Frazier did the computer-generated maps and Mike Nichols produced the index.

Spencer C. Tucker

Chapter One

The background

Impetus for a general European conflict had been building for decades. Nationalism (the triumph of statism over internationalism and the desire of subject minorities for their own nation states), two hostile alliance systems, imperialist and trade rivalries, an arms race, and economic and social tensions all led many Europeans to welcome war as a unifying and "cleansing" force.[1] Certainly all the major powers bear some measure of responsibility for the war that began in 1914.[2]

Nationalism was the major force behind the First World War, and nowhere was this more obvious than in Austria-Hungary, ruled since 1848 by Habsburg Emperor Franz Josef. Although the empire may have made sense economically, it was a racial mélange of at least a dozen minorities. Austria's defeat at the hands of Prussia in 1866 led to the *Ausgleich* (agreement) the next year. This allowed the Germans (23 per cent of the population) and the Magyars (19 per cent, the empire's next largest minority and pre-eminent in Hungary) to dominate the empire's other peoples. The Dual Monarchy was essentially two sovereign states that functioned as one in military, foreign, and tariff policies.[3]

Slavic nationalism threatened the stability of the Dual Monarchy, and Serbia was its chief champion in the Balkans. Recognized as an independent state by the 1878 Congress of Berlin, Serbia shared both the Orthodox Christian religion and Cyrillic alphabet with Russia and enjoyed its support. Serbia had long sought to be the nucleus of a large state embracing all southern Slavs.

Vienna wanted to regain prestige lost in 1866 by expanding in the Balkans. In 1908, to diminish Serb influence and cut it off from access to the sea, the Dual Monarchy annexed Bosnia-Herzegovina. This almost touched off war with Russia. Additionally, Austria-Hungary insisted on creating an independent Albania. These actions merely fired Slavic nationalism within the Austro-Hungarian Empire.

Archduke Franz Ferdinand, heir to the Austro-Hungarian throne and the strongest personality of the House of Habsburg in more than a century, intended to overhaul the constitutional structure of the Austro-Hungarian Monarchy, through force if necessary. One solution he advanced was "Trialism". This would have allowed Slavs to share power within the empire. He also toyed with recreating the Greater Austria of the 1850s with a single, centralized administration in Vienna directly responsible to the emperor.[4] It is thus impossible to say just what Franz Ferdinand would have done had he become emperor. There was a certain fatalism among the Dual Monarchy's elite. As Count Ottokar Czernin, one of the Dual Monarchy's last foreign ministers, put it: "We were bound to die. We were at liberty to choose the manner of our death and we chose the most terrible."[5]

Germany, the pre-eminent European military power, was Austria-Hungary's closest ally. The German Empire had come into being as a consequence of the Franco-German War of 1870–71. Having imposed a draconian settlement on France after that war, Chancellor Otto von Bismarck now sought to isolate France diplomatically by allying Germany with at least two of the other four great powers.

Bismarck first tried an arrangement with both Austria-Hungary and Russia, but this *Dreikaiserbund* (Three Emperors' League) shattered on Austro-Hungarian and Russian competition in the Balkans. Forced to choose between the two, in 1879 Bismarck selected Austria-Hungary as his principal ally. The Dual Monarchy was weaker and hence more susceptible to German influence; its large German minority also provided a linguistic and cultural affinity. Not prepared to cast Russia adrift, in 1887 Bismarck concluded a secret Reinsurance Treaty with that country. He promised German support in the Balkans to both powers. The potential conflict did not trouble him.

As long as Bismarck was chancellor of Germany, France remained isolated. Emperor Wilhelm I, whom Bismarck had dominated, died in 1888; his son Frederick III succeeded him. Frederick offered the promise of a new liberal era. But tragically for both Germany and Europe he died only three months later.[6] His son, 29-year-old Wilhelm II, then became emperor. Rash, headstrong, and a lover of all things military, Wilhelm soon clashed with Bismarck, who said that the impulsive new Kaiser was "like a balloon. If you don't hold fast to the string, you'll never know where he'll be off to."[7] In 1890 Wilhelm dropped Bismarck as chancellor and dramatically changed Germany's foreign policy.

Relations with Russia were already frayed over Germany's tightening of credit, but the situation was made worse when in 1890 Wilhelm ordered that the Reinsurance Treaty not be renewed. A rapidly industrializing Russia was forced to look elsewhere for foreign capital, and France was waiting. By 1894, despite Russian reluctance, the two countries had forged a military alliance against Germany.[8] Thus by 1914 there were two mutually antagonistic alliance systems in Europe. The first, headed by Germany, included Austria-Hungary and an increasingly reluctant Italy (in the Triple Alliance of 1882). During the First World War, Germany and Austria-Hungary, located in the centre of Europe, would be known as the Central Powers. France and Russia formed the second alliance, to which Britain was informally linked. These three became known as the Entente powers, the Entente, the Allied Powers, or simply the Allies.

Bismarck, the master manipulator of nations and of his own people, steered a responsible course in international affairs, but when Wilhelm II assumed his personal rule everything came undone. The Kaiser sought to play world politics (*Weltpolitik*), and repeatedly declared that he was determined to make Germany not just dominant in European affairs but in the world. His desire for a German-dominated central Europe (*Mitteleuropa*) reversed Bismarck's limited "Little German" (*Kleindeutsch*) policies. Wilhelm was not alone; many German civilian and military leaders dreamed of territorial aggrandizement that would allow Germany to compete successfully with other major world powers, particularly Britain and the United States. The treaties that Germany imposed on Russia and Romania late in the First World War indicate the steadfastness of these expansionist aims. As a latecomer to the ranks of the big powers, Germany was determined to exert its influence. Germany's policies were at the least maladroit and heavy-handed.

The Kaiser also reversed Bismarck's wise policy of not building a strong navy. A naval-building contest between Britain and Germany began in the mid-1890s.[9] Although Berlin said the larger battle fleet was purely defensive, the navy's principal proponents, Wilhelm II and Admiral Alfred von Tirpitz, actually aimed to challenge Britain, perhaps Britain and the United States together, for world mastery.[10]

Wilhelm II's precipitous actions alienated would-be allies and created a climate of uncertainty. Germans believed themselves encircled and denied their rightful "place in the sun". Tirpitz warned of a British pre-emptive strike against his fleet; General Alfred von Schlieffen wrote of a Britain envious of German economic and industrial progress, a France yearning for revenge, Slav hatred of Teutons, and Italy lining up against Austria-Hungary.[11] Bereft of allies save an increasingly weak Dual Monarchy, Germans saw their position as desperate. The theme of General Friedrich von Bernhardi's 1912 book, *Deutschland und der nächste Krieg* (Germany and the Next War) was "world power or decline". Bernhardi wrote,

3

If we look at our general political position, we cannot conceal the fact that we stand isolated. . . . England, France and Russia have a common interest in breaking down our power. This interest will sooner or later be asserted by arms. If we wish to attain an extension of our power, as is natural in our position, we must win it by the sword against vastly superior foes.[12]

Bernhardi's book went through six printings by 1914.[13]

The economic transformation that Germany experienced after 1871 brought rapid social change as well. By 1914 German political parties and social classes were polarized. Although Bismarck's constitution provided a veneer of parliamentary democracy, it actually vested power in the Kaiser and the military establishment. This produced domestic instability that included unrest among the working class, the rise of socialism, and the antagonism of most German political parties toward the government. A European war would offer the Kaiser the chance to recreate the glory days of 1871, when the nation was unified and seemed poised for a glorious destiny.[14]

France also looked forward to war. The 1871 Treaty of Frankfurt that followed the Franco-German War had stripped it of Alsace and Lorraine and imposed an indemnity of 5 billion francs – more than twice the cost of the war to Germany. Frenchmen longed to avenge that result and regain the two lost provinces. France had found immediate gratification in empire building. Imperialist ambitions almost led to war with Britain in an 1898 standoff at Fashoda on the Upper Nile River in the Sudan. But in 1904 France and Britain reached an agreement that ended decades of rivalry in North Africa and South Asia. Britain and Russia reached a similar arrangement in 1907.

Russia was beginning to flex its economic muscles and enter the modern age, although Nicholas II, tsar since 1894 and the most absolute of Europe's rulers, would make no concessions to political change. Russia sought ascendancy in the Balkans and control of the Straits to insure free access from the Black Sea into the Mediterranean. After its defeat by Japan in 1904–5, Russia had appeared incapable of waging a European war, but by 1912 it was regaining its capacity to fight. This triggered an unprecedented land-armaments race in Europe. Russian industrial and military growth, including plans for the construction of new strategic railroads, heightened the German sense of panic. In May 1914 Chief of the German General Staff General Helmuth von Moltke (the Younger) told Foreign Minister Gottlieb von Jagow that in two to three years Russia would be rearmed and the Entente powers would then be so powerful that it would be difficult for Germany to defeat them. Germany had no alternative, he reasoned, but to seek a preventive war while there was a chance of victory.[15]

Britain followed its traditional pattern of involving itself in continental affairs only when necessary to preserve vital national interests or the European balance of power, but Germany's decision to build a powerful battle fleet drove it to the side of France. With an ageing industrial plant, the British resented the surge in German industrial might and trade. By 1910 Germany produced annually some 13 million tons of steel; this was five million more than Britain and second only to the United States.[16] With Germany leading the world in the new electrical and chemical industries, Britain saw its international commercial position in jeopardy. Although aligned with France and Russia, Britain's sole military responsibility in 1914 lay in a 1912 agreement that placed it under moral obligation to protect the French coasts from German naval attack.[17]

Crises preceding 1914

Several crises almost led to general European war in the decade before 1914. Two of these, in 1904–5 and in 1911, involved the North African state of Morocco. France had been working to annex Morocco, which lay next to its territory of Algeria; Germany, with no vital interests in Morocco, threatened war if not consulted and compensated. Although it agreed only reluctantly to an international conference at Algeciras in 1906, the conferees awarded France most of what it sought.[18]

In 1908 another crisis, this time in the Balkans, almost brought war between Austria-Hungary and Russia, when the Dual Monarchy, authorized only to administer Bosnia-Herzegovina, annexed it. Russia, still reeling from its defeat by Japan, backed down and the crisis passed, but Bulgaria took advantage of the situation to declare its full independence from the Ottoman Empire (Turkey).

Balkan wars·

As a vacuum invites something to fill it, Turkey's decline invited war. In 1911 Italy invaded Tripolitania and Cyrenaica (modern Libya) and seized the Dodecanese archipelago off western Anatolia. In 1912 and 1913 two regional wars raged in the Balkans. In the first of these, the Balkan states sought to take advantage of Turkish weakness to expel it entirely from the Balkan Peninsula. In October 1912 Montenegro declared war on Turkey. Bulgaria, Greece, and Serbia followed suit. Although the Balkan states defeated Turkey they soon fell to quarrelling among themselves. In June 1913 Bulgaria, the big winner in the first war, attacked Greece and Serbia; the following month it was in turn invaded by Romania. Soon Turkey joined in against Bulgaria. A treaty in August 1913 finally put an end to the fighting, but both Balkan wars had threatened to draw in the big powers and almost led to world war.

Assassination of Archduke Franz Ferdinand

Serb nationalists, determined to prevent the possibility of Trialism in the Austro-Hungarian Empire, decided to assassinate Archduke Franz Ferdinand, a plan advanced by the secret nationalist society "Union or Death", better known as the "Black Hand". Consisting of officers, officials, and intellectuals, it was led by Colonel Dragutin Dimitriević, chief of intelligence of the Serbian General Staff. Serb government involvement remains controversial, and Premier Nikola Pašić was probably not directly aware of the plot.[19] Nonetheless, on 28 June 1914, in Sarajevo, Bosnia, a young Bosnian Serb nationalist named Gavrilo Princip assassinated both Franz Ferdinand and his consort, Sophie, duchess of Hohenberg as they rode in an open car through the city. This event touched off the Great War.

Chain of events to war

Berlin and Vienna sought to use the assassination to their advantage. They wanted a localized Balkan conflict that would restore their prestige and open Turkey and eastern Europe to economic exploitation. After all, the Franco-German War of 1870–71 had proved profitable for Germany, and in 1914 both Berlin and Vienna viewed punitive war as a viable foreign policy option. To Vienna the assassination of Franz Ferdinand seemed almost providential. Emperor Franz Josef, Chief of the General Staff General Conrad von Hötzendorf, and Foreign Minister Leopold von Berchtold believed that the time had come to settle the Serbian question once and for all.[20]

In order to embark on even a localized war with Serbia the Dual Monarchy needed German support. This was because a "local war" in the Balkans could easily become a general European war. True, Russia had backed down in 1908 over the annexation of Bosnia-Herzegovina, but Vienna could not count on Russia's continued compliance.

Wilhelm's foreign policy had isolated Germany and wedded it to the Dual Monarchy. Also French Foreign Minister Théophile Delcassé (1898–1905) had, for all intents and purposes, detached Italy from the Triple Alliance. Without Austria-Hungary, Germany would have no allies at all. Berlin had already established precedent by supporting Austria-Hungary during the crisis with Russia over Bosnia in 1908–9. On 6 July 1914, therefore Germany again pledged its support – the famous "blank cheque" – for the Dual Monarchy. In so doing, Berlin was well aware that Austria-Hungary intended to attack Serbia and that this threatened Russian involvement and a major war. German Foreign Minister Theobald von Bethmann-Hollweg tried to pressure Vienna into speedy action, believing that the Austro-Serbian war and subsequent international reaction might be over in, at most, three weeks. In any case, the "blank cheque" surrendered initiative to the Dual Monarchy.[21]

Secure in German backing, on 7 July Berchtold proposed a surprise attack on Serbia. But Hungarian Premier Count István Tisza objected. He wanted diplomatic encirclement of Serbia, with war only as an option. To cloak its intention to crush Serbia the Austro-Hungarian council of ministers then approved an ultimatum couched in terms that the Serbs would have to reject. On 22 July the terms were transmitted to Germany, where they received approval. A day later the same document was sent to Belgrade demanding a reply within 48 hours.[22]

To the world's surprise Serbia responded within the time limit, accepting all the Austrian demands save those directly impinging on Serbian sovereignty. It also offered to accept arbitration by the Hague Court or a decision of the big powers regarding the disputed items. Vienna declared the Serb response unsatisfactory. The leaders of the Dual Monarchy then severed diplomatic relations with Serbia and ordered partial military mobilization; Serbia had already mobilized. At the urgent request of Berlin, Vienna stepped up the date for war against Serbia from 29 July to a day earlier.[23]

In St Petersburg Russian Foreign Minister Sergei Sazonov hoped that he might bluff Vienna into backing down by ordering "preparatory measures" for the partial mobilization of the Odessa, Kiev, Kazan, and Moscow Military Districts. This step on 26 July was quite risky, but it had the strong support of the Russian general staff, which believed that war was inevitable.[24]

On 28 July, exactly one month after the assassination of the archduke, Austria-Hungary formally declared war on Serbia. Later that day artillery batteries began sporadic shelling of Belgrade. The Third Balkan War had begun. On 29 July St Petersburg ordered the actual mobilization of the four Russian military districts. Tsar Nicholas II made the decision only with great difficulty and after an exchange of telegrams with Kaiser Wilhelm.[25]

On 30 July Russia ordered full mobilization. Although Paris had earlier urged St Petersburg to take no action that might provoke Berlin, French Ambassador to Russia Maurice Paléologue on his own responsibility encouraged Sazonov to take a harder line.[26] While the Russian general mobilization insured that the Balkan war would become a general European conflict, German historian Fritz Fischer has pointed out that this was the final straw for Berlin only because the Central Powers were bent on a European war and, for domestic political considerations, needed a pretext for starting it.[27]

Military timetables now came into play. Germany's war plan depended on speedy action. The German General Staff believed it could not allow the Russians the opportunity to mobilize large numbers of troops. As German State Secretary for Foreign Affairs Gottlieb von Jagow put it, Germany had the speed and Russia the numbers. The German military plan, named after former Chief of the German General Staff Alfred von Schlieffen, drove events.

Germany knew that war between itself and Russia would necessarily involve France. Thus faced with the virtual certainty of a two-front war, Schlieffen had planned an overwhelming blow against France while a holding action in the east checked a slowly mobilizing Russia. Therefore the German government, at Moltke's insistence, demanded that Russia halt its mobilization. With no answer forthcoming, on 1 August Germany ordered general mobilization.[28]

The French cabinet had refused to mobilize the army but it did order troops to take up position along the Luxembourg–Vosges borders. These forces were ordered to be kept ten kilometres from the frontier, a move specifically to influence British public opinion by avoiding any French responsibility for initiating war.

The Schlieffen Plan mandated that there be no delay in opening an attack against France, and on 1 August German Ambassador Baron Wilhelm von Schoen called at the French Foreign Ministry to learn what France would do in the event of war between Germany and Russia. Berlin insisted that even if France pledged neutrality it would have to surrender certain eastern fortresses as proof of "her sincerity". No French government could survive such a concession, and Premier René Viviani in Paris replied that France would act in accordance with its interests. That same evening the cabinet ordered mobilization of the French Army.[29] On 3 August Germany declared war on France.

Four of the five great European powers were now at war. Britain held back. As early as 31 July London had demanded assurances from both Paris and Berlin to respect Belgian neutrality, guaranteed by the major powers since 1839. France sent a prompt affirmative reply but Germany declined to do so.

Again, the Schlieffen Plan drove German policy. Schlieffen had regarded the heavily fortified frontier of eastern France where the French Army would mass as a formidable obstacle. He believed the quickest way to defeat France was to strike to the north through neutral Belgium. On 2 August German troops occupied Luxembourg. The same day German diplomats demanded the right of transit through Belgium, promising to make reparations for any damages and to restore Belgian independence once the war was won. Should Belgium refuse, it would be treated as an enemy with the "decision of arms" deciding its fate. Brussels rejected the ultimatum on 3 August and early the next morning German troops invaded.[30]

The German attack on Belgium brought Britain into the war. On 29 July Germany had made a plea for British neutrality by promising not to take territory from France in Europe and to respect the neutrality of the Netherlands if Belgium did not take sides against Germany. France also courted Britain. Ambassador Paul Cambon pressed British Foreign Secretary Sir Edward Grey for the mutual military consultation provided for in their 1912 agreement if peace were threatened, but Grey refused. London promised only to honour its pledge to defend the French coasts against German naval assault. Grey was largely powerless; the cabinet was bitterly divided. Even his assurance that Britain would honour its limited commitment to France brought the resignation of one cabinet member.

Germany's invasion of Belgium dramatically changed everything. Britain had a long-standing interest in insuring that no strong power controlled the Low Countries, where many of its goods entered the continent and whence an enemy might launch an invasion of Britain itself. Upon learning of the German invasion Britain demanded that Germany reply by midnight on 4 August that it would respect Belgian neutrality. Berlin replied that "necessity knows no law" and Bethmann Hollweg accused London of going to war for "a scrap of paper".[31] With the expiration of the ultimatum London announced on 5 August that a state of war existed between Great Britain and Germany. Grey best summed up the tragedy when on the evening of 4 August, watching a lamplighter at work outside the Foreign Office, he remarked to a friend, "The lamps are going out all over Europe; we shall not see them lit again in our lifetime."[32]

Now five great European powers were at war. Italy, declaring that its treaty obligations with the Triple Alliance did not obligate it to join Germany and Austria-Hungary in an aggressive war, remained neutral. On 3 August little

Montenegro, with a predominantly Serb population of only half a million, joined its kinsmen against the Dual Monarchy. Within a few weeks Turkey joined the Central Powers and Japan sided with the Allies.

Turkey's decision resulted in a new theatre of war in the Middle East. Having Turkey as an active military opponent cut Russia off from easy access to the West and imposed heavy economic burdens, forcing it to divert military resources from the fight against Germany and Austria-Hungary. This added immensely to Russia's internal difficulties and helped bring about the Bolshevik Revolution three years later.

Japan used the First World War, as with the Second, to capitalize on the Western Powers' preoccupation with Europe. On 15 August Tokyo dispatched an ultimatum to Germany demanding withdrawal of the German fleet from the Far East and the surrender within one week of Kiaochow on the Shantung Peninsula of China. Berlin did not reply and on 23 August Japan declared war. Although Japan's entry into the war was far less important to the war's outcome than that of Turkey, the Allies did benefit from it, chiefly in the form of naval units for convoy duties and in munitions sent to Europe, especially to Russia.

Later the British agreed to cede to Japan at the end of the war all German islands north of the Equator – the Gilberts, the Marshalls, and the Carolines. At relatively little cost, the Japanese thus gained great advantage. During the war the Japanese also sought, unsuccessfully, to establish a protectorate over China.

In order to maintain the largest armies possible with the latest military equipment, governments strained their limited national resources, often at the expense of rising popular demands for social services. The continent as a whole was never as ready for war as in 1914.[33]

In August 1914 a near-universal expectation existed among Europeans that the war would be short. Almost alone British Secretary for War Lord Kitchener predicted a long conflict. "We must be prepared", he said, "to put armies of millions of men in the field and maintain them for several years."[34]

Those who believed in a short war pointed to Ivan Bloch in *The future of war* (1898) and Normal Angell in *The great illusion* (1910). Both had declared that there could be no economic winners in modern war. Europeans misinterpreted their views to mean that because a prolonged conflict would be an economic calamity for victor and vanquished alike it would not happen.

Europeans erred in another fundamental sense. The war that began in 1914 would be vastly different from the last major European conflict, the Franco-German War of 1870–71. The war of 1914–18 was total, involving entire populations. It dwarfed all previous conflicts in numbers of men mobilized and in resources expended. This great war became only in a secondary sense a conflict between soldiers. Because of its long duration, industrial output and agricultural strength more than military skill eventually determined the outcome.

Impact of technology

The war also differed from previous conflicts in the manner in which machines dominated. Tremendous advances in military technology led to important innovations in weaponry, including the tank, submarine, warplane, and poison gas. But even before these changes, technology had transformed the battlefield. Improved manufacturing techniques particularly in metallurgy made possible true machine weapons and rapid-firing artillery.

A major prewar change was the introduction of smokeless gunpowder. Utilized by the Boers against the British during the 1899–1902 South African, or Boer, War, it meant greater visibility on the battlefield. It led to changes in tactics and renewed interest in camouflage. The new powder produced less bore fouling, facilitating development of high-volume fire weapons. Smokeless powder was coupled with faster-operating bolt-action magazine rifles, solid-brass cartridge cases, and steel-jacketed bullets.

Beginning in the 1880s a revolution in small arms had also occurred with clip-fed breech-loading rifles: the German Mauser (1889), the British Lee-Enfield (1881), the French Lebel (1886), the Austrian Mannlicher (1886) and the American Springfield (1903).[35] With each new model, range was extended and velocity increased. The shape of bullets also changed; the spitzer or boat-tail bullet appeared. Smaller and aerodynamically more stable, it had longer range. These new infantry weapons had a combat effective range of 400 yards or more, and shooting matches at 1,000 yards were not uncommon. All these developments increased the superiority of defence over offence, a trend first established in the American Civil War.

Although all the rifles were roughly comparable to one another, there was a difference in their employment. Since the Boer War the British Army had stressed fast, aimed rifle fire from the prone position. With his 10-round magazine, bolt-action Lee-Enfield a well-trained British infantrymen could fire 15 or more aimed shots per minute. Although the rifles of the Continental powers were similar they lacked the Lee-Enfield's magazine capacity (the Mauser magazine held only five rounds, the Lebel eight). The Continental armies also stressed firing from the hip or standing position while advancing.[36] The British Expeditionary Force's employment of rapid, aimed rifle fire was crucial in preventing a German victory in the first few months of the war.

If any one weapon symbolized the First World War it was the machine gun.[37] The Maxim gun was the first modern machine gun. Patented in the US in 1884 by Hiram Maxim, it was a truly efficient killer. Using recoil energy, the Maxim gun was extraordinarily reliable and, weighing only 100 lb, was easily transportable.

The machine gun had proved immensely valuable in imperialist wars in Africa, but its effectiveness had also been conclusively demonstrated in the Russo-Turkish War of 1877–8 and the Russo-Japanese War of 1904–5. Surprisingly, most military theorists overlooked its implications for European fighting.

At 450 to 600 rounds per minute one machine gun could equal the fire of 40 to 80 riflemen. It also had greater range than the rifle, enabling indirect fire in support of an attack. In the German Army machine guns were deployed in companies as opposed to dispersing them among infantry formations. This facilitated their concentration in needed sectors. Light machine guns such as the excellent British Lewis Gun were developed later. Still, all armies in 1914 tended to regard machine guns as minor artillery weapons.[38]

Profound changes were also occurring in artillery. During the American Civil War artillery had been primarily a direct fire weapon used against personnel: artillerists aimed at what they could see. Improved guns changed all this. They were the result of enhanced manufacturing techniques and better knowledge of metallurgy, especially steel alloys. New smokeless, slower burning powders produced greater thrust against the projectiles and less pressure on the gun. Steel guns, which had demonstrated their worth in the Franco-German War, increasingly appeared in European arsenals. New recoil systems allowed the gun tube to recoil against springs in its carriage, which then returned it to its original position. This innovation meant that guns would not constantly have to be hauled back into position to refire, increasing their rate and accuracy of fire. New mechanical fuses, high-explosive fillers, and steel-coated projectiles all became common. The First World War also demonstrated the need for heavier artillery capable of smashing enemy bunkers.

Another important change in artillery tactics was aimed indirect fire, the first real attempt at which occurred in the American Civil War. In 1882 the Russian Carl Guk published a system for firing on an unseen target using a compass, aiming point, and a forward observer. The Japanese refined this method and, in their defeat of Russia, they used indirect fire with great success. By the 1890s most European armies had standardized the techniques of artillery fire, allowing for the massing of fire on remote targets.[39]

The howitzer also increased in importance. This mid-trajectory weapon could fire at longer ranges than mortars. It came to be the preferred artillery piece in the First World War because its high arc of fire allowed highly accurate plunging fire against enemy entrenchments. The Germans augmented their corps artillery with batteries of howitzers rather than field guns.[40]

Perhaps the finest artillery piece of its day was the French 75 mm field gun, dubbed by its proponents "the Father, Son, and Holy Ghost of Warfare". The French rejected the howitzer completely and were convinced that the 75 would give them battlefield dominance. Its mobility (it could be handled with its caisson by four horses, and if needed, by only two), rapid rate of fire (up to 20 rounds per minute), and 6,000-yard range made it a superb offensive weapon. In 1914 French Army artillery was preponderantly mobile field guns. Of 5,108 artillery pieces on hand that September, 4,098 were field guns (3,840 were 75s) and 192 were mountain guns, and only 389 were heavies. But 75 mm shells were too light to smash entrenchments and most of those on hand were in any case shrapnel. The French mistakenly believed that what the 75 mm gun lacked in hitting power it could make up for in its high rate of fire. Yet France started the war with only 1,300 rounds per gun, about three weeks' supply at best, and most of these were shrapnel. Heavier guns became increasingly important during the war. At war's end the French had 5,600 heavy guns as opposed to 6,000 field pieces.[41] Artillery was the great killer of the First World War; estimates claim artillery fire caused up to 70 per cent of battlefield deaths.[42]

Innovations at sea

There were also great changes at sea. The traditional race between armour and ordnance produced steel-armoured ships and new, more powerful breechloading guns. Whereas the largest gun in Royal Navy service in the mid-nineteenth century was the 8-inch (diameter) gun firing a 68-lb shot, by 1884 the largest gun was a 16.25-inch gun firing a 1,800-lb projectile that could penetrate 32 inches of wrought iron.[43]

The battleship underwent tremendous change in the half century before the war, reaching the apogee of its development in HMS *Dreadnought*. Launched in 1906, she immediately made all other battleships obsolete. Completed in the amazing time of just 365 days, she mounted ten 12-inch guns. The *Dreadnought* was the first all-big gun, geared-turbine battleship. Her guns could all be fired from one central fire-control location and, at 21 knots, she was the fastest ship of her type afloat.[44] The Germans soon responded by constructing their own dreadnoughts.

First Sea Lord Admiral Sir John Fisher sought to replace the battleship and armoured cruiser with the battle cruiser and increased support for submarine development.[45] Conceived on the same principles as the dreadnought of higher speed and greater armament, the battle cruiser was battleship armament on a high-speed cruiser hull. The first three British battle cruisers, authorized in 1905, were completed by mid-1908. They had a main battery of eight 12-inch guns and a speed of more than 26 knots. But battle cruisers sacrificed armour for speed, and British battle cruisers also suffered from a serious design flaw, the lack of sufficient armour on the top of the gun turrets, which became apparent in the 1916 Battle of Jutland.[46]

Other naval innovations included optical range finders, steam turbines, and a change in fuel from coal to oil. Oil had great advantages over coal; much more of it could be carried on board, refuelling was quick and easy, and even possible while underway. In 1909 the Royal Navy decided future destroyers should burn oil exclusively. Soon all ships were oil-fired, including the first battleships to be so fuelled, the *Queen Elizabeths* of 1912.[47] Oil gave Britain a special geopolitical interest in the Persian Gulf.

The modern torpedo also appeared. Developed in 1868 by Robert Whitehead for the Austro-Hungarian Navy, this weapon could sink a battleship and yet be carried by small torpedo boats. Quick-firing guns and the appearance of small escort vessels, originally known as torpedo-boat destroyers, and later simply destroyers, to accompany the battleships, somewhat countered this threat.[48]

The submarine was a delivery system ideally suited for the torpedo. The American J. P. Holland developed the first practical submarine in the 1890s. Submarines were originally believed useful largely for observation duties. Ironically in view of later events, the British and French rather than the Germans had pushed the use of submarines as weapons platforms. By 1899 the French had a submarine with torpedo tubes in service. Submarines came into their own during the First World War, but their potential as offensive weapons was already apparent.[49]

Military aviation

The United States was the first country to experiment with military aviation. In 1903 two brothers, Wilbur and Orville Wright, achieved the first manned powered flight. Five years later they built a "military flier" for the US Army

Signal Corps, and in 1913 the Army organized a squadron of aircraft to serve with General John J. Pershing in the 1916 punitive expedition into Mexico. The US Navy also experimented. In 1910 Eugene Ely flew a plane off the USS *Birmingham* and the next year he landed one on the USS *Pennsylvania*.[50]

Aircraft first went to war in the Tripolitan conflict of 1911–12. Most were unarmed and used solely for observation purposes. Although aviation made rapid strides, in 1914 generals and admirals still thought of it primarily as useful for observation and scouting. General Ferdinand Foch remarked that "aviation is a good sport, but for the army it is useless".[51] Nonetheless all the powers built aircraft. In August 1914, including seaplanes, but not airships, Britain had 270; Germany, 267; Russia, 190; France, 141; Austria-Hungary, 97; and Belgium, 24. During the war more than 161,000 were built.[52] April 1918 saw the world's first independent air force; the Royal Air Force, formed of the Royal Navy Air Service and Royal Flying Corps, had 22,000 aircraft and 291,175 personnel.[53]

Other technological changes

Other technical developments had an impact on twentieth-century war. Modern chemical industries were producing more powerful explosives. The typewriter and carbon paper assisted in the management of mass armies. The Boer War produced a realization that the traditional bright, conspicuous uniforms of Europe's armies would have to yield to the drab, utilitarian, and unconspicuous. Also the radio supplemented the telephone and telegraph and spawned development of communications intelligence. Railroads were extraordinarily important in the deployment of troops and were critical early in the war both to France on the Western Front and to Germany against Russia. Armies also experimented with motorized transport. The British Army would develop from 827 cars and 15 motorcycles in 1914 to 56,000 trucks and 34,000 motorcycles in 1918.[54] In 1914, however, all armies still relied on the horse to a considerable degree, and on the battlefield most infantrymen moved on foot. The new diesel engine proved especially useful for the submarine, which required an engine that would not give off dangerous fumes.

Medicine also experienced great change. Louis Pasteur's discovery of the germ theory of disease and the development of antiseptics heralded important advances in military medicine.

Mass armies and rapid-fire weapons created tremendous logistical problems. During the Franco-German War of 1870–71 the German Army provided 200 rounds of rifle ammunition per man, which was carried by the individual soldier and in the supply train. The average expenditure in six months of war was only 56 rounds per man. In 1914 the number of rounds per man had increased to 280, but all were gone in the first weeks of the war. In 1870–71 German artillery pieces had fired an average of 199 shells apiece. The 1,000 rounds per gun available in 1914 were all gone within six weeks of the start of the war. Horses eat about ten times as much by weight as men; simply feeding the large number of them in all armies imposed heavy demands on already strained logistics systems.[55]

By 1914 machine weapons had gained mastery of the battlefield. Small numbers of rapid-fire machine weapons supported by accurate long-range rifle fire gave dominance to the defence. Supported by artillery and barbed wire strung along the front, such weapons could sweep the ground and prevent enemy troops from attacking across open ground in any significant number.

Generals responded to this tactical dilemma by employing nineteenth-century solutions to twentieth-century warfare. Following Frenchman Henri Bergson's concept of *élan vital*, they stressed the power of individual will over machines. Later they assumed that larger and larger amounts of artillery fire would destroy all the machine guns and artillery emplacements, allowing the infantry to advance. But sufficient numbers of machine guns and their crews survived even the most prolonged bombardments.

There were four military ways to solve this dilemma. One was to exhaust an enemy with formidable defences and firepower. A second approach, the strategy of offensive attrition warfare, advocated continued conventional attacks to wear down the enemy. A third option utilized new technology, such as the tank, poison gas, or airplane to achieve a breakthrough. The fourth was an indirect strategy that avoided the enemy's major defensive lines, attacking elsewhere, as in the 1915 Dardanelles Campaign. For the most part the generals chose the second method, with disastrous results for the men they commanded.[56] During the war all armies experimented to a lesser or greater degree with new tactics, but only after the conflict's sheer carnage forced innovation.

Chapter Two

1914: the war of movement

Balance of forces

In August 1914 each side had certain advantages. Germany, with a population of 65 million, was among the world's leading industrial nations.[1] Her 880,000-man standing army was the world's finest.[2] Generations of Prussia's best and brightest had entered the military, and this trend continued after the unification of Germany. Well-trained and led, especially at the junior officer level, the German Army was ready to the smallest detail. It also had more artillery per corps and was the best supplied army in technical equipment.[3] Conscription and lengthy reserve service until age 45 also gave Germany an important advantage in trained men in the initial battles. Although Germany would have to fight on two fronts, her railroad net, built with military considerations in mind, partially offset this disadvantage.

Germany also had the world's second largest navy, the result of the Kaiser's decision to build a powerful battle fleet. In capital ships the Imperial German Navy had 15 dreadnoughts, 5 battle cruisers, and 30 pre-dreadnoughts and coast-defence ships.[4] Although designed to operate only at short range from their bases, German warships were in many respects among the best in the world.

The Dual Monarchy's military was not nearly as well trained, led, or equipped as Germany's. Although Austria-Hungary had a population of 50 million and a conscription system on the German model, financial constraints limited her peacetime army to 480,000 men, far smaller than that of either France or Germany. Based on "skeletonizing", the Austro-Hungarian Army could expand rapidly in times of crisis; during mobilization infantry companies would triple in size. The Dual Monarchy also had the excellent Škoda arms production complex. Located at Plzeň (Pilsen), it provided superb heavy

17

howitzers and mortars that would prove immensely valuable in 1914 in reducing Belgian fortresses.

Unfortunately for the Dual Monarchy its polyglot nature made for inefficiency in war. The army contained more than a dozen nationalities of dubious loyalties and there was outright hostility between them. Troop dispositions were often made on the basis of ethnic rather than military considerations. Most of the officers were of German ethnic background and German was generally the language of command, although one Slovak regiment received its commands in English. The language problem remained a major hurdle. The army was also poorly trained, with many of its officers promoted on the basis of social connection rather than ability.[5]

In 1914 the Austro-Hungarian Navy had 3 dreadnought battleships, 3 *Radetzky*-class semidreadnoughts, and 9 pre-dreadnoughts and coast-defence ships. Naval construction on the eve of the war claimed 20 per cent of Austro-Hungarian defence spending and, to the dismay of Chief of the General Staff General Franz Conrad von Hötzendorf, siphoned off scarce resources from the army.[6]

From sheer power and organization, therefore, it was inevitable that Germany would dominate the Central Powers. Working against Austro-Hungarian military cooperation with Germany, however, was Vienna's lingering resentment from the humiliating defeat Prussia had inflicted on her in 1866.

France had a population of some 40 million and a well-trained army of 823,000 men. Her manpower pool was considerably smaller than Germany's, but France expected the war to be over quickly with reserves likely to be of little service. Located predominantly in the Mediterranean, the French Navy had 4 dreadnoughts, 6 *Danton*-class semidreadnoughts, and 15 pre-dreadnoughts and coast-defence ships.

Unfortunately for the Allied cause, Russia was unprepared for offensive war in 1914. The most populous of all European nations with 167 million people, she had on paper a pre-war army of 1,400,000 men. But the effectiveness of any organization begins at the top, and Russia's military leadership was inept. Army field commander Grand Duke Nicholas Nikolaevich, one of the Tsar's uncles, had never actively commanded troops. Chief of Staff General N. N. Yanushkevich, a protocol officer at court who had been promoted for political reasons, readily admitted total ignorance of his responsibilities. The real work of military planning fell to unimaginative Deputy Chief of Staff General V. A. Danilov.[7]

Russia had, after her humiliating military performance in the war with Japan (1904-5), embarked on an ambitious programme to improve her military capabilities, including heavy investment in new strategic railroads that would enable her to mobilize her vast resources more quickly. In 1910 Russian mobilization could proceed at 250 trains a day; by 1914, 360; the figure projected for 1917 was 560. Rapid Russian troop deployments would nullify the German war plan – one reason the German military favoured war in 1914.

On the eve of the war Russia was actually spending more on her military than Germany – the Germans calculated 1.57 billion marks to 1.496 billion – although getting less for it. Part of the problem was the misapplication of resources to defensive purposes. Instead of investing in field artillery the Russians concentrated on costly fortresses and heavy stationary guns. In 1914, fortresses had 2,813 modern heavy guns; the field army only 240 heavy howitzers and cannon.[8] The army also had few trucks; the bulk of supplies would have to be moved from railheads by horse-drawn carts. Lacking the industrial base of the other major warring powers, Russia required imports to be able to fight effectively. Her 1914 conscripts were fervent and courageous, and they deserved better officers.

Throughout the war the Russian army suffered severe shortages of virtually everything, including food, shells, and even telegraph wire to enable head-quarters to communicate with units in the field. Too much emphasis was placed on cavalry, and merely supplying fodder for the horses imposed a tremendous burden on the already strained rail net.

Russia also had a powerful navy. It was, however, divided by geography into separate forces in the Baltic, the Black Sea, and the Far East. In 1914 the Russian Navy had 11 pre-dreadnoughts and coast-defence ships.

Great Britain, with 46 million people, differed from the other major powers in that she had neither conscription nor a large standing army. Her small professional army of 235,000 men was fashioned for colonial require-ments. The British Expeditionary Force (BEF) sent to France numbered barely 160,000 men. It was also woefully unprepared and hardly an instrument for total war. Historian Basil Liddell Hart, however, called the BEF "the most highly trained striking force of any country – a rapier among scythes". In contrast to the other armies, it had experienced protracted warfare, albeit in the colonies.[9]

Britain's strength was in her navy. With 22 dreadnoughts, 9 battle cruisers, and 40 pre-dreadnought battleships, it was by far the world's largest. The Royal Navy, assisted by those of France, Russia, and Japan (2 dreadnoughts, 1 battle cruiser, and 14 pre-dreadnoughts and coast-defence ships), gave the Allies domination at sea. Britain also had the world's largest merchant marine. At 19 million tons it had half the world's total.[10] Maritime superiority not only secured for the Allies their own overseas resources but enabled them to

19

utilize the industrial production of leading neutral countries, especially the United States.

Britain's naval superiority also allowed her to blockade Germany by sea. This vital factor in the defeat of Germany has not received the attention it deserves. The blockade, it should be noted, violated the 1909 Declaration of London according neutrals the right to trade with belligerent states. Britain classified as contraband all foodstuffs intended for German consumption.[11]

Germany and Austria-Hungary did enjoy the important advantage of interior lines. From their central location they could shift resources where needed over the efficient German railroad net much more easily than could the Entente powers on the periphery.

In contrast to the compact Central Powers, the Allies were widely separated geographically. British troops had to be transported to the continent by ship. Russia was cut off from her western allies save by sea, and Japan was far removed from the fighting in Europe. The Allies also did not have a unity of command; too often there was little or no coordination or planning, especially in the early fighting. It was not until April 1918 that a unified command structure came into being.

All points considered, the Allies were much stronger than the Central Powers. One calculation is that in August 1914 the Allies fielded 199 infantry divisions to 137 for the Central Powers, and 50 to 22 cavalry divisions. Their combined population was also much larger: 279 to 120 million.[12] The Allies were also much better placed economically than the Central Powers. If the war could be prolonged and all other factors remained equal, economics and demography could bring victory.

War plans

Germany's war plan called for quick military victory. It had been developed by Count Alfred von Schlieffen (1833–1913), chief of the German General Staff from 1891 to 1905. Schlieffen knew that in a European war Germany would have to fight France and Russia simultaneously and to choose where to place emphasis. It would be many weeks before Russia could fully mobilize and that meant that decisive victory against her would be not be possible in the early going; furthermore, the western part of the Russian empire had no vital objectives for the German Army. The Germans were also concerned about the vastness of Russia and its ability, amply demonstrated in 1812, to swallow up an invading force.

Schlieffen therefore chose to concentrate first on France, the country posing the most immediate threat. A massive German blow delivered at maximum speed would knock her from the war in six weeks. After this resources could be shifted east over Germany's excellent railroad net to deal with a slow-mobilizing Russia held at bay by minimal German defensive forces. Indeed, it was the Russian mobilization, which threatened to upset the German timetable, that triggered Berlin's ultimatum to Russia and her subsequent declaration of war. In short, Germany staked everything on a quick, victorious campaign against France.

But how to defeat France quickly? The heavily defended French frontier between Luxembourg and Switzerland was a formidable obstacle, especially as the Germans were well aware that the French planned to position the bulk of their forces there for an offensive to retake Alsace and Lorraine. Schlieffen decided, therefore, that the best way to defeat France lay through Belgium. His plan called for a massive five-army scythe-sweep through Belgium to gather up the Channel ports ("the rightmost soldier will brush the English Channel with his sleeve", he is alleged to have said), encircle Paris from the west, and drive the French back eastward against their own fortress line to destruction in a giant battle of annihilation. To make this massive operation possible Schlieffen planned to use reserves along with regular troops in the attacking force.[13]

Two weaker German armies would defend in Lorraine against the expected French thrust there, perhaps even withdrawing so that the French would follow and be unable to shift resources north to intervene against the German envelopment. Everything depended on overwhelming pressure from the German right wing, which would have to move more swiftly than the rest of the army. When Schlieffen died in 1913 at the age of 80 his last words were supposed to have been "It must come to a fight. Only make the right wing strong."[14]

Schlieffen's plan would, of course, violate Belgian neutrality and that of little Luxembourg. The Great Powers in 1839 had guaranteed Belgian neutrality. Undoubtedly this act would bring Britain into the war. The Germans, though, believed the British regular army was too small to present a serious obstacle. By the time Britain could make a major contribution to the fighting the war would be over. The Germans made the same miscalculation with the United States in early 1917.

The allocation of German forces exemplifies the bold nature of Schlieffen's plan. He would leave only ten divisions, with supporting local troops, to face the Russians while 68 divisions marched west. Of the divisions committed against France 59 would comprise the right wing and only nine the left wing.[15]

In 1906 General Helmuth von Moltke (the Younger) succeeded Schlieffen as chief of the general staff. The War Ministry opposed the appointment, pointing out Moltke's lack of combat experience and leadership abilities; Moltke himself suspected the post was beyond his abilities. It was said that the Kaiser insisted because of the association of the Moltke name with Prussia's victories in the Wars of German Unification.

Moltke made key modifications to the German war plan. Fearing the threat to his communications and the impact on morale of a French invasion of Germany, he weakened the ratio between right- and left-wing forces by adding eight of nine new divisions to the left wing and only one to the right wing. The genius of the original plan had been that Schlieffen was prepared to sustain temporary defeat in Lorraine, even draw the French into Germany, to secure overall victory. Moltke also dropped Schlieffen's idea of sending troops through Holland, opening up the possibility of a right-wing bottleneck. He also made a key modification when the campaign was in progress. Because the Russian Army moved faster than anticipated, Moltke sent two corps from the right wing to reinforce East Prussia.[16] Moltke's changes to the Schlieffen plan violated Frederick II's dictum: "He who defends everywhere, defends nothing."

German historian Gerhard Ritter has noted that the Schlieffen Plan, while bold, failed to take into account the French rail net. German troops would have to move by foot along their great arc. Schlieffen's plan allowed no deviations in timetable, yet the invaders would inevitably be slowed by blown bridges and lengthened supply lines. French defenders inside the arc, meanwhile, would be able to utilize railroads to shift resources quickly along lateral lines. The Schlieffen Plan might have worked either earlier or later: in Napoleonic times, before the advent of the railroad; or later during the Second World War, when mechanized vehicles could rapidly transport large numbers of men and supplies across open country and aircraft could disrupt enemy mobilizations and troop movements.[17]

The French strategic plan lacked the imagination of the Schlieffen Plan and played to its strengths. The French High Command believed Germany would attack France from Lorraine and perhaps through eastern Belgium. But in January 1911 General Victor Michel became vice president of the Supreme War Council and commander-in-chief designate. Michel opposed the High Command's decision to concentrate French forces along the Alsace-Lorraine frontier and the eastern portion of the Franco-Belgian border. He proposed instead reducing French troops facing Alsace and Lorraine and placing some 700,000 men along the entire Franco-Belgian border. To defend this broad front, Michel, as in the Schlieffen Plan, planned to utilize reserves on the front lines. The French Army would then be in position to stop the German sweep and, once the main axis of the German attack had been identified, could launch its own massive counterattack.

The existence of the Schlieffen Plan was known before the war and most observers believed in the certainty of a German violation of Belgium. Nonetheless, much of the French high command rejected Michel's proposals and in December 1911 he was forced to resign as vice-president of the Supreme War Council.[18] Convinced by their own bitter experience in the Franco-German War of 1870–71 that defence would not win a future war, a doctrine based on the offensive came to the fore in France. Its theorists, including Louis Loizeau de Grandmaison and Ferdinand Foch,[19] clung to faith in an all-out offensive (*offensive à outrance*). Only such an offensive immediately on the outbreak of war would allow the French to break through the German lines and produce a victorious ending to the short war so universally anticipated.

Michel's successor was General Joseph Jacques Césaire Joffre. His plan called for a massive easterly offensive to secure the lost provinces of Alsace and Lorraine. Joffre stated that "whatever the circumstances, it is the commander-in-chief's intentions to advance with all forces united to attack the German armies".[20] Because the British told him that in the event of their involvement they would send to France at most only six divisions in the early stages, in contrast to 85 French and an estimated 110 German, Joffre did not assign them a major role.[21] Despite his acceptance of the fact that the Germans were likely to attempt a strong thrust through Belgium in the event of war, Joffre's Plan XVII[22] (unveiled in 1913) located three of the five French armies on the borders of Alsace and Lorraine. First and Second Armies on the right wing were to invade Lorraine. Third Army, in the centre, would strike toward Metz and Thionville. Joffre was reluctant to shift resources to the left flank for fear of uncovering the easiest German invasion route, from Alsace, toward Verdun. Only one army, the Fifth, was in the critical area of the Belgian frontier. Between Montmédy and Mézières, it could follow Third Army or, should the Germans really come through Belgium, strike them on the flank. Fourth Army, concentrated as a reserve near St.-Didier, would be available to support either flank as the campaign developed.[23]

Plan XVII failed to take into account the vast increases in defensive firepower. Joffre concluded, falsely as it turned out, that the Germans would not use their reserves on the front lines, and that without them they would lack sufficient manpower for a broad-front attack. He therefore expected the main German attack to originate from Lorraine. But because the overall plan stressed mobilization and concentration it left Joffre considerable flexibility to determine the best axis of attack.[24]

Joffre therefore committed his forces to the attack as Moltke hurled his own right wing against the virtually denuded French left. Plan XVII met complete defeat, but had Moltke not reinforced his left wing the French attack would have taken longer to crumble and it would have been far more difficult for Joffre to extricate his forces and shift them to meet the main German blow to the north.

Austria-Hungary entered the war with a series of contingency plans drawn up in 1906 by Chief of the Imperial General Staff Franz Conrad von Hötzendorf. Austria-Hungary faced multiple potential enemies: Russia, Serbia, Italy, and Romania. She was also divided in her immediate offensive ambitions; her treaty obligations to Germany required that she oppose Russia, yet she considered her immediate goal to be crushing Serbia. Austria-Hungary also had to guard against the possibilities of Italy and Romania entering the war. In his planning Conrad recognized Russia as the greatest threat but, inexplicably, minimized it. He seemed to rely upon Germany to deter a Russian attack or, failing that, on German military intervention to defeat Russia.

Conrad devised four alternative plans for the deployment of Austria-Hungary's six armies, the second-echelon Second Army being the swing element in each. Plan B (for the Balkans) dealt with war only against Serbia. It called for an offensive by Fifth and Sixth Armies based in Bosnia while Second Army attacked from Vojvodina, north of Belgrade. Plan I (Italy) called for an attack against Italy while maintaining a minimum defensive posture against Russia. Plan A dealt with war only against Russia. It called for Fifth and Sixth Armies to guard the Serbian frontier while First and Fourth Armies attacked northeastwards from Galicia into Russian Poland in combination with the Germans. At the same time, Third and Second Armies would drive from Eastern Galicia into Russia itself. Plan R, based on Russian intervention after Austria-Hungary had attacked Serbia, would be the most difficult to execute. In it Second Army would be deployed against Russia.

In July 1914, when she hoped for war only against Serbia, Austria-Hungary partially mobilized her Balkan forces and second echelon troops. After it became clear that Russia would not remain quiescent, Conrad sought to concentrate resources in East Galicia for Plan R in the hopes of a double envelopment east of Warsaw with the German Eighth Army. Poland was a potential springboard for a Russian strike into the industrial centre of German Silesia, which Conrad hoped to turn into a trap by a simultaneous German and Austro-Hungarian attack. He wanted the German Eighth Army to strike south while his First and Fourth armies moved north. Third and Second Armies would, meanwhile, protect the Dual Monarchy's vulnerable eastern flank.

Although Conrad recognized the dangers of prematurely committing resources against Serbia, in 1914 he did so anyway. In shifting to Plan R, Conrad was handicapped because Second Army was not immediately available and the Germans failed to support his opening offensive. Even if Second Army had been available it is doubtful this would have changed events, however. Austria-Hungary was incapable of fighting effectively on two fronts simultaneously; her resources were hopelessly split and too many troops were in transit and unavailable to either front, the result of poor planning and Conrad's mismanagement.[25]

The Russian strategic dilemma was simpler than that of her opponents because she would fight on only one front. The problem was the vastness of that front, along which she would have to face both Austria-Hungary and Germany. Pre-war Russian planning envisioned two options, with dispositions for each essentially the same. Two armies, First and Second, were positioned in the north facing East Prussia, while three armies, Third, Fifth, and Eighth, were stationed in the southwest facing Austria-Hungary. The Fourth Army would be deployed either north or south, depending on circumstances.

If the Germans launched their main offensive against Russia, the Russian General Headquarters (*Stavka*) envisioned a broad retreat, much in the fashion of 1812 against Napoleon, followed by a counterattack when the opportunity presented itself. If Germany's main blow fell against France, Russia planned immediately to attack Austria-Hungary in Galicia. Only after her mobilization was completed would Russia attack East Prussia. Providing both attacks went well, the two army groups might then be combined for a drive into central Germany to end the war. As it turned out, French pleas for help led the Russians to attack both Germany and Austria-Hungary simultaneously.[26]

Invasion of Belgium

In the First World War the Western Front was the crucial theatre. On 2 August the Germans moved into Luxembourg. The next day they began crossing the frontier into Belgium. Belgium had a population of only 7.5 million people and in July 1914 her army was only 48,000 men. With war she mobilized 217,000 more.

The German build-up of forces was rapid. Within the first week of the war 1.5 million German troops were in position for the offensive. To the north were the two armies comprising the right wing charged with encircling Paris:

near Aix-la-Chapelle (Aachen) in northeast Belgium was General Alexander von Kluck's First Army; on its left near Limburg was General Karl von Bülow's Second Army. These two armies held Germany's fate in the war and were by far her strongest in terms of manpower. Kluck had 320,000 and Bülow 260,000 men. General Max von Hausen's Third Army, by comparison, had only 180,000 men.[27] To the left of Second Army was Third Army, Duke Albrecht of Württemberg's Fourth Army, Crown Prince Wilhelm of Prussia's Fifth Army, and Crown Prince Rupprecht of Bavaria's Sixth Army. General von Heeringen's Seventh Army held the far left and had the task of defeating any French invasion of Alsace.

On 4 August the Germans encountered their first major resistance as Kluck's First Army approached the Belgian fortress city of Liège on the Meuse River, 15 miles inside the frontier. Liège dominated the narrow Meuse corridor between the Dutch frontier and the Ardennes, so its prompt reduction was vital in the German plan. It had six major and six minor forts, but rifle trenches to protect the intervals between the forts were not ready and the guns of the forts were obsolete.[28] By 12 August the Germans had brought up heavy 305 mm Škoda siege howitzers on loan from the Austrians as well as their own less numerous 420 mm pieces. The large armour-piercing shells easily penetrated the concrete and steel forts, turning them into death traps. By the 16th the Germans had taken all 12 forts.

On 20 August much of the Belgian Army took refuge in the fortress city of Antwerp, where it posed a danger to the flank and rear of the German advance. On the same day the Germans arrived at Namur, the last Belgian fortress barring access up the Meuse River valley into France. Heavy howitzers reduced it in two days.

Belgian resistance, however, forced Moltke to leave troops behind at Antwerp and elsewhere, further weakening the German armies invading France. Belgium also provided an example and cause for the Allies. German atrocities, exaggerated by Allied propaganda and discounted in the interwar period, were real. The Germans adhered to a policy of *Schrecklichkeit* (frightfulness) in order to cow the Belgians into submission. The German destruction of the medieval cultural treasure city of Louvain with its priceless medieval manuscripts and their execution of individual snipers (*francs-tireur*) and hostages belied the notion of "civilized" war.[29]

French offensive into Alsace and Lorraine

As the Germans prepared to deliver their major blow from the north, Joffre struck east into Alsace and Lorraine. French infantry clad in blue coats and red trousers (the officers wore white gloves) attacked with flags flying and bugles blaring. The troops did not lack enthusiasm; what they needed was heavy mobile artillery to prepare their way. The broken terrain also deterred the attackers.

On 6 August General Bonneau's VII Corps attacked southern Alsace. Three days later the Germans drove them back. A second attempt on 14 August by General Pau's special Army of Lorraine was more successful. It took Mulhouse before Joffre withdrew it to utilize it elsewhere. The French were able to retain only a tiny portion of the province.[30]

Joffre continued to regard the German thrust through Belgium as a feint.[31] On 14 August he launched his main attacks into southern Lorraine and the Ardennes by General Auguste Y. E. Dubail's First Army and General Noël Joseph Edouard de Curières de Castelnau's Second Army. The fighting in Lorraine, the Ardennes, at Charleroi, and at Mons during this period is collectively known as the Battle of the Frontiers.

In Lorraine the Germans fell back, but their machine gun and artillery fire forced the French to pay a high cost for very small gains. Crown Prince Rupprecht of Bavaria secured permission from Moltke for his Sixth Army and von Heeringen's Seventh Army to counterattack. On the 20th they hit the French on the flank. The resulting Battles of Sarrebourg and Morhange were German victories; they were in fact the first great demonstrations of the power of machine-gun fire against massed formations of advancing troops. Although the French First Army retreated in good order, Second Army almost disintegrated before regaining its original starting point. The two armies then successfully defended Nancy and the Moselle line.

Despite his defeat in Lorraine, evidence of the overwhelming German drive developing through Belgium, and his shifting of Fifth Army north to the Sambre River, Joffre persisted with his Ardennes attack. On the 21st General Ruffey's Third Army and Langle de Cary's Fourth Army drove northeastwards toward Virton and Neufchâteau, but the combined German Fourth and Fifth armies outnumbered the attackers. The rugged terrain also forced the French to channel their advance and made them easy targets for German artillery, leading to heavy French casualties and a retreat to defensive positions behind the Meuse River.[32]

With his troops now back in their original positions, Joffre was able to utilize the French railroads to shift units northward to meet the German sweeping movement developing through Belgium. The German success against the French offensive into Alsace and Lorraine, therefore, had decisive, if unforeseen, consequences for the campaign and for the war.

Deployment of the BEF

Between 9 and 22 August the British Expeditionary Force arrived in France. The British transported to France some 160,000 men in six infantry divisions, one cavalry division, two cavalry brigades, and support troops. Wilhelm II, with his penchant for unfortunate phrases, is said to have referred to the BEF as a "contemptible little army",[33] but all British troops were volunteers and most were battle-tested. Under the command of Field Marshal Sir John French, the "Old Contemptibles", as the men now proudly referred to themselves, soon proved their worth in battle.

There was disagreement among British leaders over where the BEF should be deployed. Some, including Field Marshal Lord Roberts, one-time commander of the British Army, wanted it sent to Antwerp. Newly appointed Secretary of State for War, Field Marshal Lord Kitchener, thought it should concentrate near Amiens. In the end the BEF assembled farther east than Kitchener thought prudent, on the extreme left wing of the Allied line in the Mauberge–Le Cateau area.[34]

Allied retreat

Meanwhile Charles-Louis Lanrezac's Fifth Army had moved into the angle formed by the Sambre and Meuse rivers between Givet and Charleroi. The BEF concentrated to its left in the area between Maubeuge and Le Cateau. The Germans not only greatly outnumbered the Allied forces but also were moving in a wider arc than their opponents supposed. Fifth Army and the BEF were in danger of being cut off from the north by the German First and Second Armies and from the east by Third Army.

Fortunately for the Allies, Lanrezac sensed the danger. The four infantry and two cavalry divisions of the BEF then in France had arrived at Mons in Belgium on 22 August expecting to join an Allied offensive, but the day before, the Germans had attacked the French Fifth Army and crossed the Sambre. On 23 August, having been told of the fall of Namur and the arrival of the German Third Army at Dinant on his exposed right flank, Lanrezac correctly ordered an immediate withdrawal. Although this was the only way to save Fifth Army from destruction, Joffre believed Lanrezac lacked fighting spirit and on 5 September replaced him with General Louis Franchet d'Espèrey.

The Russians at this point affected the fighting in the West. Acting faster than the Germans thought possible, on 17 August two Russian armies invaded

East Prussia. On 25 August, just as the Western Front was nearing its crucial point, Moltke detached two army corps and a cavalry division from the German right wing, sending them east to reinforce the province of East Prussia, which Schlieffen had deemed expendable.

On the morning of 23 August the BEF first encountered Kluck's army at Mons while covering Lanrezac's left. That day the Germans attacked in close formations and came under accurate British rifle fire. The British retired several miles to pre-selected positions, but with Lanrezac having withdrawn that day they could no longer remain at Mons.[35]

Although the French right wing was holding, all armies in the centre and on the left, including the BEF, were in steady retreat. The German right, led by Generals Kluck and Bülow, moved inexorably southwest toward Paris. On 26 August General Sir Horace Smith-Dorrien's II Corps turned and fought Kluck's First Army at Le Cateau. This action, a dramatic day-long delaying action against a German force more than twice as large, allowed the rest of the BEF to withdraw. It cost the British 7,812 casualties (2,600 POWs) and 38 guns.

As the French and British fell back toward the Marne "Papa" Joffre provided a critical element of calm. He may have lacked imagination and flair but he had the unflappable temperament essential in defensive war. Retreats are notoriously difficult to execute, and his leadership was critical. His "appetite for three regular meals remained steady and his ten o'clock bed-time inviolable. . . he maintained an even tenor, a solid control".[36] Vital also was the ability of France's much-maligned reservists to make a difficult withdrawal without breaking order.

Equally important was Joffre's rapid transfer of significant numbers of men from Lorraine. Just north of Paris near Amiens he organized a new army, the Sixth, commanded by General Michel Maunoury and composed largely of men brought from the eastern fortresses. It also was forced to retreat and soon came under the authority of General Joseph Galliéni, since 28 August military governor of Paris and designated successor to Joffre if the latter were killed or incapacitated.

The Germans now made their last, fatal, diversion from the Schlieffen Plan. By 28 August Kluck's forces were north and east of Paris and lacked the strength for a sweep west of the city. Kluck was convinced that the BEF had been destroyed and that the French Fifth Army was the Allied left flank. He wanted to wheel inward and push Fifth Army away from Paris. Bülow, whose Second Army had been badly mauled in a counterattack by Lanrezac's Fifth Army, appealed for help and this gave Kluck the excuse he needed. On 30 August, without first getting Moltke's permission, he changed direction so that his First Army would pass northeast of Paris, not west as originally planned. Kluck's goal was to catch the French centre and right armies from the rear. On 2 September Kluck made another fateful decision. On his own authority he ordered First Army to pursue the French southeast of Paris. Soon a gaping hole developed between his right flank and that of the Reserve Corps following him and screening that flank.

Aircraft monitoring enemy movements now proved their worth. On 3 September a French aviator confirmed enemy columns "gliding from west to east" toward the Ourcq valley. French cavalry patrols and documents found on a dead German officer subsequently verified the change of direction. In sharp contrast to excellent Allied intelligence the Germans were largely unaware of their opponents' actions.

First Army, advancing down the Ourcq valley and the corridor between Meaux and Chateau-Thierry on the Marne, would be vulnerable to a thrust from Paris by Galliéni's forces. Galliéni at once saw the possibilities and pressed Joffre for permission to launch an immediate counterattack, despite the fact that Sixth Army was designated specifically to defend Paris.[37]

Gloom and defeatism held sway in Paris. The government fled to Bordeaux in the south and half a million Parisians also left. Word was also received of a catastrophic Russian defeat at Tannenberg. The only positive development for the Allies was an agreement on 5 September whereby France, Great Britain, and Russia transformed their entente into an alliance. In the Pact of London each country declared it would not sign a separate peace. Japan adhered to the treaty on 19 October.

Battle of the Marne

But armies alone would decide whether the alliance survived, and in early September that appeared unlikely. By 4 September five German armies pressed along a line that sagged below the Marne River, but these forces, thinned by men left behind in Belgium or siphoned off for service on the Eastern Front, were far weaker than those envisioned by Schlieffen. Along the Marne the Allies actually enjoyed a slight numerical advantage.

Galliéni wanted a counterattack along the entire front. Field Marshal French, however, discouraged by developments, was actually contemplating a retreat back on the Channel ports. Galliéni went to French's headquarters to plead his case but only saw French's chief of staff, who declined to commit his chief. Galliéni then returned to Paris, where he won approval from Joffre for an attack by Sixth Army north of the Marne. Joffre himself went to French's headquarters and secured British support.[38]

Meanwhile Kluck, believing that the French and British were still in retreat and as yet unaware of the French Sixth Army's presence, continued to press his advance and disregarded an order from Moltke to protect Bülow's right flank, which he knew would halt his advance for two days. Battle was joined on the afternoon of 5 September when Sixth Army's advance guard clashed with part of Kluck's First Army on the Ourcq River north of Meaux. The Battle of the Marne, 6–12 September, was one of history's most decisive battles. Ranging from Belfort to north of Paris it involved more than two million men.

On the night of the 5th, Joffre ordered all the Allied left-wing armies to turn and launch full-scale attacks on the Germans. His order, read to the men at first light on the 6th, was as follows:

> Now, as the battle is joined on which the safety of the country depends, everyone must be reminded that this is no longer the time for looking back. Every effort must be made to attack and throw back the enemy. A unit which finds it impossible to advance must, regardless of cost, hold its ground and be killed on the spot rather than fall back. In the present circumstances, no failure will be tolerated.[39]

Kluck, with his army now split and facing south on the Marne River and west on the Ourcq, finally became aware of his grave situation. He ordered the rest of his army north to the Ourcq and turned to deal with Sixth Army. During 7–9 September he forced the French onto the defensive.[40]

With Maunoury's Army fighting desperately to hold, Galliéni commandeered some six hundred Paris taxicabs to transport 6,000 men 30 miles to the front in what historian Barbara Tuchman called "the last gallantry of 1914, the last crusade of the old world".[41] Although the actual impact of these reinforcements does not match the post-event mythology, the event symbolized the linkage between Paris and the battle 30 miles away.[42]

When Kluck manoeuvred on 7 September to meet Maunoury's threat a gap of some thirty miles opened between his army and Bülow's. Into this gap moved 20,000 men of the BEF, along with elements of Franchet d'Espèrey's Fifth Army. The next day Moltke at German headquarters in Luxembourg sent a trusted young staff officer, Lieutenant Colonel Richard Hentsch, to visit commanders in the field and assess the situation. He instructed Hentsch that, if he discovered that the BEF had crossed the Marne and was moving into the gap between First and Second Armies, he was to order Bülow back to the Aisne River. Hentsch had sweeping powers to make whatever adjustments seemed appropriate. It is a compliment to the German staff system that so junior an officer could have such authority. On 9 September, after Hentsch had reviewed the situation with a deeply pessimistic Bülow and other commanders, he concurred with Bülow's decision to order Second Army to withdraw to the Aisne. Kluck's position was now untenable and he too had to withdraw to the Aisne.[43]

By 9 September the Germans had fallen back all along the front. Although Germany never published her losses in the First Battle of the Marne, she lost at least 15,000 prisoners and 36 guns. The British sustained 1,700 casualties and the French around 80,000.

The tragedy of the Marne from the French point of view was that Joffre was unable to exploit his victory. The Germans retreated in good order; French troops were always too few and too late. Nevertheless, what the French soon called the "Miracle of the Marne" upset the Schlieffen Plan and changed the course of history by denying Germany the quick victory she needed to win the war.

The Germans halted along the Aisne. They had an excellent natural barrier in the Chemin des Dames, a ridge four miles north of the river and running parallel to it. On 13 September all three corps of the BEF (III Corps had been constituted on 30 August) and French Fifth Army got across the Aisne but a German reserve corps managed to seal off the Allied penetration the next day. The chance for a breakthrough had been lost.

Moltke's health and nerves were shattered and, in any case, failure at the Marne made his replacement inevitable. On 14 September the Kaiser named Minister of War General Erich von Falkenhayn to take over direction of German military operations. Moltke continued in his post in name only until 3 November when Falkenhayn formally succeeded him as chief of the German General Staff.

"Race to the sea"

From mid-September the battles on the Western Front extended northward. Both sides engaged in attacks and counterattacks in an effort to turn the other's flank. In the process, they extended their fronts from the Aisne to the coast. Falkenhayn massed strength on the right flank in a belated effort to capture Channel ports that the Germans might have had earlier at little cost.[44] These actions are known collectively as the "race to the sea".

First Battle of the Aisne

In mid-September, meanwhile, the Allies initiated what became known as the First Battle of the Aisne (15–18 September). Attempting to envelop their enemy's right flank, they were rebuffed by the Germans fighting from hastily constructed field fortifications. Heavy, inconclusive, fighting also occurred in Picardy during 11–26 September. Farther south, during 22–25 September, the French repulsed repeated German attacks against Verdun, although the Germans did manage to punch a salient into the French lines south of Verdun at St-Mihiel, which they held until September 1918.

The Allies also made both a key personnel move and a change of frontal responsibility. During the Battle of the Marne General Ferdinand Foch's Ninth Army had held a crucial sector of the front against repeated German attacks. Foch demonstrated the importance of counterattacks to defensive operations and gained a reputation for both optimism and determination under pressure. While it is legend that during the battle he reported: "My right is driven in; my centre is giving way, the situation is excellent, I shall attack",[45] it nonetheless summed up his fighting qualities. On 4 October Joffre appointed Foch the French Army deputy commander-in-chief and gave him the task of coordinating operations of the northern wing. This did not give Foch direct power over the BEF, but he did secure British cooperation.[46]

The change in frontal responsibility came at the request of Field Marshal French. In order to shorten supply lines to Britain he wanted to shift the BEF from the Aisne to Flanders and resume position of the extreme left of the Allied line, and Joffre agreed. On 1 October the BEF began to relocate to Flanders, the region with which it would be closely identified for the rest of the war.[47]

Siege of Antwerp

The Belgian Army, meanwhile, was trying to hold the port of Antwerp, now reinforced, on the insistence of Kitchener and First Lord of the Admiralty Winston Churchill, by three British Royal Marine brigades.

Allied forces there tied down German troops and heavy artillery that might have participated in the fighting in France. Falkenhayn had to take Antwerp not only to prevent a possible Allied assault on the flank of units trying to secure the Channel ports but to free German resources there.

Antwerp came under bombardment by Austrian and German siege howitzers on 28 September, two of its outer ring of forts suffering magazine explosions. The city surrendered on 10 October. Two of the three Royal Marine brigades escaped, as did most of what remained of the Belgian Army. The British intervention helped delay the fall of Antwerp for up to five days, purchasing time for the BEF to establish itself in Flanders.[48]

Battle of the Yser

King Albert I brought his army out along the coast to positions behind the Yser River. In the 18 October–30 November Battle of the Yser, the five divisions of the Belgian Army and French forces supported by British and French naval gunfire fought off German attacks. They accomplished this through hard fighting and ingenuity. On 25 October, on Albert's order, they opened the sluice gates at Nieuport to flood the countryside. The slowly rising waters on 30 October forced the Germans to retire behind the Yser to avoid being trapped by flooding behind them.[49] The flooding made inevitable the Battle of Ypres, as it forced the Germans to shift their northern efforts from the coast southward there.

Belgian and British troops continued to hold a small 10×25-mile sector in northwestern Belgium for the rest of the war. It included La Panne, Furnes, and Ypres. Albert set up his headquarters at La Panne and remained there for the duration.

First Battle of Ypres

The final action of the "race to the sea" took place in farm country around Ypres, the only place remaining where each army might outflank the other. The result was the bloody First Battle of Ypres (22 October–22 November).

As additional British and Indian troops arrived in France, the German numerical advantage in the West was fast disappearing. Ignoring General Paul von Hindenburg's pleas for reinforcements on the Eastern Front, Falkenhayn deployed his five newly organized reserve corps on the Western Front in an effort to take the Channel ports. He now had available the heavy artillery released from the siege of Antwerp, but the soldiers in the new corps were largely 17- to 20-year-olds, whose patriotism could not compensate for a lack of training.

The extreme north of the Allied line was held by the Belgian Army. To its south was the French Eighth Army, the BEF, and then the French Tenth Army. The BEF had only recently redeployed from the Aisne. During the second week in October it held a line extending from a salient around Ypres south to La Bassée.

Neither General Joffre nor Field Marshal French anticipated the German thrust in Flanders. Outnumbering British forces at the point of attack 2 to 1, the Germans began their drive on 22 October. The fighting was soon desperate. Although accurate British rifle fire decimated the close ranks of the advancing German infantry, their superior numbers forced I Corps commander General Sir Douglas Haig to assemble men regardless of unit or assignment in order to halt several German breakthroughs.

Both sides brought up reinforcements, the BEF assisted by an Indian corps and French troops. In a 1 November night assault the Germans captured the important Messines Ridge on the south side of the salient. The following morning French troops bolstered the line, but Allied counterattacks failed to dislodge the Germans. Bad weather brought the battle to a close at the end of November.

The month of savage fighting at Ypres was particularly costly to the Germans. They called it the *Kindermord von Ypren* ("The Massacre of the Innocents at Ypres") for the 134,000 men, most of them young draftees, lost there.[50] British casualties were also heavy. The BEF suffered 58,000 casualties at Ypres, including many young professional officers and veteran NCOs. French losses were about 50,000 men; Belgian about 19,000. But the Channel ports, vital for British resupply, had been saved.

Stalemate and trench warfare

First Ypres ended the war of movement on the Western Front and began the struggle of stalemate. The front now extended for some 350 miles without interruption from the Channel to the Swiss border. As the theatre of fighting shifted to the east, both sides improved their defences – extending trench lines, deepening rifle pits, constructing dugouts, and laying miles of barbed wire.

Trench construction grew more sophisticated and, as time went on, temporary positions took on an air of permanence. Originally the trenches consisted of a ditch or, if that was not possible (because of a high water table as in Flanders), of a raised breastwork of sandbags and wood six to seven feet above ground, with defensive walls up to twenty feet thick.

"Dug-outs" or caves were cut into the walls of the trenches but most soldiers had to make do at night with a waterproof sheet and a small sleeping area carved out of the side of the trench. Earthen buttresses or "traverses" built at regular intervals in the trenches prevented enfilading fire. The troops also constructed support and communication trenches, and they laid belts of barbed wire in the area separating their trench from that of the enemy. This area, which varied between 90 and 2,400 feet, was known as "No Man's Land".[51]

German defensive works on the Western Front were always more sophisticated than those of the Allies. This was in part because of the German decision to assume the strategic defensive in the West. The French and their allies, on the other hand, did not intend their positions to be permanent. As the war lengthened, the Germans constructed deep defensive belts of obstacles, wire, and minefields. They also installed concrete pillboxes for machine guns and prepared immense dugouts up to 40 feet below ground to protect whole platoons and companies when not on the front line or preparing for an assault. Some of these even had electricity.[52]

The same reasoning that led Allied commanders not to give undue attention to their trench lines also led them to the mistaken decision to defend all territory regardless of terrain, fields of fire, or vulnerability to attack. Joffre and French also insisted on holding all recaptured terrain. If lost, it had to be regained at all costs. The Germans were much more flexible in their defensive tactics, experimenting with such tactical innovations as the flexible defence and reverse-slope defence.[53]

Conditions in the trenches, worse in bad weather, were generally hellish, a fact of which the generals were too often unaware or insensitive to. Exposed to both frostbite and "trench foot", the men had to fend off lice and rats and endure shelling, grenades, snipers, patrols, wire-laying, and occasional trench raids. They also had to be ready for gas attacks.

Artillery fire became increasingly important. Installed in prepared emplacements to the rear, the big guns were carefully registered by firing them against known enemy positions. Once this was accomplished, new targets were located by spotters in balloons or aircraft, or by ground observers. (As aircraft proved their worth for observation purposes, it became necessary for the other side to shoot them down, and pursuit, or "fighter" aircraft were born.) Artillery changed from light guns useful in open mobile warfare to trench mortars, howitzers, and heavy siege guns capable of long-range fire against the reinforced obstacles that now appeared along the front. Shrapnel, useful only against troops and horses in the open, was largely ineffective against entrenchments, and every effort was made to produce more high-explosive rounds. Ammunition demands vastly exceeded pre-war estimates, and both sides experienced shortages of projectiles. They also maintained large numbers of the largely useless horse cavalry in order to exploit possible breakthroughs.

Thanks largely to artillery, the machine gun, and barbed wire, from the end of 1914 until early 1918 there was no change of more than ten miles in the front lines on the Western Front. The sole exception was the 1917 voluntary German withdrawal in the Noyon salient. Until 1918 defenders were always able to plug breaks in the line by rushing reinforcements to the threatened point.

New German commander General Erich von Falkenhayn believed that the war could be won only on the Western Front, and he dismissed Hindenburg's and Erich Ludendorff's suggestions that the Eastern Front receive priority. But he knew that the only opportunity for manoeuvre warfare lay in the east where H–L (Hindenburg and Ludendorff) had registered brilliant successes. By December Falkenhayn shifted some resources there to support a limited offensive to protect Silesia and Austro-Hungarian forces. He did this "reluctantly and meagerly; enough to secure success, but never in sufficient quantity or time for decisive victory".[54]

Joffre, meanwhile, pressed the offensive, convinced that with adequate artillery support his armies could break through the German lines. He targeted the Noyon salient between Arras and Reims, pointing toward Paris. Joffre's strategy, essentially that which the Allies successfully employed in the second half of 1918, was to strike both sides of a salient. A thrust from the Artois plateau against its western side would push the Germans across the Douai plain and threaten the major German railroad line to their forces in northern France; an advance northward from Champagne would cut the rail lines supplying the German centre armies. Once successful these would be followed by a third push from the Verdun–Nancy area, in which the French right-wing armies might take the war into Germany in a modified version of Plan XVII. At the very least Joffre believed these attacks would provide the Russians needed relief. They did not succeed in 1915, however, because of inadequate resources and poor execution.

First Battle of Artois

On 8 December Joffre issued orders for simultaneous offensives by General Louis Maud'huy's Tenth Army in Artois in the vicinity of Arras and General Ferdinand de Langle de Cary's Fourth Army in Champagne in the vicinity of Reims. In order to divert the Germans from his real intention, Joffre planned a series of Belgian, British, and French secondary thrusts at various points from the North Sea coast to the Vosges Mountains.[55] From 14 to 24 December the Allies attacked from Nieuport to Verdun. Logistical problems prevented the simultaneous attack Joffre sought. Winter weather and inadequate roads in Champagne delayed Fourth Army's assault.

The attack in Artois began on 17 December when Tenth Army struck units of Crown Prince Rupprecht's Sixth Army on Vimy Ridge, a dominating geographic feature. The attackers were plagued by a lack of heavy artillery, heavy rains, and fog. Although General Henri Philippe Pétain's XXXIII Corps captured a portion of the German front line, the overall assault failed. To the north, Belgian, French, and British diversionary attacks around Ypres also met with little success. By Christmas Day stiff German resistance and poor weather led French commanders to restrict operations in Artois to besieging the German-held village of Carency. French attacks continued until 4 January, when Joffre allowed Maud'huy to suspend the Artois offensive until Tenth Army could lay new plans, stockpile supplies, and replace casualties.

First Battle of Champagne

The Champagne offensive began on 20 December. In what was later known as the First Battle of Champagne (20 December–17 March) Langle de Cary's Fourth Army struck between the Suippe River (a small tributary of the Aisne) and the Argonne Forest. Initially the French made progress against divisions of General Karl von Einem's Third Army. Hopeful of exploiting these slight gains, on Christmas Day General Langle de Cary committed a fresh corps between the other two, but the three, advancing on a very narrow front, quickly became entangled. The attack, hampered by fog, defective artillery shells, and German counterattacks, faltered, as did a renewed effort on 30 December. The second phase of the offensive began on 16 February and lasted until 17 March.[56]

Five months of war on the Western Front in 1914 cost the Germans 667,000 men, the Belgians around 50,000, the French 995,000, and the British 96,000. The British were especially hard-hit; their old professional army virtually ceased to exist. At the end of December the BEF reorganized into two armies – the First commanded by Haig, and the Second by Smith-Dorrien. Until a large volunteer army could be trained Britain relied on Empire troops – Indian Gurkhas, Sikhs, and Muslims – and the Territorials. The latter were the American equivalent of the National Guard: volunteer part-time soldiers, for the most part poorly trained. They took the field as the old regular army was being consumed at Ypres and held it while the large British volunteer force of some 2.5 million men, dubbed "Kitchener's Army", was trained.[57]

Hopes on each side for a quick, decisive victory in the war now lay in ruins. Entrenching tools, machine guns, and barbed wire had transformed the fighting in the West. The war of manoeuvre became one of stalemate and attrition.

Eastern Front

Simultaneously with the German invasion of Belgium and France, fighting had begun in the East where the front ran north–south from the East Prussian marshes to the Carpathian Mountains. In contrast to the Western Front, partly because of the length of the lines there, the Eastern Front was quite fluid.

French and Russian military planning was based on the war being decided within six weeks and Germany deploying the vast bulk of her military strength west. Both powers agreed that Russia would have to strike fast and hard in order to divert German strength east.[58] In July 1912 the two general staffs had agreed that in the first weeks of a war each would launch a massive offensive against Germany. Russia promised to do this on the twelfth day of her mobilization. She also agreed to push construction of her strategic rail net.[59] The Russians continued to stress their need for more time to mobilize, and in 1913 the two allies agreed that Russia would move as soon as possible 15 days after mobilization began.[60] This was perilous for Russia, the least sophisticated logistically of the principal antagonists.

There has been speculation that the rapid Russian offensive actions were evidence of their self-sacrifice, but in reality they reflected only common sense.[61] An immediate Russian invasion of east Prussia nonetheless carried substantial risk for Russia. Even though Russian infantry and cavalry units were nearing full strength and outnumbered the Germans in east Prussia by almost three to one, the Russians lacked logistical support – a sharp contrast to the Germans and the Austro-Hungarians.

General Yakov Zhilinsky, commander of the Northwest Front Group, had at his disposal two large armies: First Army, commanded by General Pavel K. Rennenkampf, an undistinguished cavalry officer who had seen service against the Japanese in 1904; and Second Army, commanded by General Aleksandr V. Samsonov, an aged officer who had found it difficult to lead even a division in the Russo-Japanese war. Each of their armies contained five corps totalling some 300,000 men, but many of the men did not have rifles and others lacked boots.[62] East Prussia, however, seemed vulnerable to invasion from both the east and the south.

The German strategic plan in the East assumed a slow Russian mobilization delayed further by the poorly developed Polish road network. The badly outnumbered German Eighth Army in East Prussia consisted largely of garrison troops and reserve units numbering only 13 divisions. Its commander, General Maximilian von Prittwitz und Gaffron, was obese to the point of near immobility. As with most of his Russian counterparts, he was incompetent. Fortunately for the Germans his deputy chief of staff, Colonel Max Hoffmann was an officer of great ability. Although at the time he received little credit for it, Hoffmann formulated the plan for the resultant German victory.

Prittwitz's orders called for him to defend East Prussia in the unlikely event of a Russian attack. If that proved impossible, he was to retreat to the Vistula River, where a permanent defence line could be held until help arrived from the West. In other words the worst-case scenario had the German High Command (OHL or *Oberste Heeresleitung*) temporarily ceding to the enemy much of East Prussia.

At dawn on 17 August the northern arm of the two Russian pincers, Rennenkampf's First Army (6.5 infantry and five cavalry divisions), began crossing the East Prussian border on a 35-mile front. Its objective was the fortified city of Königsberg to the west. On 19 August Samsonov's Second Army to the south also attacked. It was to keep pace with First Army and make its way around the heavily wooded Masurian Lakes region in the direction of Danzig. The two armies would join at Allenstein. Once the German defenders had been destroyed in the ring, the united Russian forces could drive into the heart of Germany toward Berlin. The Germans had known the outline of the Russian plan as early as 1910.[63]

Russian hopes for success in this offensive, however, were hampered by the fact that her two invading armies were, largely because of the Masurian Lakes, too widely separated to be mutually supporting. In any case, chance of the two armies cooperating seemed remote since Rennenkampf and Samsonov were bitter enemies. Russian blunders, geography, and superior German leadership all played a part in the outcome.

The first fighting occurred on the afternoon of 17 August just inside the frontier when units of the German I Corps under General Hermann von François blocked the Russian advance. François deliberately disobeyed Prittwitz's instructions to retire to Gumbinnen, where the Germans had established a preliminary defensive line, and rashly attacked three Russian corps at Stallupönen. While inconclusive, the Battle of Stallupönen heightened Rennenkampf's sense of caution.

During the fighting the Germans had an advantage in intelligence gathering. Not only did they receive information via aircraft reconnaissance, which the Russians lacked, but they were also able to intercept Russian radio communications. The poor training and illiteracy of Russian radio operators precluded their mastering codes, and there was insufficient wire. As a result, Russian Army communications were broadcast by radio "in the clear". The Germans knew Stavka's plans as soon as the Russian field commanders.[64]

On the 19th Rennenkampf halted his advance to restore order and allow Samsonov to catch up. At the same time there was growing dissension at German headquarters between Prittwitz, who was showing signs of panic, and Colonel Hoffmann, who recognized Russia's weaknesses and urged offensive action. Prittwitz gave way to François and Hoffmann and authorized an attack against Rennenkampf, which took place on 20 August at Gumbinnen. Despite initial German success, the Russians held. Perceived as a Russian victory, the battle nonetheless revealed major Russian weaknesses in leadership and logistics.

Prittwitz, faced with the decision of either resuming the attack the next day or withdrawing, learned that Samsonov's forces had invaded from the south and were advancing west of the Masurian Lakes. Conflicting intelligence reports led him to believe that a third Russian army had invaded as well. Sensing impending disaster, he ordered a retreat to the Vistula. He also informed German Army headquarters at Coblenz that he might not be able to hold even there.[65]

Battle of Tannenberg

Hoffmann understood that Rennenkampf's army was in disarray and posed no threat and he thought it feasible to turn the entire German force against Samsonov in the south. Ignoring Prittwitz, Hoffmann and chief of staff General Ernest Grünert drew up a plan to take advantage of their interior lines and superior railroad network. This plan, to which Prittwitz consented, became known later as the "Tannenberg Manoeuvre", a classic example of the military principles of mass, surprise, and economy of force combined.[66] It involved sending the bulk of German forces opposing Rennenkampf south to encircle and destroy Samsonov's army before Rennenkampf became aware of what was happening and reacted. If successful against the Russian Second Army, German forces could then reconcentrate in the Insterburg Gap and destroy the Russian First Army.

The final act preliminary to the main battle came from German Army headquarters. Unaware of Prittwitz's change of heart, Moltke sacked both him and Grünert. Eighth Army's new commander was 68-year-old General Paul von Beckendorff und Hindenburg, a Prussian Junker recalled from retirement. General Erich Ludendorff, famous for his role in the capture of Liège, became Hindenburg's chief of staff. The two men, who worked in harmony throughout the war, became known as "the Duo" or simply H–L, although the duo was actually a trio, since Hoffmann played a key role. Their staff called them *das Hünentrio* (the Three Giants).[67]

Hindenburg and Ludendorff drew up a plan nearly identical to that already devised by Hoffmann. Ultimately three German corps – I (François), XVII (General August von Mackensen), and I Reserve (General Otto von Below) – comprising the bulk of German forces in East Prussia, were entrained and moved south to join XX corps (General Friedrich von Scholtz) already in position near the southern border. The plan was extraordinarily daring; it left only a single cavalry division in the north to keep watch on Rennenkampf. Had he moved his army west and then south there would have been nothing to prevent it taking Eighth Army from the rear. If he had simply moved the two combined Russian armies south, they would have greatly outnumbered the German Eighth Army. But Rennenkampf sat in place.

The resultant Battle of Tannenberg, fought between 26–31 August, was named after one of the towns in the area to reverse a 1410 defeat of the Teutonic Knights at the hands of Polish and Ukrainian forces.

Russian front commander General Yakov Zhilinsky, whose headquarters was well behind the lines, was unaware of German intentions. He blithely assumed that Rennenkampf and Samsonov were coordinating their movements when, in actuality, the two armies had lost contact with each other. Zhilinsky repeatedly urged Samsonov to drive to the Vistula and close the pincers around the Germans. Samsonov replied that his troops had no rations and were near exhaustion. Samsonov also assumed that Rennenkampf protected his northern flank.[68]

The opposing forces came into contact on 23 August. The Germans outnumbered Samsonov's Second Army by 180 battalions to 150; Second Army was also dangerously spread out over a 60-mile front with its two wings separated from its centre. The main German attack opened on 26 August when Mackensen's and Below's corps attacked Samsonov's exposed northern flank. François' corps then struck from the south. By the 28th the Germans had turned both Russian flanks, dooming Second Army.

The ever-cautious Moltke, apprehensive about the battle's outcome, offered reinforcements from the Western Front. Ludendorff protested that reinforcements were not needed, correctly pointing out that in any case they would arrive too late. Moltke insisted, and on 25 August withdrew three corps from the critical German right wing and sent them east, inadvertently helping to save France.[69]

Rennenkampf, meanwhile, was totally oblivious to what was happening to the south. Zhilinsky, who read Samsonov's dispatches, suspected the worst and repeatedly urged Rennenkampf to attack the Germans from the north, but to no avail. Rennenkampf continued to inch forward, oblivious to the fact that only a light cavalry screen opposed him.

On the 29th Samsonov ordered his two central corps to retreat through the woods to the Russian frontier, but it was too late. Only one 15-mile wide escape corridor along the Omulev River remained open. The three Russian corps in the centre were literally destroyed by German artillery. On the afternoon of 30 August a despondent Samsonov committed suicide. Exhausted and starving his men surrendered by the thousands. On the night of 30/31 August some Russian units, without food or water for several days, tried repeatedly to break out but, illuminated by searchlights, were mowed down by machine gun and artillery fire.[70] The battle of Tannenberg was a Russian disaster. They sustained 122,000 casualties, including some 90,000 prisoners, and lost 500 guns. German losses were between 10,000 and 15,000.

First Battle of the Masurian Lakes

The German Eighth Army, now significantly reinforced by Moltke's Western Front additions, wheeled north to re-engage the Russian First Army. Although the Russians still held a numerical advantage this was offset by the psychological lift the Germans gained at Tannenberg and their knowledge of Russian plans through radio intercepts. For the Germans the one moderating factor was that the Austrians had suffered alarming reverses in Galicia and Serbia. Conrad was pleading for reinforcements, which OHL for the moment refused. Hindenburg was more concerned about his own front.

Rennenkampf dug in, taking advantage of natural obstacles in rivers and the Masurian Lakes. H–L's plan called for a wide envelopment of the Russian Army's southern flank while frontal holding attacks pinned First Army in place. Yet H–L assigned the bulk of their forces to the holding attacks. The I and XVII Corps under François and Mackensen, the two most aggressive German commanders, carried out the envelopment.

What is known as the First Battle of the Masurian Lakes opened on

7 September, the fighting becoming general two days latter. François' I Corps, which had played a leading role at Tannenberg, was again critical to the outcome, forcing back the Russian left flank. But Rennenkampf disengaged under cover of a two-division counterattack, thereby preventing an envelopment. On 13 September his forces regained the Russian border.[71] In this battle alone the Russians lost 100,000 men killed and wounded, 45,000 prisoners, and 150 guns. German casualties were around 70,000.

Although Zhilinsky was sacked Rennenkampf retained his command. The Russians could easily replace the men lost, but it would be a long time before they could replace trained officers and non-commissioned officers. Russian victories against the Austrians disguised the immediate impact of the disaster, although Allied confidence in Russia was badly shaken. On the German side there was renewed hope and confidence in victory and the Hindenburg myth had begun.

Operations in Poland

While the Germans were smashing their two northern armies the Russians had met with success against the Austrians. When the war began Conrad opted to dispatch two armies, plus his second-echelon Second Army, across the Danube and Sava rivers to finish off Serbia; his remaining three armies would be employed in operations against Russian Poland. However, the surprising success of the Serbs in repulsing the Austrian invasion, the unexpectedly rapid Russian invasion of East Prussia, the Russian concentration of large numbers of troops along the Galician frontier, and the quiescence of Italy and Romania all led Conrad to change his plans. Motivated by the need to recoup the Dual Monarchy's military prestige after the rebuff by the Serbs, the desire to secure additional defensive terrain and manoeuvring room north of the Carpathian Mountains, and the need to demonstrate solidarity with his German ally, Conrad decided to transfer Second Army from the Serbian front to reinforce Galicia. Conrad also hoped to draw Russian strength away from East Prussia, relieving pressure on the German Eighth Army and, perhaps, enabling it to hold East Prussia by itself, enhancing German chances of success on the Western Front. Also the longer he waited to strike, the greater would grow the numerical disadvantage between his forces and those of the Russians.

The fighting in Galicia began as a large general engagement along the frontier. The Austrians had about one million men, the Russians some 1,200,000. Russian Southwestern Front commander General Nikolai Ivanov, expecting the Austrians to attack due east from the fortress of Lemberg, had positioned Nikolas Ruzski's Third and Aleksei Brusilov's Eighth Armies to defend in depth between Dubno and Proskurov. Meanwhile Baron Salza's Fourth and Pavel Plehve's Fifth Armies would strike south from Poland, cutting the Austrians off from Cracow and taking the enemy fortresses of Lemberg and Przemyśl. Ivanov's reunited forces would then clear the Carpathian passes for an advance on Budapest and Vienna. Unfortunately for his plans, the Austrians did not follow the expected scenario.

Conrad ordered General Viktor Dankl's First Army to advance to Lublin to cut the Warsaw–Kiev railroad, secure control of the road to Brest-Litovsk, and threaten Russian positions east of Warsaw. General Moritz von Auffenberg-Komarów's Fourth Army was to the right of First Army; to its right was General Brudermann's Third Army. Left-flank security was provided by Baron Heinrich Kummer von Falkenfeld's Army Group. Baron Hermann Kövess von Kövessháza's Army Group provided right-flank security.

The Austrian attack, launched on 23 August, collided at once with Ivanov's advancing Fourth and Fifth Armies. Neither side was doing what the other expected. As the fighting evolved the Austrians made limited gains to the northeast while the Russians advanced to the south. Full battle was finally joined in the vicinity of Lemberg (Lvov), the major city of eastern Galicia.

Fought between 23 and 24 August, the Battle of Kraśnik, as well as the 26 August–1 September Battle of Zamosc-Komarów, were Austrian victories. In the first case Dankl's Austrian First Army rebuffed Salza's Russian Fourth Army; in the second, Auffenberg's Austrian Fourth Army did the same to Plehve's Russian Fifth Army.

On the southern part of the front, however, things went differently. On 26 August Ivanov advanced his left wing, precipitating the Battle of Gnila Lipa. By the 30th Ruzsky's Russian Third and Aleksei Brusilov's Russian Eighth Armies had defeated the Austrian Kövess Group and Third Army so thoroughly that, despite a two-day Russian halt necessitated by poor roads and the need to reform, the Austrians were unable to regroup.

Ivanov threw Plehve's Russian Fifth Army back into the fray north of Lemberg. The Austrians, who had assumed that Plehve had been defeated, were caught off guard shifting forces to the south and were forced to retreat. The Austrians in the north were defeated yet again at Rava-Ruska between 3 and 11 September. Although the Austrian Second Army, transferred from Serbia to Galicia by the end of August, now went into action, it too was forced back.

The entire Austrian front now collapsed. Suffering the loss of some 130,000 men, Conrad abandoned Lemberg. The Russians pushed the Austrians back more than 100 miles to the Carpathian Mountain passes. While the withdrawal was for the most part orderly, many Slavs in the Austro-Hungarian Army surrendered and offered to switch sides. In late September the Russians trapped more than 100,000 enemy soldiers in the great fortress of Przemyśl, although it held out until 22 March 1915.

The extent of the Austrian defeat was staggering. Of the million men with whom the Austrians had begun the offensive, at least 300,000 were lost, including 100,000 prisoners and 300 guns. The Austro-Hungarian Army never recovered from the blow. Austrian morale was at a nadir, her armies having been defeated by both the Serbians and Russians. Furthermore, the Russians now held most of Galicia and were poised for further strikes into Silesia and Hungary. Had their pursuit been more determined they might have secured the crucial passes to the interior of Austria and Hungary. But Russia had also suffered heavily, losing some 255,000 men (45,000 of them POWs) and 182 guns.[72]

The Austro-Hungarian defeat in Galicia posed a major problem for the Germans because Silesia, one of Germany's main industrial centres, stood in danger of being outflanked from the south. Also Russian Army commander Grand Duke Nicholas Nikolaevich had done much to rebuild the Russian Army.

By the end of September both sides were busy preparing new offensives. Hindenburg requested reinforcements from Falkenhayn, but the latter, then mounting his own drive on the Channel ports, had none to spare. Hindenburg then withdrew four of the six German corps in East Prussia and formed them into the new Ninth Army. Again utilizing their superb railroad net, the Germans shifted by train within 11 days Ninth Army's more than 220,000 men, horses, artillery, and equipment over 450 miles south to the vicinity of the Polish city of Czestochowa. Here they linked up with the Austrian First Army in order to protect Silesia. Hindenburg and Ludendorff took direct command of Ninth Army while retaining operational control of the Eighth.

Stavka was divided over its next objective. Grand Duke Nicholas favoured another offensive into East Prussia; General Ivanov, along with Chief of Staff General Mikhail Alekseev, argued for Silesia, where the possibility existed of forcing Austria from the war. In the end Nicholas compromised by detaching the Russian Ninth Army from the northern force in order to attack Cracow. This left only General Sievers' Tenth Army and General Rennenkampf's First Army for a northern offensive.

On 29 September the German Ninth Army (Mackensen) opened its Polish offensive. The Germans had reached the Vistula River by 9 October but then slowed because of inferior numbers, supply problems, exhaustion, and unfamiliarity with the terrain.[73] Despite knowledge from a captured Russian order that Stavka was planning to invade Silesia, Hindenburg continued Mackensen's attack. The Germans got to within 12 miles of Warsaw before Hindenburg finally ordered a withdrawal on 17 October. By 1 November Ninth Army was back at its starting point and Hindenburg was faced with the prospect of an invasion of Silesia by four Russian Armies.

Hindenburg, on 1 November designated commander-in-chief of the Eastern Front, continued to benefit from intercepts of uncoded Russian radio messages. On 3 November, privy to Russian plans, he made his decision. Based on a plan developed by Hoffmann he sought to replicate Tannenberg. Between 4 and 10 November Mackensen's entire Ninth Army was again moved, this time 250 miles north from Czestochowa to Torun at the northern tip of the Polish salient. There it was in position to strike the Russian's right flank if they invaded Silesia. Conrad, acting in concert, moved the Austrian Second Army north from the Carpathians into Mackensen's former positions.

On 11 November Below's German Ninth Army attacked the hinge between the Russian First and Second Armies. Oblivious to the German presence, the Russians began their Silesian offensive. Mackensen's troops, therefore, caught Rennenkampf's First Army on its northern flank as it was moving to its staging areas, capturing 12,000 prisoners and 15 guns in the first two days. This led Stavka to relieve Rennenkampf of his command and replace him with General Litvinov. The Germans, meanwhile, smashed into the flank of Scheidemann's Russian Second Army.

In the ensuing Battles of Lódz and Lowicz (16–25 November) it was again Russian manpower against German firepower as the Russian Second Army sought to extricate itself. It was saved only by hard fighting and the arrival of Plehve's Russian Fifth Army, which made a forced march north to its rescue. Both Russian armies now quickly fell back on their supply centre at Lódz. When the pursuing Germans arrived there they found seven Russian corps on the town's perimeter and were surprised by the Russian Fifth Army's attack. Briefly the Russians were in position to envelop the Germans but were unable to exploit the opportunity.

Fighting continued until early December. On the 6th the Russians evacuated Lódz and retreated to the Bzura-Rawka River line before Warsaw. While the Battle of Lódz could be counted a Russian tactical victory, strategically it went to the Germans because the Russians called off their Silesian offensive. It would not be renewed.[74]

German losses in the campaign totalled approximately 35,000; Russian casualties approached 95,000, including 25,000 POWs and 79 guns. It resulted in a widespread perception that the Russian Army was no match for the Germans.

Serbia invaded

Fierce combat also occurred in Serbia.[75] In August 1914 Serbia, with only five million people, seemed at an immense disadvantage. Austro-Hungarian forces outnumbered Field Marshal Radomír Putnik's 200,000-man Serbian Army (three armies totalling 12 divisions) three to one. The only immediate help for Serbia was Montenegro's 3 August declaration of war on her side. A major disadvantage for Serbia was the location of her capital, Belgrade, immediately across the Danube River from Austria-Hungary. The Austrian plan was to occupy swiftly both Belgrade and Valjevo, a key city of western Serbia, before the Serbian Army could be fully mobilized. On 29 July an Austrian Danube River flotilla began bombarding Belgrade.

The first hitch in Conrad's plans came when Russia entered the war, forcing him to implement Plan R by ordering the Austrian Second Army to Galicia. Nonetheless, to Austrian commander Oskar Potiorek, the conquest of Serbia seemed an easy matter. On 12 August General Frank's Fifth Army crossed the Sava River in the north while Potiorek's Sixth Army crossed the Drina from Bosnia in the west. Putnik shifted forces northeastward to meet them. The 16–25 August Battle of the Tser Mountains, involving a quarter of a million men on each side, ended in Austrian defeat. The Austrians then withdrew back across the Drina and Sava.

In early September the Serbs crossed the Sava into Serb-populated Syrmia, and on 10 September cut the railway between Hungary and Romania. Farther west, with Montenegrin support, the Serbs captured Višegrad, and in early October besieged Sarajevo. Serbian and Montenegrin forces under General Vaković decisively repulsed two Austrian relief attempts.

Despite their successes the Serbs, short of supplies and, especially, ammunition, were steadily pushed back. The Austrians concentrated on taking Belgrade but, despite a five-to-one local superiority, they were repelled in three attempts to outflank the city by crossing the Drina 50 miles west. On 10 November the Austrians switched their efforts east of Belgrade. Aided by river monitors, they gained a foothold on the Serbian side of the Danube, but a Serb counterattack forced them back.

The third Austrian attempt to take Belgrade was successful. On 5 November General Potiorek crossed the Sava with four divisions southwest of

Belgrade and advanced along the south bank. He took the deserted Serb capital on 2 December. The Serbian government had relocated south to Niš.

The fall of Belgrade was the low point in Serbia's 1914 fortunes. Death, disease, and desertion reduced her army to only 100,000 men, and ammunition was in short supply. Also, while Serbian attention was focused on defence of the capital, Austrian forces had taken Valjevo in northwest Serbia. Four months into the war, therefore, the Austrians had at last achieved their initial aims.

The Austrian advance continued in the general direction of Niš, but after French ammunition finally reached the Serbs through Salonika, Putnik's three Serb armies defeated the Austrians in the Battle of Rudnizk-Souvoba that lasted from 5–8 December and retook Valjevo. They defeated the Austrians yet again north of the city on 11 December. The Austrians now attempted an orderly withdrawal north to Belgrade and west to Višegrad and Sarajevo, but it turned into a rout. Near Belgrade whole units, caught against the Danube, abandoned their equipment and surrendered. On 15 December the Serbs retook Belgrade with King Peter and his sons riding at the head of their troops. By the end of the year no Austro-Hungarian soldiers remained on Serbian soil and the Serbs held a strip of enemy territory near Višegrad. Vienna dismissed Potiorek.[76]

Between August 12 and mid–December 1914 Austria-Hungary had lost 227,000 men (including POWs) and 179 guns in the Serbian campaign. Serbian losses were around 70,000 men (including 15,000 POWs) and 42 guns. The Serbs noted with some pride that they were the only victorious Allied power.

War at sea

Although in 1914 land engagements held centre stage, there were also fights at sea. Despite Germany's naval building programme, in August 1914 the Royal Navy held a considerable advantage over the German Navy in modern capital ships:[77]

	British	German
Dreadnoughts in service	22	15
Dreadnoughts under construction	13	5
Battle cruisers in service	9	5
Battle cruisers under construction	1	3

British superiority was even more pronounced in terms of other warships:

	British	German
Pre-dreadnoughts	40	22
Coast-defence ships	NA	8
Armoured cruisers	34	7
Protected cruisers	52	17
Scout cruisers	15	NA
Light cruisers	20	16
Destroyers	221	90
Torpedo boats	109	115
Submarines	73	31

For the British Grand Fleet and the German High Seas Fleet, the most important forces on each side most likely to come to blows at the beginning of the war, the numbers were as follows:

	Grand Fleet	High Seas Fleet
Dreadnoughts	21	13
Pre-dreadnoughts	8	8
Battle cruisers	4	3
Armoured cruisers	NA	1
Light cruisers	11	7
Destroyers	42	90

The Royal Navy was so spread over the world that its actual advantage in home waters was lessened. It could, however, count on the French, Russian, and Japanese navies, whereas Germany was assisted only by that of Austria-Hungary.

Battle of Heligoland Bight

These favourable circumstances, along with their own penchant for the offensive at sea, led the British to initiate the 28 August 1914, Battle of Heligoland Bight. Heligoland Island, located in the North Sea to the west of Schleswig-Holstein, guarded the anchorages of the German High Seas Fleet. It also protected the western entrance to the Kiel Canal, the important waterway that allowed German ships to move undisturbed between the North and Baltic Seas. The British sent two destroyer squadrons, along with some submarines, to the bight in the early morning hours of 28 August to attack the light German warships and depart before heavy German ships could arrive.

The action was timed to cover the transport of 3,000 Royal Marines to Ostend.

Although the entire operation was rife with confusion and lack of communication, it was successful. The British had one light cruiser and two destroyers badly damaged, but they sank three German light cruisers and one destroyer and damaged three other cruisers. The British lost 35 men killed, the Germans over 1,000. The battle's real significance lay in the fact that the Kaiser placed even greater restrictions on the High Seas Fleet's freedom of action.[78]

Other actions at sea

The Royal Navy had been actively engaged in capturing German merchant ships or driving them into neutral ports; 109 German ships, including the 54,000-ton *Vaterland*, were interned in US ports alone.[79] The British also hunted down isolated German warships and gradually cleared the seas of surface threats to Allied shipping, although the battle cruiser *Goeben* and light cruiser *Breslau* reached Constantinople (see Chapter 3). The light cruisers *Königsberg* and *Emden* also for a time eluded the British.

In August 1914 the *Königsberg* was the station ship at Dar-es-Salaam in German East Africa. After she carried out commerce raiding in the Indian Ocean, British warships blockaded her in the Rufiji River delta. In July 1915, after one of the most prolonged naval engagements in history, her crew scuttled her (see Chapter 7).

The *Emden* was by far the best known of German surface raiders. Commanded by Captain Karl von Müller, she was active in the Pacific Ocean. In a three-month rampage she bombarded Madras and sank or captured 23 merchant ships, a cruiser, and a destroyer. At one time or another the *Emden* tied down nearly 80 Allied warships. On 9 November, while raiding Direction Island in the Cocos (Keeling) group, the more powerful Australian cruiser *Sydney* intercepted her, forced her aground on a reef, and destroyed her.

Battle of Coronel

More spectacular were two naval battles off the coast of South America. The first of these, the Battle of Coronel, was fought on 1 November 1914, off

Chile between British Vice Admiral Sir Christopher Cradock's North American and West Indies Station Squadron and German Admiral Maximilian Graf von Spee's East Asia Squadron.

Spee had two heavy cruisers, the *Scharnhorst* and *Gneisenau*, and the three light cruisers, the *Nürnberg, Dresden,* and *Leipzig*. At the outbreak of the war he moved his squadron from Qingdao (Tsingtao) in China to Easter Island where, in mid-October, he learned that Cradock's force was nearby. Cradock had only four ships: the elderly heavy cruisers *Good Hope* (his flagship) and *Monmouth*, the light cruiser *Glasgow*, and the converted merchant ship auxiliary cruiser *Otranto*.

Cradock had requested significant reinforcement but Admiralty headquarters at Whitehall ordered out only the old battleship *Canopus* with four 12-inch guns. These were bigger than anything in Spee's squadron, but they were capable of only relatively short-range fire and were manned by reservists who had not conducted firing practice. Cradock warned that the *Canopus* would slow down his squadron speed to only 12 knots and thus it would be unlikely he could chase down Spee's 20-knot squadron.

The *Canopus* arrived at Port Stanley in the Falklands on 22 October. Cradock left her at this coaling and wireless station while he took the rest of his ships to search for what he assumed was a lone German ship, the *Leipzig*. At the same time Spee's ships were hunting the *Glasgow*, which Cradock had detached with orders that she later rendezvous with the rest of the squadron.

Late on the afternoon of 1 November the opposing forces met off the Chilean coast. Although the two sides were approximately equal in total firepower, the Germans had a clear advantage in long-range guns. Cradock had only the two 9.2-inchers of his flagship to oppose sixteen 8.2-inch guns on the *Scharnhorst* and *Gneisenau*. The Germans opened the battle near the extreme range of Cradock's guns and refused to close. Both the *Good Hope* and *Monmouth* went down: the former with 895 of its total complement of 900 men, including Cradock. None of the *Monmouth*'s 675-man complement survived. The *Glasgow* and damaged *Otranto* obeyed Cradock's order to escape and managed to get away.

Battle of the Falklands

The Battle of Coronel, the first major Royal Navy reverse at sea in a century, was a shock to the British. There was real concern that Spee would steam his squadron around Cape Horn and attack vulnerable British naval installations in the South Atlantic. London now sent a powerful naval force under Vice Admiral Sir Frederick Doveton Sturdee to Port Stanley, where the *Canopus* was scuttled on a mud flat near the harbour's entrance to serve as a stationary fortress.

Sturdee arrived at Port Stanley on 7 December. His squadron consisted of eight ships: the modern battle cruisers *Invincible* and *Inflexible*; the cruisers *Caernarvon, Bristol, Kent, Glasgow,* and *Cornwall*; and the auxiliary cruiser *Macedonia.*

Spee, meanwhile, received an erroneous report that no British warships were in the Falklands and decided to attack Port Stanley. Early on 8 December he detached the *Gneisenau* and *Nürnberg* to conduct the raid while his remaining ships remained at sea to search for British ships. The Germans found the British ships coaling and undergoing maintenance. Smoke, produced by British crews desperately trying to get up steam, warned the Germans, who turned away just as salvos from the *Canopus* splashed near them. All of Sturdee's ships, except the *Kent* and *Macedonia*, were soon in pursuit.

The Battle of the Falklands opened early in the afternoon of 8 December. Spee ordered his slower light cruisers to attempt to escape, but Sturdee dispatched his own cruisers to pursue them while his heavy ships chased the *Scharnhorst* and *Gneisenau*. The *Invincible* and *Inflexible*, faster than the two German warships, soon overtook them. The circumstances of Coronel were now reversed. In the Battle of the Falklands it was the British who chose to engage in a long-range battle that the Germans could not win. Each of the two British battle cruisers had eight 12-inch guns, with decided range and striking advantages over the 8.2-inchers of *Scharnhorst* and *Gneisenau*. Sturdee's cruisers were also superior to the German light cruisers.

In the battle both German heavy cruisers were sunk, as were the *Leipzig* and *Nürnberg*. The last German cruiser, the *Dresden*, escaped and remained at large until the following March when she was scuttled off Chile. Sturdee's ships sustained only light damage and 21 casualties, while some 2,000 Germans perished. Not only did the Battle of the Falklands restore British pride, it removed the German naval threat to the South Atlantic.[80]

German Navy raids against Britain

Despite the Kaiser's attitude, Admiral Tirpitz continued to advocate offensive German naval action, in part for political reasons. He observed, "If we come to the end of a war so terrible as that of 1914, without the fleet having bled and worked, we shall get nothing more for the fleet, and all the scanty money that may be will be spent on the army."[81] The rest of the naval leadership supported a defensive strategy, except for offensive minelaying and bombardment of the British coastal towns, important for morale reasons.

Commander-in-Chief of the German High Seas Fleet Admiral Friedrich von Ingenohl now ordered Vice Admiral Franz von Hipper's battle cruisers to bombard the British coast and lay mines along the coastal shipping route. The Germans conducted two such raids at the end of 1914: against Yarmouth on 3–4 November; and Hartlepool, Whitby, and Scarborough on 15–16 December. Bad weather (on three occasions the opposing forces passed each other just out of view) and signal mishaps prevented either side from inflicting a serious reverse on the other.

The shelling of Yarmouth by Hipper's battle cruisers, while a German cruiser slipped in close ashore to lay mines, resulted in little damage. It did cause Whitehall to transfer the Third Battle Cruiser Squadron from Scapa Flow to Rosyth, where it would be in a better position to meet a future German attack.

Meanwhile one of the great counter-intelligence coups of the war almost brought disaster for the Germans. On 26 August the German light cruiser *Magdeburg* ran aground off Odensholm Island off the coast of Russian Estonia. The arrival of Russian warships foiled German attempts to destroy her, and the Russians salvaged three copies of the German naval code book along with the current key. The Russians passed one copy to the British, and by early December 1914 the cryptographers of Admiralty Room 40 could decipher German naval signals.[82]

When Ingenohl ordered out five battle cruisers under Vice Admiral Franz von Hipper the British intercepted and decrypted the signal to begin the operation. Ingenohl's goal was to lay minefields into which the Germans would lure a part of the Grand Fleet. Whitehall dispatched Vice Admiral David Beatty's battle cruiser squadron and a cruiser squadron. They were ordered to a point roughly off the southeast corner of the Dogger Bank, midway in the North Sea between Britain and Denmark, where they could intercept the German ships as they returned from their raid. Whitehall also sent out Vice Admiral Sir George Warrender's Second Battle Squadron with six of its best dreadnoughts and eight destroyers, and it instructed the Grand Fleet to follow on the night of the 16th from Scapa Flow while a squadron of eight predreadnought battleships would sally out from the Firth of Forth. What Whitehall did not know was that the entire German High Seas Fleet had come as far as the Dogger Bank to act as a covering force. That would place 22 German capital ships in close proximity to Warrender's six dread- noughts. The German concentration remained undetected because their ships observed strict radio silence.

Early on the 16th, Warrender's destroyers clashed with destroyers and cruisers of the High Seas Fleet, but bad weather limited visibility. Convinced that he had encountered the destroyer screen of the Grand Fleet, Ingenohl ordered the High Seas Fleet to turn away, missing a chance to inflict a crushing defeat on the British. This also left Hipper in the lurch, as the High Seas Fleet was to have remained in place until the coastal bombardment was completed.

The German battle cruisers bombarded Scarborough, Hartlepool, and Whitby, inflicting considerable damage ashore while one of their cruisers laid about 100 mines. The British were unable to intercept them on their return because of bad weather and human error. By late afternoon the German ships were beyond reach of the Royal Navy.

The German bombardment, which killed 40 civilians and injured several hundred, was a shock to the British people. It was the first time civilians had been killed in Britain from enemy action since 1690. British propaganda portrayed the Germans as the "baby killers of Scarborough".

On 17 December First Lord of the Admiralty Winston Churchill under- went tough questioning in Parliament. While his capital ships had almost trapped five German battle cruisers, what Churchill did not know was how close they had come to an encounter with a more powerful German force. Never in the following years did the Germans come as close to the "Kräfteausgleich" (decisive encounter) sought by Tirpitz.[83]

Submarine warfare

The submarine was by far Germany's most potent weapon against the Allies at sea. The *Unterseeboot* (U-boat) could arrive on station undetected and attack without warning. At the beginning of the war both sides failed to anticipate the potential of this new weapon; most admirals regarded submarines as useful only for gathering information on enemy fleet movements. Even those who thought submarines might be used as offensive weapons against enemy war- ships failed to think in terms of the submarine as a commerce destroyer. In fact, Germany entered the war with few submarines because Tirpitz was busy building a balanced surface fleet. He rejected a June 1914 recommendation that Germany build 222 submarines for a blockade of the British Isles.[84] At the start of the war Germany had just 31 U-boats.

The submarine phase of the war did not begin well for Germany. On 9 August in the North Sea the British cruiser *Birmingham* rammed and sank the *U15*, which was on the surface for engine repair. On 5 September, however, *U21* sank the British destroyer *Pathfinder* off the Firth of Forth, the first warship sunk by a submarine in the war. She went down with 259 men. A far more graphic illustration of the submarine's potential, however, came on 22 September when *U9* sank three old British cruisers, the *Cressy*, *Hogue*, and *Aboukir*, off the Dutch coast. The *Aboukir* was the first to be torpedoed. The captains of her sister ships, believing she had been the victim of a mine, stopped their ships dead in the water to take aboard survivors, making them easy prey. While the loss of 1,459 seamen (837 others were rescued) and three cruisers hardly upset the naval balance, it did signal the arrival of a new age in naval warfare.

Situation at the end of 1914

As 1914 came to an end it was clear that the Germans had failed to achieve their objectives. Although they occupied about a tenth of France they had failed to achieve the quick victory anticipated. The rough parity of forces on the Western Front, as well as the substitution of trench warfare for the war of movement, led many German officers to believe that victory might come first in the East and that it would be best to concentrate there. The vastness of the Eastern Front made trench warfare unlikely, and Stavka obliged the Germans by learning little about the realities of the new offensive and defensive war. Russian commanders continued to send large numbers of men to their deaths in massed charges against machine guns and artillery fire.

Within the German Army the "Easterners", those who favoured concentrating against Russia to drive her from the war, were outnumbered in the High Command by "Westerners". Although the latter included German Army commander Falkenhayn, increasingly the Easterners influenced the Kaiser and Chancellor Bethmann-Hollweg, who instructed Falkenhayn to give the war against Russia priority in 1915.[85]

Although Russia had lost the bulk of her trained officers and non-commissioned officers and was chronically short of war matériel, she was resilient and had the resources to replace her huge manpower losses. The British and French were also confident. Their navies and those of their allies controlled the seas, and the Allies were in a position to use the resources of the rest of the world to their advantage. By merely surviving they could have confidence in ultimate victory, but they were not prepared simply to remain on the defensive. After all, the Germans were still in France.

Chapter Three

1915: stalemate and trench warfare

The hallmark of 1915 on the Western Front was the stalemate of trench warfare. All the major offensives of 1915 and 1916 including Artois, Champagne, and the Somme were failures. Nevertheless both Joffre and Falkenhayn continued to believe that a breakthrough in the West was possible. With the Germans occupying a tenth of France, including important industrial districts, it was politically impossible for any French commander to remain on the defensive. Joffre later justified his costly offensives by maintaining that they convinced Italy to join the Entente in 1915, that they took pressure off Russia on the Eastern Front and off the French at Verdun in 1916, and that such attacks wore down defenders as much as attackers. Reportedly one of Joffre's favourite phrases was, *"Je les grignote"* (I keep nibbling at them).[1] Attrition warfare continued to absorb the attention of Allied Western Front commanders throughout the war.

First Battle of Champagne continued

Although the Allies had failed to break through the German lines during the December 1914 First Battle of Champagne, Joffre renewed the offensive there on a much broader front on 15 February. The attacks gained some ground but could not be exploited because of the lack of surprise and poor weather. Conditions at the front were appalling. On 2 February General Brulard of 2nd Division reported, "First-line units . . . stand knee-deep in water."[2]

Newly arrived German reserves enabled German General Karl von Einem's Third Army to carry out a series of counterattacks, primarily at night, along La Bassée Canal and near Soissons. By early February the German lines were stabilized. Langle de Cary brought up fresh troops and attacked again in late February and early March but made little headway. By mid-March, with the French Fourth Army exhausted, the offensive was for all practical purposes over. Joffre formally halted it at the end of the month although for morale purposes he ordered Langle de Cary to maintain an offensive posture.[3] Overall the French suffered 94,000 casualties, the Germans only 46,000.

Battle of Neuve Chapelle

To the north on 10 March, meanwhile, the British struck at Neuve Chapelle in their first big set-piece attack of the war. The previous October the Germans had forced a bulge in the line there that enabled them to enfilade British positions on either side. Haig proposed retaking Neuve Chapelle and capturing Aubers Ridge, thus threatening the important rail centre of Lille. The first major offensive of the war launched from a trench system, it was carried out by British and Indian units.

Haig insisted on thorough planning. Utilizing aerial photography the British drew up detailed plans for the attack. They also prepared assembly trenches and advanced ammunition dumps and established precise artillery timetables. The battle saw the first large-scale artillery preparation of the war from 342 British guns. The howitzers and heavy guns shot indirect fire against the German trenches while the lighter field guns concentrated direct fire on the enemy barbed wire. To achieve surprise and because of a shell shortage, the preliminary bombardment lasted only 35 minutes.[4]

The attack achieved complete surprise, the British easily overrunning the first German line. They took Neuve Chapelle and eradicated the salient north of the village, but the British failed to get past German strong points and the attack collapsed. IV Corps commander General Sir Henry Rawlinson, concerned about a possible counterattack, chose not to commit his reserves, British communications broke down, and the Germans rushed up reinforcements and easily curtailed this narrow-front attack. Haig ordered the assault renewed on the 12th, but the Germans pre-empted it with an attack that morning. The British repulsed that but their own assault failed. That night Haig cancelled further attacks. In the Neuve Chapelle battle the British sustained some 13,000 casualties, the Germans about 12,000.[5]

Each side learned important tactical lessons. The Allies understood the need for more accurate preparatory artillery fire by heavier guns (much of the heavier fire was inaccurate, the consequence of improper registration). They chose to focus on the destruction of obstacles and concluded that artillery needed to destroy everything in the infantry's path. This led to larger and larger artillery preparations.[6] The British also concluded that the attack showed the need to mount attacks on a broad front to allow commitment of reserves and to maximize striking power by assigning each division a relatively narrow assault front. The Germans in turn became convinced that properly entrenched troops, supported by machine guns, artillery, and reserves, could repulse a numerically superior enemy. To solidify their defences they built a secondary trench system all along the Western Front.

Battle of the Woëvre

German defensive abilities were again demonstrated in April in the Battle of the Woëvre (5–30 April). General Auguste Dubail, commander of the French Eastern Army Group, ordered seven corps of his First Army to attack both sides of the St Mihiel Salient. His goals were to straighten out the French lines, produce a shorter front, ease the threat to Verdun, divert German reserves from Artois and Champagne, and sever German rail communications in the Metz area.

Joffre suspended the offensive on 30 April. It was halted by poor weather, inadequate artillery support, ammunition shortages, rugged terrain, German defence and counterattacks, and three fresh German divisions reinforcing the nine already in place. The French sustained nearly 64,000 casualties, including those lost in supporting attacks west of Verdun. Sporadic fighting continued into the summer months, after which St Mihiel became a quiet sector until the Americans attacked it again in September 1918.[7]

These failures did not deter Joffre and the French High Command. With the Germans concentrating against Russia in 1915, Joffre and Ferdinand Foch, commander since January of the Northern Army Group, sought to exploit the Allies' numerical advantage in the West by a breakthrough in Artois. Their goals were the same as in late 1914. By taking Vimy Ridge, Artois' dominant geographic feature, they would command the Douai plain and be in a position to sever key German railroads in the Douai–Lille area, forcing a German withdrawal from northern France.

Second Battle of Ypres

To maximize the chance of success Joffre convinced a reluctant Field Marshal French to participate. Although the BEF lacked adequate heavy artillery, ammunition, and reserves, its commander agreed to relieve two French corps in the Ypres salient and to attack at Aubers Ridge in what would be the largest in a series of supporting assaults all along the front.[8]

Allied preparations were disrupted on 22 April 1915, by the first successful use of poison (chlorine) gas in the war.[9] This initiated the Second Battle of Ypres (22 April–25 May).[10]

At the end of October 1914 the Germans had fired shells with an irritant gas in the Neuve Chapelle sector, but without apparent effect. They first used tear gas, xylyl bromide (codenamed "T-Stoff"), on the Eastern Front on 31 January 1915, when they fired some 18,000 gas shells against the Russians at Bolimov. The weather was so cold that the gas failed to vaporize; it froze and sank into the snow.[11]

The Germans then decided to try chlorine gas on the Western Front. Chemist Fritz Haber, in charge of the new weapon there, was certain it would be successful and urged his army superiors to exploit it. Sceptical about the project and strapped by the shift of significant German manpower to the Eastern Front, they regarded it largely as an experiment and refused to allocate reserves to Duke Albrecht of Württemberg's Fourth Army to exploit any breach it might effect in the enemy line. Falkenhayn's goals at Ypres were in fact quite modest: to reduce the salient and to mask his transfer of reinforcements to the Eastern Front for the Gorlice–Tarnow Offensive.[12] Haber was also forced to release the gas from commercial metal cylinders and depend on the wind for dispersal, delaying the attack.

There had been clear warnings of an impending gas attack. In March the French took prisoners who described preparations for such an attack, and on 13 April a German deserter described to his French interrogators "tubes of asphyxiating gas . . . placed in batteries of twenty . . . along the front". This information was ignored as was the deserter's crude respirator gas mask. Accurate reports reached Second Army commander Smith-Dorrien, but he neither issued a general warning nor ordered precautionary measures.[13]

At about 5.30 p.m. on 22 April, after a brief German bombardment, Allied pilots overhead and French Algerian troops holding a section of line in the salient around Ypres spotted an advancing greenish yellow cloud. The Germans had opened 5,000 gas cylinders, releasing 168 tons of chlorine gas. The resultant cloud wiped out two French divisions manning a four-mile section of front, killing and incapacitating the defenders or causing them to flee from their positions. German troops cautiously advancing behind the cloud captured 2,000 prisoners and 51 guns. By the end of the day 15,000 Allied soldiers were casualties, 5,000 of them dead. Still, the Germans lacked sufficient manpower to exploit the situation and Allied reserves soon sealed the breech. A second gas attack on 14 April was less successful. Canadian troops used handkerchiefs soaked in water or urine as crude respirators.

British counterattacks were not successful and Smith-Dorrien sensibly suggested withdrawing to a more tenable line along the Yser Canal and Ypres ramparts. Field Marshal French took this as a lack of will and transferred responsibility for Ypres to General Herbert Plumer. Smith-Dorrien was sacked and sent home to Britain, a loss for the BEF. Ironically, French allowed Plumer to pull back as Smith-Dorrien had urged, but three miles short of Ypres.[14] After another month, fighting there died down. Casualties in the Second Battle of Ypres through 25 May were 60,000 British, 10,000 French, and 35,000 German.

The Allies thereafter developed their own poison gases; the British employed gas for the first time at Loos on 25 September 1915.[15] First World War gases were of three main categories: chlorine; phosgene, which attacked the lungs and caused them to fill with fluid, literally drowning the victim; and mustard gas. The latter, introduced in 1917, burned and blistered the body, resulting in great pain and, in some cases, temporary blindness. Both sides also introduced gas masks, which by 1916 had become standard issue, and the result was a stalemate of sorts.[16]

The poison gas of the First World War incapacitated or wounded far more men than it killed. From the standpoint of the attacker, this was an advantage because each wounded enemy soldier neutralized other additional soldiers and increased the burden on enemy logistical and medical systems.

Second Battle of Artois

With the Ypres front stabilized the French began what became known as the Second Battle of Artois (9 May–18 June). Manning the German line in Artois were 13 well-entrenched divisions of Rupprecht's Sixth Army. To defeat them Foch and Tenth Army commander General Victor d'Urbal sought to incorporate lessons learned in earlier offensives. To secure the flanks of the main four-mile wide thrust against Vimy Ridge they planned a broad five-corps assault on a 24-mile front between Notre Dame de Lorette and Arras, with five infantry and six cavalry divisions in reserve. The French also prepared a 1,200-gun, 700,000-round preliminary bombardment against targets selected by intensive aerial reconnaissance.

The French began their preliminary bombardment on 4 May. Their infantry attack on the 9th met with initial success. Within 90 minutes General

Henri Philippe Pétain's well-prepared XXXIII Corps advanced 2.5 miles and reached the crest of Vimy Ridge near Souchez; but the nearest French reserves were about 7.5 miles in the rear and it took eight hours for them to reach the fighting, allowing German counterattacks to push the exhausted French off the crest. None of Tenth Army's other corps made appreciable gains. Although the fighting continued until 18 June, the chance for a quick breakthrough was gone.

The BEF diversionary attack by Haig's First Army to reduce the salient around the village of Neuve Chapelle and reach Aubers Ridge two miles east was a disaster. It was a larger version of the March assault and Haig hoped to replicate the earlier success of a short, intense bombardment of only 40 minutes, although this was partly attributable to lack of ammunition.

British gains were limited to the first few hours of the assault and Haig was forced to break it off after only one day. The British failed because of inaccurate artillery fire, poor communication between the infantry and supporting artillery, and lack of heavy guns capable of destroying the well-constructed German bunkers. The Germans quickly brought in reserves and their artillery broke up the attack. The British suffered some 12,000 casualties and failed even to prevent Prince Rupprecht from shifting units from this sector to Vimy Ridge.[17]

On 16 May d'Urbal renewed his offensive in an effort to widen Pétain's constricted salient, but he achieved only small gains in heavy fighting. Haig's two-division supporting attack of 15 May at Festubert, just north of La Bassée Canal, attempting to combine a night attack with a massive five-day artillery bombardment, also failed despite initial gains because of British artillery ineffectiveness (many shell fuses failed) and rigorous German counterattacks. The British committed three additional divisions on 16–18 May to no avail. By 27 May the BEF halted its attacks with nothing more to show than 17,000 additional casualties. In fact, the BEF did more to assist the French Tenth Army by taking over responsibility for some five miles of trenches between La Bassée Canal and Lens than by its Festubert operation.

The final French effort to salvage the Artois Offensive came on 16 June when d'Urbal launched an 18-division push all along his front. Hoping to correct the fatal mistakes of 9 May, he opted for a brief, intensive bombardment of known German positions and concentrated his reserve formations immediately behind the first wave. This proved disastrous. German artillery and machine-gun fire slaughtered the densely packed French infantry formations and their counterattacks quickly eliminated French gains. With the offensive stalled, on 18 June the British and French suspended it.

The Second Artois Offensive ended in complete failure. The Allies, despite gaining about five square miles of ground, neither took Vimy Ridge nor forced the Germans to retreat or to divert units from Russia.[18] The Northcliffe press railed against Kitchener and the War Office because of the BEF's artillery and ammunition shortages and failures. Britain was producing only 22,000 shells a day, versus 100,000 in France and 250,000 in Germany and Austria-Hungary.[19] The "Shells Scandal", while it did not create the May cabinet crisis, led to a coalition government and creation of a Ministry of Munitions under energetic David Lloyd George.[20]

German losses in the offensive numbered about 73,000 men but Allied casualties totalled more than 102,000 French and 37,000 British. In spite of this, British and French commanders still maintained that a breakthrough required only massive and well-targeted preparatory barrages, wider attack frontages, reserves advancing close behind the first wave, and thoroughly detailed plans of attack. Confident in these beliefs, Joffre planned to renew the offensive in Artois and Champagne in the autumn. But the Second Battle of Artois heightened German confidence that a strong defence in depth, backed by sufficient reserves, could repel any offensive. The Allies were much slower to adopt the concept.

Renewed Allied offensives in Artois and Champagne

Joffre remained determined to take advantage of the favourable manpower ratio in the West created by the German decision to concentrate against Russia. He was convinced that converging French infantry attacks from Artois and Champagne could overcome German defences, sever their rail communications, and force their withdrawal from the Noyon salient. At the very least, Joffre expected the attacks to relieve the hard-pressed Russians.

His autumn offensive scheme called for minor diversionary attacks along the length of the front to support simultaneous offensives in Champagne by Pétain's Second Army and Langle de Cary's Fourth Army, and in Artois against Vimy Ridge by General d'Urbal's Tenth Army. The British were to support these with an attack near Loos, while the Italians – who had joined the Allied cause in May – attacked Austria-Hungary along the Isonzo River.

Joffre believed previous offensives had failed because of the inability to achieve simultaneous attacks and from insufficient artillery preparation, poor infantry–artillery coordination, an overly narrow front, and inadequate planning. He believed that careful planning and preparations would bring success. The French Army was reorganized into Northern (Foch), Central (de

Castelnau), and Eastern (Dubail) Army Groups, and Pétain was promoted to command Second Army.[21]

The BEF prepared to attack near Loos in order to support Tenth Army's left flank in Artois. French and Haig had protested Joffre's plan, as the area assigned to them was difficult terrain and the BEF was deficient in heavy artillery. But Kitchener ordered them to comply, "even though by so doing we may suffer very heavy losses".[22]

The BEF, meanwhile, continued to increase in size. Between February and September it added six Territorial and 15 New Army (Kitchener) divisions. A second Canadian division also arrived, and with the first formed the Canadian Corps. A third British army under General Sir Charles Monro held the 20 miles of trenches taken over from the French in May and August.[23]

In preparation for the coming offensive Joffre created new army formations by reducing the size of infantry companies, reorganizing territorial units, and calling up men of the class of 1915. French Central Army Group commander General de Castelnau sought to minimize exposure to enemy fire by having his men construct protective bunkers in which they could wait out the initial bombardment; he also narrowed the distance they would have to traverse before engaging the Germans by having his men push their trenches forward to less than 300 yards from the main German line. In order to maximize chances of maintaining communication, French troops laid double and triple phone lines. Second and Fourth Armies also expanded their road and rail network in order to ensure greater logistical support. Finally, to improve the preliminary bombardment, the French carefully sited some 700 heavy guns and stockpiled 800,000 shells. The guns were older models, however; many of them had only recently been removed from unoccupied fortifications. Most lacked recoil systems, which meant they had to be repositioned after each round.

The Germans were also active. Outnumbered, they had constructed interconnected fallback defensive entrenchments two to four miles behind the entire Western Front. With few reserves – only six infantry divisions and four infantry brigades for the entire front – Falkenhayn was so certain that low French morale and British shortages would prevent any massive Allied offensive that he refused to believe von Einem's reports of an Allied build-up or to dispatch reserves to Champagne or Artois until early September.

On 21 September the French began their Champagne offensive with a four-day preliminary bombardment. Although this nullified any chance of achieving surprise, Joffre and his subordinates were convinced that their detailed planning, superior firepower, and élan would bring victory. On the morning of 25 September, French infantrymen "went over the top" in Champagne and, that afternoon, in Artois along a 24-mile-front.

Second Battle of Champagne

The Second Battle of Champagne (25 September–16 October) began promisingly enough. The 18 divisions (along with ten infantry divisions and two cavalry corps in reserve) of the French Second and Fourth Armies heavily outnumbered von Einem's German Third Army (eight divisions with one in reserve) and the right-wing corps of Fifth Army. The heavy four-day French bombardment badly damaged German defences and cut their wire in many places. In the centre the attacking troops advanced nearly 2,500 yards in less than two hours before they came up against the second German defensive line five hours ahead of schedule. French artillery, following the carefully prepared schedule, opened fire on the German second line just as the French 10th Colonial Division reached it. The French infantry, unable to contact their artillery, fell back in disarray. To hold the second line Einem called up all available reserves, including dismounted cavalry and recruits.

News of the French near-breakthrough in Champagne caused Falkenhayn to rush reserves, including two corps recently arrived in Belgium from Russia, to Artois and Champagne. On 26 and 27 September the French renewed their attack with five fresh divisions and, confident they were close to a break-through, called up cavalry. They reached the second German line on a front of nearly eight miles and, on the 28th, briefly penetrated it; but German counterattacks drove them back. Later that day substantial German reserves began to reach Third Army and the French assault stalled.

On 30 September Castelnau ordered a pause to allow his Second and Fourth Armies to rest and regroup. On 5–6 October the French renewed the attack with 19 divisions, focusing primarily on the centre of the enemy line. The Germans held because reinforcements arrived and persistent fog impeded French artillery fire. The French scored only minor gains and the struggle degenerated into a series of limited attacks and counterattacks. On 3 November Joffre ordered Second and Fourth Armies to suspend operations.

The Champagne Offensive gained only about 15 square miles and a maximum penetration of 2.5 miles at a cost of some 144,000 French casualties to only 85,000 for the Germans. Given planning, resources committed, and the generally favourable strategic situation, it was a major French defeat.[24]

Third Battle of Artois

Concurrent with Foch's Champagne Offensive, the Third Battle of Artois raged between 25 September and 16 October. It followed the same pattern as its two predecessors – a main thrust against Vimy Ridge supported by attacks on both flanks. In order to strain the enemy's meagre reserves the attack was launched simultaneously with the French offensive in Champagne and diversionary assaults elsewhere.

To improve chances for an Artois breakthrough Foch and d'Urbal massed 420 heavy guns, 130 more than in the May assault. They also planned close infantry–artillery coordination and broadened the attack frontage. To overcome the lack of reliable battlefield communications, Allied commanders tried to plan every detail and schedule everything to the minute.

Despite emphasis on careful preparation and coordination, Anglo-French liaison was lacking. Left to his own resources Haig, whose British First Army would make the Loos assault, concluded from the initial German success at Second Ypres that he might compensate for his weak artillery support – 110 heavy guns with scant ammunition – with a surprise gas attack. He believed the release of nearly 150 tons (5,500 cylinders) of chlorine gas, quickly followed by a six-division assault by his I and IV Corps against the two German divisions on their front, would rupture the enemy lines. If these troops could then quickly seize Hill 70 just east–southeast of Loos the British reserve of I Cavalry Corps and XI Corps could exploit the penetration. To tie down German reserves other BEF formations were to launch lesser attacks north of La Bassée Canal and east of Ypres.

Crown Prince Rupprecht's German Sixth Army opposed the Allied forces. His men were thinly spread – only 17.5 divisions for 35 miles of line – but they were well entrenched and supported by carefully positioned machine guns, and they were backed by a second defensive line for the most part beyond Allied artillery range. The primary German problem here, as along the entire front, was a lack of reserves.

Once again Joffre elected for firepower and élan over surprise. On 21 September the French began a four-day preliminary barrage, after which Tenth Army began its assault. Quickly seizing the fortified town of Souchez, the French also took the area known as "the Labyrinth"; but nowhere did they breach the Germans' second defensive line. All attempts to advance farther were thrown back. Joffre and Foch then opted to focus on the more promising Champagne push. On 29 September, therefore, d'Urbal suspended offensive operations in Artois.

Battle of Loos

Early on 25 September Haig's British First Army, just to the north of Tenth Army, launched its Loos attack, preceded by gas released from cylinders. Haig had almost postponed the attack because of lack of wind, but a slight late-afternoon breeze was deemed sufficient to carry the gas toward the German lines. Much of it dissipated harmlessly, and some even came back on the British to down troops in the first wave, but enough reached the German trenches to help the British overrun the German front lines. One division reached Hill 70. Another seized the mining town of Loos itself. A third penetrated the German second line near Hulluch. Farther north, two divisions breached German front trenches but stalled at the second line. The northern-most attacks failed from ineffective artillery and gas attacks. Nevertheless, the BEF had, on a front of four to five miles, penetrated the German lines to a maximum depth of about 4,000 to 5,000 yards.

Although the initial gains were impressive, first-wave units suffered heavy losses and were soon exhausted. A breakthrough was still possible if reserves could be brought up quickly, but French had positioned his reserve, XI Corps, seven to ten miles to the rear, despite protests from Haig who had been supported by Foch.

XI Corps's two divisions were the first of the newly raised "Kitchener" units to see offensive action in France. Thrown into battle between Hill 70 and Hulluch on 26 September without artillery support, they were shattered by fresh German troops. XI Corps suffered 8,229 casualties and had to be relieved by the Guards, the last available British infantry division, and the Third Cavalry Division. On the 27th and 28th, the Guards Division renewed the offensive at Loos but the chance for success had passed.[25]

Vimy Ridge

To reinvigorate the stalled British offensive, Joffre sent his French IX Corps for a joint assault with the British I Corps, supported by a renewed attempt by the French Tenth Army against the northern end of Vimy Ridge. But Rupprecht's Sixth Army, now heavily reinforced, launched counterattacks that delayed these assaults until 10 and 13 October. Only near the apex of Vimy Ridge, at Givenchy, did the renewed Allied attacks make even temporary gains. With his troops stalled and exhausted, on 14 October

French suspended the BEF offensive and two days later d'Urbal followed suit.

Public debate now erupted over French's handling of the battle, focusing on his poor placement of XI Corps. French did not get on well with his Allied counterparts or with his subordinates and superiors. Haig, along with General Sir William Robertson, French's chief of staff, reported unfavourably on French to King George V. French's attempt to alter his orders releasing XI Corps to Haig's control to show that he had turned it over earlier than was the case was the last straw. French was dismissed on 17 December and replaced by Haig, who kept command of the BEF on the Western Front for the remainder of the war. On 23 December Robertson became Chief of the Imperial General Staff.[26]

Although British communiqués called Loos a tactical success, the streams of casualties told a different story. The British took roughly 8,000 yards of German trench frontage and made a penetration of about two miles but suffered approximately 62,000 casualties. The French also made minor gains at a cost of over 48,000 mem. The German Sixth Army reported just over 51,000 casualties.

New weapons and tactics

The failure of Joffre's offensives were a serious blow to French morale and caused many commanders, including ardent disciples of offensive operations such as Joffre and Foch, to modify, though not abandon, their faith in offensives. There were also calls for extended training and for new equipment, such as mortars, better suited to trench warfare.

By early 1915 the Germans had excellent trench mortars (*Minenwerfer*), most of which were rifled, at the front. They ranged in size from a 76 mm bore, weighing 312 lb and firing a 9 lb shell, to a 245 mm bore (1,693 lb), utilizing a 210 lb projectile. Range varied from over 600 yards to more than 1,200. Such weapons were ideally suited for firing against front-line trenches. The Allies were slower to develop trench mortars, although the 1915 British smooth-bore Stokes, available in 3-inch and 4-inch models firing 10 lb and 25 lb shells respectively, was probably the most famous such weapon of the war. Rifle grenades, of which the British Mills and French "VB" (for Viven-Besières) were the best known, also came into general use.[27]

The Germans primarily, but also to some extent the French, began to explore new tactics. By the end of the year the Germans were experimenting with special squad-sized assault detachments as opposed to linear formations;

these men would bypass strong points and employ grenades, carbines, flamethrowers, and trench mortars. French infantry Captain André Laffargue expressed similar ideas in his pamphlet, *The Attack in Trench Warfare*, which came to Foch's notice.[28]

There were political repercussions from the failures on the Western Front. French Premier René Viviani's government fell and Aristide Briand became premier. Massive casualty lists and minimal results also led the Chamber of Deputies to demand increased civilian control over the war effort, including the right to examine the performance of generals. As a result, the French Army confined offensive efforts to the upcoming Salonika Expedition.

Western Front in 1915 in sum

In sum, the 1915 Allied offensives on the Western Front demonstrated the increasing lethality of artillery and machine-gun fire and the consequent superiority of the defence over the offence. The continuous line forced frontal assaults, which invariably encountered heavy enemy defensive firepower, thus producing higher casualties for the attackers. The Germans were quicker than the Allies to realize this; during 1915 they learned a great deal about the power of an elastic defence in depth with two or more widely separated defensive lines. Advancing troops might break through the first line but invariably they were caught in the belt before the second line. Here, beyond the range of or out of communication with their own guns, they were pounded by enemy artillery. By early 1916 the entire German Western Front was four to six miles deep. Dual interlocking defence lines and safe, comfortable troop bunkers eliminated the need to rotate front-line units frequently. Despite the demonstrated superiority of the defensive, in 1916 both sides undertook offensives. These culminated in the massive bloodlettings of Verdun and the Somme.

Altogether 1915 was a year of carnage on the Western Front. The French suffered 1,292,000 casualties and the British 279,000. The Germans, standing on the defence, lost only 612,000 – less than half the Allied total.

Italian Front

In 1915, however, the Germans had to contend with another war front in Italy. Although primarily impacting Austria-Hungary, this development further drained German resources. The Allies had hoped that the Italians would enter the war, expecting them to relieve the pressure of Austro-Hungarian forces facing Russia. They also hoped that Italy might contribute troops against Turkey.

Although both sides courted Italy, the Allies offered what the Central Powers could not – lavish territorial gains along the Adriatic at the expense of Austria-Hungary. Accordingly, on 26 April Britain, France, and Russia signed the Secret Treaty of London with Italy. The Allies promised her the Trentino and southern Tyrol (the subsequent Alto Adige) up to the Brenner Pass; Gorizia and Gradisa; Trieste and the Istrian Peninsula; North Dalmatia and the islands facing it; Vlorë in Albania; the Dodecanese Islands in the Aegean; some Turkish territory should that country be partitioned; and, if the Allies gained territory in Africa at the expense of Germany, the expansion of Italy's possessions of Eritrea, Somaliland, and Libya. On 23 May Italy declared war on the Dual Monarchy.[29]

The Italian Army under General Luigi Cadorna numbered some 875,000 mem but was short of heavy guns, ammunition, and motor transport. Politics dictated that Italian troops attack the Dual Monarchy rather than reinforce the Western Front, and geography controlled the location of these operations. The border between Austria-Hungary and Italy followed the southern slopes of the Alps, limiting any Italian offensive to the narrow and extremely rugged Isonzo River front projecting into Austria to the east. Cardona's plan was to stand on the defensive on the Trentino front while making the major attack along the Isonzo. The Italians would attack toward Trieste with their immediate objective the seizure of Gorizia. Fortunately for the Austrians, commander of the Italian Front Archduke Eugene had heavily fortified the frontier.

First, Second, Third, and Fourth Battles of the Isonzo

On 23 June the Italians began their offensive. In what became known as the First Battle of the Isonzo (23 June–7 July 1915), General Pietro Frugoni's Second Army and Emanuele Filberto the Duke of Aosta's Third Army – about 200,000 men and 200 guns – attacked the 100,000-man Austro-Hungarian Fifth Army commanded by General Svetozar Borojević von Bojna. Complicated by Isonzo flooding, the Italians did not have all their divisions ready at the beginning of the attack, and Borojević demonstrated a mastery of defensive warfare. Consequently the Italian attack was beaten back, and fighting on the Italian Front soon resembled Western Front trench warfare.

With mobilization finally completed, from 18 July to 3 August Cardona tried again in the Second Battle of the Isonzo. He brought up more artillery, but the Austrians had deployed two additional divisions and held their lines. In the First and Second Isonzo battles the Italians sustained perhaps 60,000 casualties and the Austrians about 45,000.

The Italians and Austrians fought two other battles along the Isonzo before the year ended: Third Isonzo, from 18 October to 4 November; and Fourth Isonzo, 10 November to 2 December. Again the Austrians held the Italians to insignificant gains.[30] Italian losses in these two battles were 117,000 men; the Austrians lost 72,000.

Although terrain in the area was difficult, these attacks showed, as on the Western Front, that well-prepared defensive positions were more than a match for massed frontal assaults. Unfortunately for the Allies, in 1915 the Italians did not significantly relieve the pressure on Russia.

Italy's entry into the war did facilitate Allied military cooperation. On 7 July 1915, General Joffre convened at Chantilly, France, the first Inter-Allied Military Conference. The Allies agreed only that each national army would act on its own and that there should be more such meetings. On 6–8 December, the Allies held a second conference at Chantilly. Military representatives of France, Great Britain, Italy, Russia, and Serbia agreed to Joffre's plan for simultaneous maximum–effort attacks as soon as practical against the Germans and their allies in order to break the military stalemate. It was also agreed that the war would be won only in its principal theatres: the Western, Russian, and Italian Fronts.[31]

The Eastern Front: Hindenburg's winter offensive

In the East in 1915 the Central Powers took the offensive. The long front helped produce a war of movement rather than static trench warfare. Handicapping lengthy advances, however, were the region's primitive transportation network and harsh winter conditions, which inevitably brought attacks to a halt.

Under pressure from H-L, former chief of the general staff Moltke, and other Easterners, the Kaiser ordered that Germany's major effort in 1915 be in the East. As a result, in the winter of 1914–15 the Germans strengthened their forces there. To support an Austrian offensive in the

Carpathians region and to forestall a Russian attack, Falkenhayn authorized a new formation, the composite Südarmee (South Army) commanded by General Alexander von Linsingen. Composed of both German and Austrian troops, it was to cooperate with forces of the Dual Monarchy. To the north Hindenburg formed a new army, the Tenth under General Hermann von Eichhorn, and positioned it near Tilsit. It comprised four corps recently arrived in the East.

The German High Command (OHL) was divided over where to strike. Hindenburg wanted the major effort against the Russians in the north, while Falkenhayn insisted it should be in the south. As the Germans discussed their options, the Russians formed a new army, the Twelfth commanded by Pavel Plehve, to renew their drive into East Prussia. Their offensive was scheduled for 20 February, but the Germans pre-empted it.

In effect the German strategic dilemma resolved itself in two offensives. The first, a southern drive in which Linsingen's composite Südarmee would push northwest through the Carpathian Mountains, was directed toward Lemberg. To its left Austrian General Borojević von Bojna's Third Army (Borojević was on this front before the Italian declaration of war) would relieve the besieged fortress of Przemyśl; while to its right an army group under Austrian General Karl von Pflanzer-Baltin would support the main effort. The second offensive was a northern drive, involving Eighth and Tenth Armies, to attack the Russians from the Masurian Lakes region of East Prussia.

In order to distract the Russians, at the end of January the German Ninth Army feinted an attack in the direction of Warsaw. During this operation the Germans employed poison gas for the first time in the war. The attack did succeed in drawing Russian attention from German preparations in East Prussia.

Second Battle of the Masurian Lakes

Hindenburg opened the northern offensive on 7 February. Known to history as Second Masurian Lakes (7–22 February), this bloody battle began in a snowstorm when the German Eighth Army struck the left flank of the Russian Tenth Army. The next day the German Tenth Army struck the Russian right, driving it back in desperate fighting. On 11 February the Germans reached Stallupönen; three days later they took Lyck. On 21 February the surrounded Russian XX Corps (General Bulgakov) surrendered in the Augustow Forest, but its heroic stand enabled three other corps to escape. On 22 February Russian Plehve's Twelfth Army counterattacked, bringing the battle to an end after a German advance of some 70 miles.[32] Although total Russian casualties ran to 200,000 (90,000 of them prisoners), Russia remained very much in the war. The campaign marked the last German attempt to support Austro-Hungarian operations in the south indirectly by offensives in the north. Hereafter OHL realized the necessity of joint operations.

Surrender of Przemyśl

The southern part of the Central Powers' 1915 offensive did not meet with similar success. As Falkenhayn had predicted, the Carpathian advance of Linsingen's Südarmee became bogged down in poor weather and the inadequate road network. On 17 February Pflanzer-Baltin's Austrian Second Army took Czernowitz and 60,000 prisoners, but a Russian counterattack halted his advance and Borojević's Austrian Third Army was unable to relieve Przemyśl. On 22 March, after a 194-day siege, the Austrian fortress and its 110,000-man garrison surrendered, freeing three Russian corps. The Russians then resumed their Carpathian advance against the Austro-Hungarians, but Linsingen's Südarmee checked them by the end of April.

German spring–summer offensive

General Falkenhayn, meanwhile, went to the Eastern Front to assume personal command. Hindenburg argued for another northern thrust in the direction of Kovno and Vilna, which could then turn south and trap the more westwardly positioned Russian Second and Tenth Armies. He argued that this could produce the most enemy casualties, perhaps driving Russia from the war.

More sensitive to Austro-Hungarian problems than Hindenburg, Falkenhayn supported Conrad's pleas for the next effort to be in the south. His plan called for Hindenburg to tie down Russian forces north of Warsaw while the main drive occurred in the sector between Gorlice and Tarnów in Galicia; there the Austro-Hungarian Fourth and Second armies would support the flanks of General August von Mackensen's new Eleventh Army. Eleventh Army's ten infantry and one cavalry divisions were formed by stripping units on the Western Front. Opposing them from north to south were the Russian Fourth, Third, Eighth, and Eleventh Armies.[33]

On 2 May, after a preliminary four-hour bombardment, the Central Powers seized Tarnów. The Russians, who lacked both heavy guns and shells, were forced back, and their entire Carpathian line rolled up. Russian Third Army commander General Radko-Dmitriev reported that his army had "bled to death".[34] By 14 May the advance had covered 80 miles.

Italy's entry into the war on 23 May, however, forced Conrad to relocate some units, but on 3 June the Central Powers retook Przemyśl. They then occupied Lemberg (22 June) and crossed the Dniester River (23–27 June). The Russians fell back all the way to the Bug River. The Carpathians had now been cleared and all of Galicia recovered. In their two-month campaign the Central Powers retook all the territory Russia had captured in 1914.[35]

Conrad pleaded with Falkenhayn to maintain the southern offensive, but Hindenburg ordered the northern drive on Vilna to begin on 1 July. Conrad, however, convinced Falkenhayn to allow Mackensen to renew the southern offensive. When the Kaiser approved, Hindenburg again had to postpone his plans.

The offensive resumed on 13 July with General Max von Gallwitz's new Twelfth Army attacking the northeastern edge of the Polish Salient. To prevent Hindenburg from controlling the initiative, Falkenhayn created a new German Army Group, comprising the Woyrsch Corps and Ninth Army under Prince Leopold of Bavaria, which took its orders directly from him.

Falkenhayn then began a broad advance from Mlava, southwest of the Masurian Lakes, to Czernowitz near Romania. The Russians, again taken by surprise, failed to coordinate their efforts. By the end of July the Germans had taken Lublin. General Gallwitz's Twelfth Army drove toward Warsaw, which the Russians abandoned during 4–7 August. On 18 August Tenth Army took Kovno and on 19 August Ninth Army took Novo Georgievsk. The Russians did not defend Brest-Litovsk; it fell on 25 August as they retreated across the Niemen River into the Pripet Marshes. By early September the Polish Salient ceased to exist and the Germans stood on Russian soil. The culmination of the drive came on 19 September when Vilna was taken.

In mid-August Falkenhayn, certain that his own objectives had been accomplished, finally unleashed Hindenburg to the north. This offensive continued until the end of September. Mindful of the onset of bad weather and increasing transportation problems, Falkenhayn halted it on a line running from Dvinsk in the north to Khotin on the Dniester in the south. Here the front stabilized.

Although the Russians gave up a phenomenal 300-mile deep swath of territory, Grand Duke Nicholas carried out the retreat with skill. Seriously handicapped by shortages of weapons, shells, and supplies of every kind, he managed to avoid attempts to envelop his armies and preserved the bulk of them. He was rewarded by being relieved of command on 21 August and assigned to the Caucasus Front. Tsar Nicholas II now assumed personal command of Russia's armies with General Mikhail V. Alekseev as his chief of staff, a change which adversely affected officer morale. Russian losses had been staggering, totalling a million men. For the year casualties reached some two million, half of them prisoners. Germany and Austria-Hungary had lost more than one million men.[36]

Turkish Front

Yet another front developed in 1915 when the Western Allies tried to break the stalemate in the West by an attack on Turkey through the Dardanelles. The addition of Turkey on the side of the Central Powers was a major coup for Berlin, the significance of which the Allies failed to understand at the time. In the decade before the First World War Turkey had been a major focus of German foreign policy, evidenced by the Berlin-to-Baghdad Railroad Project and Germany's Drive to the East (*Drang nach Osten*).

The shift in Turkey's international alignment had coincided with growing pressure within that country for change. Turkey's Arab subjects were restless, and a reformist group of young intellectuals and army officers known as the "Young Turks" were bent on modernizing Turkey. In 1909 the young Turks deposed Sultan Abdul Hamid. To modernize their country they invited the British to reform their navy and the Germans their army. In June 1913 General (later Field Marshal) Otto Liman von Sanders arrived to head the German military mission.

London, meanwhile, dragged its feet in modernizing the Turkish navy and, in a very important development, on 28 July 1914, First Lord of the Admiralty Winston Churchill sequestered two dreadnoughts Turkey had ordered in 1911 and paid for by popular subscription. This aborted contract played a key role in enabling the pro-German faction in the Turkish government to achieve an alliance with Germany.

On 3 August 1914, Turkey had declared its armed neutrality. The Turkish leadership was sharply divided, with a majority favouring continued neutrality. The Central Powers desperately needed Turkey in the war on their side, especially with Italy neutral. Turkey was well situated for attacks on British-controlled Cyprus and the vital Suez Canal. The claim of Sultan

Mohammed V (1909–17) to be the leader of Islam and his proclamation of a *Jihad* (holy war) had implications for millions of Moslems within the British and French Empires and in southern Russia. Most importantly, Turkey controlled the vital water passageway to the Black Sea. Through this could pass military aid to Russia and Russian goods – chiefly grain – to pay for that aid. Without this, trade would have to pass through the Arctic or go through the Far Eastern port of Vladivostok, and then overland 5,000 miles along the trans-Siberian railway. With Turkey on their side the Central Powers could greatly inhibit Russia's capacity to wage war.

While the Turkish government vacillated, two German warships, the battle cruiser *Goeben*, the most formidable warship in the entire Mediterranean (commanded by Admiral Wilhelm Souchon), and the light cruiser *Breslau*, changed the course of the First World War. Although British and French naval units heavily outnumbered his own ships, Souchon succeeded in getting them to the Dardanelles and then to Constantinople. The presence of two German warships off the capital was of immense benefit to the pro-German faction. Without Berlin's concurrence, Souchon arranged to "sell" both warships to Turkey as replacements for the Turkish dreadnoughts sequestered by Britain. Renamed, the two warships retained their German crews and Souchon became commander of the Turkish navy while retaining his position in the Germany navy.

With the secret support of Turkish Minister of War Enver Pasha, the leading supporter of the German alliance, Souchon used his warships to provoke war between Russia and Turkey. On 29 October he carried out a bombardment of Russian bases under the guise of training exercises in the Black Sea. The Turkish cabinet was not informed in advance, and Souchon even reported that the Russians had attacked him first.[37]

The Dardanelles

Turkey's entry on the side of the Central Powers severed French and British access to the Black Sea and bottled up 350,000 tons of shipping there.[38] Driving her from the war would reduce pressure on Russia and allow her to move troops from the Caucasus Front facing Turkey. But because Britain and France initially focused on the Western Front, reopening the Dardanelles was at first not a high priority. The French, especially, opposed any plan other than pushing the Germans out of France. But stalemate on the Western Front led British leaders to consider resorting to their traditional strategy of indirect approach through sea power.

Perhaps the most controversial campaign of the war, the Dardanelles operation was also one of its great missed opportunities.[39] Early in the war First Lord of the Admiralty Churchill and Secretary of State for War Kitchener discussed a plan to involve Greece in the war. The Allies would support a Greek landing on the Gallipoli peninsula at the northern entrance of the Dardanelles in order to silence land batteries guarding the Straits; this would allow Allied naval forces to steam past and threaten Constantinople. The Greeks, who were to receive Cyprus as a reward, turned down the project.

At the end of December 1914 Lieutenant Colonel Maurice Hankey, Secretary of the British War Council, submitted another plan. He argued that, while French armies held the deadlocked Western Front, Britain should send three corps of Kitchener's newly raised army against Turkey in a combined operation, hoping both Greece and Bulgaria would support them.[40]

Most French generals, including Joffre, opposed Hankey's plan. They believed that a decision in the war could come only in its main theatre – France – and that all available forces should be massed on the Western Front. Churchill embraced the idea of an operation against Turkey and became its chief proponent because it offered "the only opportunity to use naval power by itself to win the war".[41] Churchill's plan differed from that of Hankey, however, in that it foresaw only a naval operation. British First Sea Lord Fisher went along on condition that the attack be "immediate" and involve land troops. Originally sceptical, Kitchener was persuaded by a plea from Russian commander Grand Duke Nicholas for a diversionary naval attack against Turkey to relieve pressure on the Caucasus Front. Kitchener also believed that no breakthrough in the West was possible until British war industries could provide much greater output. If Britain were to enjoy success in the short run, it would have to be outside Europe. Chancellor of the Exchequer David Lloyd George also supported the plan as an alternative to the slaughter of the Western Front and a means to boost British morale.[42]

The British Admiralty and Imperial General Staff had studied such an operation before the war, concluding that to succeed it would have to be a joint army–navy amphibious action. Kitchener, however, opposed drawing troops from France. He insisted on a purely naval operation. Churchill sold the plan to the War Council principally by excluding the need for troops and insisting that "surplus" naval forces would suffice. The War Council therefore decided on naval action alone against the Dardanelles, with Constantinople as its objective.[43]

Churchill and the plan's other advocates envisioned great gains from the operation. They believed it would drive Turkey from the war and possibly bring some of the Balkan states in on the Allied side. It would diminish the possibility of a Central Powers attack on the Suez Canal, Cyprus, or Aden, as well as expose the Central Powers to a new southwestern front. Churchill saw it as a means to break the costly deadlock on the Western Front. He also minimized the difficulties. He did not appreciate the need for training and specialized equipment, the vulnerability of ships to shore fire, and the necessity of amphibious operations to silence that fire.

At the beginning of January Churchill queried Admiral Sackville Carden, commander of the blockading squadron off the Dardanelles, whether he thought the Dardanelles might be forced by ships alone. "I do not consider Dardanelles can be rushed", Carden replied. "They might be forced by extended operations with large number of ships."[44] Carden wanted a methodical reduction of Turkish defences. His plan called for a task force of 12 battleships, 3 battle cruisers, 4 light cruisers, 16 destroyers, 6 submarines, and 12 minesweepers, along with auxiliary vessels and 4 seaplanes.

The heavy guns and armour of the battleships would be essential in reducing the shore batteries, while the battle cruisers were thought necessary to deal with a possible sortie by the former *Goeben*. The Admiralty added its newest dreadnought, the *Queen Elizabeth* (eight 15-inch guns), which was already scheduled to go to the Mediterranean for gunnery trials. France contributed a battleship squadron with supporting vessels under Admiral Émile Paul Guépratte.

On 13 January Britain's War Council unanimously ordered the Admiralty to "prepare for a naval expedition in February to bombard and take the Gallipoli peninsula with Constantinople as its objective".[45] Admiral Carden believed that, weather permitting, he could do the job in about a month. The assumption was that once the fleet reached Constantinople the mere threat of naval bombardment would drive Turkey from the war. If the *Goeben* had brought Turkey into the war, surely a powerful fleet would force her out.

Carden's task force was the most powerful ever assembled in the Mediterranean. It consisted of the dreadnought *Queen Elizabeth* (flagship), the battle cruiser *Inflexible*, 16 old battleships (four of them French), and 20 destroyers (six French). A flotilla of 35 minesweeping trawlers and a seaplane carrier were also sent out; and cruisers and submarines were also available.

General Otto Liman von Sanders, head of the German Military Mission and Inspector General of the Turkish Army, had been alerted to the possibility of a British attack when the Royal Navy had shelled the Dardanelles defences the previous November. In early 1915 the Turks had about 100 land guns defending the Dardanelles, 72 of which were in fixed emplacements in 11 different forts. Although most were old, the Germans had supplied two dozen new 5.9-inch (15 cm) howitzers capable of quick redeployment as well as some other modern pieces. The heaviest guns, along with torpedo tubes, searchlights, and minefields were at the entrance of the Dardanelles. The key was the Narrows, where the shores were only about a mile apart. There the Turks had located the bulk of their defences. They were, however, short of shells. Only two divisions of Turkish infantry, one on each side of the Narrows, were available to oppose a landing. Liman held that if the Allies had attempted one as late as March they would have been successful.[46]

Delayed by bad weather, the bombardment of the outer Turkish forts at Cape Helles did not begin until the morning of 19 February. The forts, although hit, did not return fire. That afternoon the British ships then closed to approximately 6,000 yards, whereupon some Turkish batteries returned fire, forcing them to withdraw. The encounter proved the need to close to decisive range in order to engage the shore guns in direct fire. Bad weather the next day forced an interruption.

The bombardment recommenced on 25 February. In two days it silenced the outer Turkish forts, allowing minesweepers to begin clearing a path for the larger ships. The next day demolition parties, accompanied by Marines, went ashore to complete destruction of the outer forts. The fleet then steamed into the Straits as far as had been swept and began bombarding the inner forts. On 2 March Carden signalled London that, unless bad weather intervened, he expected to be off Constantinople in two weeks.

His optimism, however, proved unfounded. Although the inner forts could be hit with the aid of spotter planes adjusting naval gunfire, damage was not significant. Turkish troops soon reoccupied abandoned positions. Turkish howitzers, which could fire from behind the crests of the hills, were not easily accessible to flat trajectory high-velocity naval guns, and these highly mobile pieces scored a growing number of hits on the ships from both sides of the Narrows. Although their fire did not bother the battleships it did affect minesweeping. Until troops could be landed to destroy the howitzers, their fire would prevent minesweeping; and until the minefields were cleared the big ships could not be brought close enough to destroy the Turkish earthworks.

On 3 March Carden's second-in-command, Admiral John de Robeck, reported that the operation would not succeed unless troops were landed to control one or both shores of the Straits. London resisted the demand for troops. Kitchener contemplated a large-scale land force only in the event of the fleet failing to get through.

The blame for this was largely Churchill's. He had assured the War Council that the navy would be able to do the job alone. Refusing to involve land forces at the beginning, he had not sent out the Marine division, which was available.[47]

Churchill kept up pressure on Carden. On 11 March he informed Carden that the goal was great enough "to justify loss of ships and men if success cannot be obtained without it".[48] Churchill also urged speed before the Germans sent submarines and passed along intelligence information that the Turks were running out of ammunition. Carden was terrified of taking responsibility for the destruction of any ships, and on 16 March his health broke. de Robeck then assumed command of the grand assault planned for two days later.

The naval effort to force the Narrows began on schedule on the 18th when Allied battleships opened a heavy bombardment of Turkish batteries in the Narrows. Although three ships sustained damage, most shore batteries were hit hard. Then disaster struck. The French battleship *Bouvet* was hit in one of her magazines and blew up, sinking in less than two minutes with the loss of 640 men. Allied shelling continued throughout the afternoon when de Robeck ordered his minesweepers forward, but they withdrew after coming under fire. Then the *Inflexible* hit a mine and had to be withdrawn. A few minutes later, a mine also disabled the battleship *Irresistible*. The shore gunners concentrated on her, and most of her men were taken off.

De Robeck then ordered a withdrawal for the night, instructing his chief of staff, Captain Roger Keyes, to stay behind in the Straits with the destroyers to organize the *Irresistible* for towing with the help of two other battleships, the *Ocean* and *Swiftsure*. Instead of concentrating on the salvage operation, however, the captain of the *Ocean* shelled shore installations. Soon she, too, was hit by an explosion, which disabled her steering. Keyes ordered the *Swiftsure* to retire with the crew of the *Ocean*. He then met with De Robeck aboard the *Queen Elizabeth* to secure permission to sink the *Irresistible* by torpedo and to determine if the *Ocean* could be salvaged. As Keyes returned, there was a great explosion. No trace of the *Irresistible* and *Ocean* was found. Only later was it learned that both had succumbed to a small belt of 20 mines laid parallel with the shore by a small steamer only ten days before the assault. Allied seaplane patrols had failed to detect them.

De Robeck was depressed by the loss of the capital ships, but Keyes and other senior officers believed that one more determined push by the fleet would be decisive. The shore batteries had used up half their ammunition that one day and were down to their last armour-piercing shells. The Turks had also expended virtually all their mines.[49]

A great storm now blew in and damaged some ships, but preparations went forward. On 19 March Whitehall ordered de Robeck to renew the assault, promising a reinforcement of five battleships (four British and one French). On 20 March de Robeck had 62 vessels ready for minesweeping and announced that the offensive would be renewed in a few days. Two days later de Robeck changed his mind. Back in London in an acrimonious session the War Council decided to let the views of commanders on the spot prevail. The naval offensive was not renewed.[50]

The attempt to force the Dardanelles with warships alone cost the British and French 700 lives, three battleships sunk and two crippled, and damage to other ships. Turkish War Minister Enver Pasha correctly pictured the repulse as a great victory for his country.

Gallipoli

For political reasons the campaign had to be continued, but it now shifted to land operations on the Gallipoli Peninsula. Naval activities then consisted chiefly of gunfire support and resupply. The decision for a land operation entailed the diversion of additional naval assets, which caused Fisher to resign as First Sea Lord. Subsequent reshuffling of the government also saw Churchill removed as First Lord of the Admiralty; not long afterward he was a lieutenant colonel commanding a British Army battalion on the Western Front. In 1917 he returned to the cabinet as minister of munitions.

London had decided before the 18 March naval bombardment to send out land forces. On 1 March Prime Minister Eleutherios Venizelos of Greece had offered three divisions, but the Russians vetoed this plan as threatening their war aim of controlling the Straits. When this news reached Athens the Venizelos government fell and a pro-German ministry replaced it.[51]

On 19 February Kitchener released the well-trained 29th Division for Gallipoli, but opposition from British and French generals caused him to substitute the new Australian and New Zealand Corps (ANZAC) of two divisions then in Egypt. On 10 March Kitchener restored the 29th and added the Royal Naval Division. The French also agreed to send a division.

General Sir Ian Hamilton, commander of this "Mediterranean Force" of some 70,000 men since 12 March, arrived at the Dardanelles in time to watch the naval bombardment six days later. In spite of the probability of employing troops, there had been little preliminary planning. Maps were few and inaccurate and information on Turkish forces was virtually non-existent. Hamilton also lost valuable time by choosing to stage his forces in Egypt.

Liman von Sanders, ably assisted by Turkish Colonel Mustapha Kemal, had meanwhile been active. He had six widely dispersed divisions of the Turkish Fifth Army. The Gallipoli Peninsula was hilly and rocky, ideal defensive

terrain, and Liman von Sanders organized strong positions in the hills immediately behind the likely invasion beaches. He placed the bulk of his troops at
central points from which they could be quickly shifted to invasion sites.

Frantic efforts by the Allies finally led to the collection, off Mudros on the
island of Lemnos, of an armada of 200 ships supported by 18 battleships, 12
cruisers, 29 destroyers, 8 submarines, and a host of smaller craft. On 25 April
Allied troops landed on the Gallipoli Peninsula from barges towed by motor-
boats in two main lodgements. The 29th Division went ashore on five
beaches at Cape Helles on the end of the peninsula, while the ANZAC Corps
landed about 15 miles farther up (about a mile farther north than planned)
near Gaba Tepe at a beach still called Anzac Cove.

Turkish opposition was fierce, machine-gun fire in particular producing
heavy Allied casualties, but by nightfall the invaders were established ashore.
At the same time French troops went ashore at Kum Kale on the Asiatic side
of the Straits where they encountered a larger Turkish force. Advance there
proving impossible, on the 27th the French were extracted and transferred
to Helles.[52]

By the first week in May the Gallipoli fighting developed into trench
warfare similar to that on the Western Front, save that opposing lines were
often only yards apart. The reinforced Turks were well dug in and could easily
detect any Allied moves to drive them from their almost impregnable positions. Turkish artillery was also ideally positioned to shell the beaches.

Early in May the Allies reinforced the bridgeheads with two additional
divisions – one each from Britain and France – and a brigade from India.
Some ground was gained on 6 May, but stalemate followed. The British then
dispatched five additional divisions, monitors for shore bombardment, more
aircraft, and a number of armoured landing barges. But Turkish strength also
increased to 16 (albeit smaller) divisions.

A new naval attack was abandoned in mid-May after the Turks sank the
British battleship *Goliath*. Only submarines could make the passage through
the Narrows to interfere with Turkish shipping. Of 12 sent (nine British and
three French), seven were lost. One British submarine, the *E-14*, reached the
Sea of Marmara and sank a Turkish troopship with 6,000 men aboard, all of
whom perished. German submarines were also active. The *U-21* sank two old
British battleships, the *Triumph* and *Majestic*.[53]

The Allies now decided to employ two of their new divisions at Suvla Bay
north of Anzac Cove to outflank Turkish defenders there and draw them
away from Anzac. At the same time Allied units at Anzac were to break out
and seize the high ground to the east of Suvla dominating the landing areas.
Diversionary attacks would take place at Cape Helles.

Although the British successfully landed at Suvla Bay on the night of

6–7 August, Mustapha Kemal, now a corps commander, contained the landing to little more than a toehold. Liman von Sanders shifted resources north to Suvla Bay; inept Allied ground commanders at Anzac wasted the opportunity to break through the weakened lines.

At the end of August the French offered to send out a whole army, and the British found two additional divisions for yet another invasion, planned for November. This had to be postponed, however, when Bulgaria entered the war on the side of the Central Powers. This immediate threat to Serbia impacted the situation at Gallipoli. Hamilton was forced to send two of his divisions to Salonika in northern Greece. Bulgaria' entry into the war also aided Turkey in that after Serbia was overrun it provided a direct rail link for Central Powers munitions to reach her.

By the middle of September Paris concluded that there was no hope for the Gallipoli campaign. But London persisted, unwilling to sacrifice a venture on which so much had been invested. General Hamilton also strongly opposed evacuation. But much criticism appeared in the Australian and British press based on reports by war correspondents about incompetent British land commanders.[54]

In October 1915 General Sir Charles Monro replaced Hamilton. Monro concluded that Allied positions ashore were unsatisfactory. With little prospect for improving them without substantial reinforcements, the army would run serious risks in trying to cling to its positions in winter without a major supply base.

Kitchener then went to Gallipoli to see for himself. A blizzard at the end of November caused enormous suffering among the Allied troops on the peninsula, and Kitchener advised evacuation as the only reasonable course. With both the French and Russians arguing for the Salonika front as an alternative, on 7 December the British Cabinet decided to evacuate Gallipoli. Monro predicted up to 40 per cent losses.

On 8 December orders went out to Monro to withdraw his forces from Suvla and Anzac, retaining the lodgement at Helles. Night after night the Allies withdrew vast stocks of supplies; and on the night of 18–19 December the troops were taken off from Suvla Bay and Anzac Cove. The Turks caught unawares, awoke to find their enemy gone.

Liman von Sanders decided to concentrate his resources against the last redoubt at Cape Helles. Here the Allies had four divisions totalling 35,000 men. On 17 December the British Cabinet decided to evacuate them as well. French troops withdrew unscathed on 1 January 1916. On successive nights the remaining men and equipment were gradually withdrawn. The weather was poor and Turkish shells caused a number of casualties on the beaches. On 7 January the Turks launched a determined assault but failed to pierce the

British lines. The difficult evacuation of the Helles Beaches was carried out on the night of 8–9 January, again without loss, although bad weather prevented some ordnance and ammunition from being evacuated. Its demolition by the British informed the Turks that the evacuation at Helles was over.

The evacuation of the Gallipoli Peninsula was the largest operation of its kind prior to Dunkirk in 1940. It was also the only well-executed part of the entire campaign. There are no accurate casualty totals for the 259-day campaign. Total Allied losses were some 252,000 men. Turkish records are incomplete, and their official figure of 251,309 is undoubtedly low.[55]

The Allied failure at the Dardanelles meant that Turkey continued in the war. The Strains remained closed, cutting off Russia from Western aid, which undoubtedly helped bring about her military collapse and the Bolshevik Revolution. The Gallipoli landing was much studied in the years following the war. It led to considerable experimentation in naval aviation and landing and resupply techniques, all of which proved influential in the development of US Marine Corps amphibious doctrine in the Second World War. If the Allies had been prepared to commit at the beginning of the campaign the resources ultimately deployed they probably would have been successful.

The Balkan Front

As stated earlier, developments in the Balkans greatly influenced the decision to withdraw from Gallipoli. Although overshadowed by more dramatic fighting elsewhere, the Balkan Front was nonetheless an important theatre. In order to continue in the conflict, Turkey needed supplies from Austria-Hungary and Germany. But the direct Berlin-to-Constantinople railroad line through Serbia had been disrupted immediately on the start of the war, and in June 1915 neutral Romania halted the flow of arms through its territory. If Turkey were to continue in the war the Central Powers had to defeat Serbia.

Sickness now proceeded to do what Austro-Hungarian arms had earlier failed to accomplish. At the end of 1914 typhus broke out among Austrian troops in Valjevo. This quickly spread to the civilian population and, when it recaptured the town in December, to the Serbian Army. By May Allied medical units and the American Red Cross had brought the epidemic under control but not before some 100,000 people had died. To add to Serbia's troubles, a rebellion encouraged by Bulgaria broke out in Macedonia, which had come under Serbian rule as a result of the Balkan Wars. The Serbs suppressed the revolt only with difficulty and after granting political concessions. Serbia, which the Western Allies were either unwilling or unable to strengthen with technical assistance, artillery, and munitions, was extremely vulnerable.[56]

Balkan Front

The Allies had long pressed Bulgaria to join them but her price was the acquisition of Macedonia. The Allies regarded this as reasonable on ethnic grounds, but Serbia refused to consider it. The Central Powers, however, were prepared to cede what Bulgaria wanted – Serb and Greek territory. In July the Germans persuaded the Turks to cede to Bulgaria a strip of territory along the Maritza River. In August Bulgaria obtained a sizable loan from Germany and the Dual Monarchy. Also influencing Bulgaria's decision were the success of the Central Powers on the Eastern Front and the failure of the Allies at the Dardanelles and Gallipoli. On 6 September, therefore, Bulgaria concluded an alliance with Germany and Austria-Hungary and two weeks later began to mobilize. The alliance provided for a joint attack on Serbia, with the two Central Powers providing six divisions each and the Bulgarians four. In return the Central Powers guaranteed Bulgaria Macedonia. If Romania joined the Allied side Bulgaria would receive the Dobrudja from her and, should Greece prove hostile, the Kavalla region.[57]

When Bulgaria mobilized, Serbia appealed for assistance to Britain and France. She also sought the aid of Greece under terms of a 1913 treaty between those two states.[58] Greek Premier Venizelos, who had returned to power only in August, wanted to join his country to the Allied side but insisted that the Entente provide the 150,000 men that Greece was bound to send to the Bulgarian frontier according to its 1913 treaty with Serbia. The Western Allies agreed and Venizelos acceded to their request to land troops at Salonika. But the Allies were in no position to send 150,000 men immediately. In early October one French and one British division reached there, with two additional French division landing at the end of the month.

In the meantime London and Paris continued frantic efforts to get Athens to join the war on their side, even promising Cyprus in the bargain. Since Greece was treaty bound to help Serbia in the event of a Bulgarian invasion, Venizelos mobilized the army. But with Constantine and popular opinion opposed to the mobilization and to foreign troops at Salonika, on 5 October Venizelos resigned. Greece would remain neutral.

Falkenhayn had given overall command of the Serbian invasion to capable and energetic Eighth Army commander August von Mackensen, now a field marshal. Command of the German Eleventh Army passed to General Max von Gallwitz. Falkenhayn insisted that Hindenburg provide the bulk of the troops for the upcoming Serbian invasion. Hindenburg resisted but the Kaiser intervened in Falkenhayn's favour.

Austria-Hungary's desperate military position (five of her divisions were engaged against the Russians east of the Bug River) mandated that Germany furnish not six but ten divisions. Mackensen's plan was simple yet effective. It called for Gallwitz's German Eleventh Army and General Baron Hermann Kövess von Kövessháza's Austro-Hungarian Third Army to strike from the north, after which Bulgaria would send its First and Second armies from the east to cut off any Serbian retreat south.

On 6 October the Germans and Austro-Hungarians invaded Serbia, crossing the Danube and Sava Rivers on a wide front. Five days later the Serbs were caught by surprise when the two Bulgarian armies invaded from the southwest.

Serbia's situation was now desperate. She could expect little help from either the Western Allies or Russia. Weakened by her military efforts the previous year and the typhus epidemic, she faced four invading armies, the combined strength of which – 330,000 men – was nearly double her own.

The northern offensive went forward with ruthless efficiency. The Serbs fell back, fighting desperately and managing to evade envelopment. Belgrade fell on 10 October and Kragujevac, 50 miles south of the Danube and Serbia's principal arsenal, on 21 October. By the end of the month the northern invasion force had linked up with the Bulgarians on the Danube. The Bulgarian thrust in the south also had gone well. On 22 October the Bulgarians severed communications between the Serbian Army and Salonika, and Niš fell on 5 November. Half of Serbia was in enemy hands and its army was disintegrating.

The British and French in Salonika belatedly tried to halt the Bulgarian advance. In early November General Maurice P. E. Sarrail, in command of the French contingent, made a tentative advance up the Vardar Valley into Serbia. But it was both too little and too late. Three weeks later the Allies withdrew back to Salonika. Serbia was lost.

On 8 November Greece declared herself a "Benevolent Neutral" favouring the Allies, She agreed to allow them to continue at Salonika in return for a pledge that they would eventually restore her territory. Despite this agreement, the Greek Army did all it could, short of actual fighting, to obstruct the Allies in Salonika. The Allies' actual intervention was a bombardment of the Bulgarian port of Dedeagach on 21 November, but this had no effect on land operations.

The Serb government, army, and refugees now retreated into Albania. General Putnik supervised an epic Serb retreat across the Albanian mountains, carried out in winter at great human cost by starving and inadequately clothed soldiers over ice-bound mountain passes. Medicine was also in short supply.

There was no relief when the Serbs arrived at Shkodër. With the Austrians launching air attacks on the town, the Serbs continued another 60 miles south to Durrës on the coast where, under protection of an Italian garrison, British, French, and Italian ships evacuated survivors to the Greek island of Corfu, which the French had occupied on 11 January without Greek consent. By 10 February the evacuation was complete. The Central Powers now occupied all of Serbia, Montenegro, and Albania (except for the area around Vlorë, controlled by the Italians). Sporadic mountain warfare between the Italians and Austrians continued in Albania until the end of the war.

The Serbian Army, 300,000 men at the start of the war, was reduced to only 75,000, and the Central Powers had a secure overland link with Turkey.[59] In these circumstances London favoured evacuating Salonika but, because General Sarrail had powerful allies in the Chamber of Deputies, French Premier Briand advocated remaining there. He presented his reasons in diplomatic and military terms. If France and England allowed Germany to have a free hand in the Balkans, he argued, Russian and Italian interests would be threatened and Entente solidarity endangered. Also, 150,000 Allied troops could not only protect Salonika but pin down 400,000 Bulgarian and German troops in the Balkans. On 9 December Kitchener agreed that the Allies should remain. The French and British armies were now committed to a campaign that they both disliked and that tied down needed resources. British forces occupied a line to the north of Lake Doiran; the French the line of the Vardar River.[60]

War at sea

The war at sea, although inconclusive, went closer to Allied expectations. The year began badly for the British when, early on the morning of 1 January in the English Channel, the *U24* sank the unescorted battleship *Formidable* with the loss of 571 men.

The Royal Navy did increasingly tighten its naval blockade of Germany. London added items originally omitted from the contraband list, including copper, cotton, and oil. Finally, in March 1915, the blockade became total with the inclusion of foodstuffs.

Dogger Bank

On 24 January the long-awaited first fleet action of the war occurred off the Dogger Bank in the North Sea. This engagement sprang from the 1914 German cruiser raids against east coast British towns. To facilitate future interception of such forays, in December the Admiralty had moved Admiral Sir David Beatty's battle cruiser squadron from Scapa Flow to Rosyth.

Hopeful of destroying British light surface ships, German navy commander-in-chief Admiral von Ingenohl directed Admiral Franz Ritter von Hipper to patrol the Dogger Bank area with 3 battle cruisers (his flagship the *Seydlitz*, *Derfflinger*, and *Moltke*), the slow armoured cruiser *Blücher*, 4 light cruisers, and 19 destroyers.

After the British intercepted and decoded Hipper's orders Whitehall ordered the Grand Fleet to rendezvous at the Dogger Bank. At 7.15 am on 24 January, in good weather conditions, Beatty made contact with the Germans. His squadron consisted of the battle cruisers *Lion* (flagship), *Tiger*, *Princess Royal*, *New Zealand*, and *Indomitable*; 17 light cruisers; and 35 destroyers.

Recognizing that he was outgunned, Hipper immediately reversed course for home, his squadron slowed by the *Blücher*. At about 9.00 am Beatty's ships caught up with the Germans, opening fire at 20,000 yards. But his order that his ships engage their "opposite number" led to confusion and unequal fire distribution, while the Germans concentrated their fire on the *Lion* in the British van.

The *Blücher* and the *Seydlitz* were badly damaged, and the Germans were saved only because their gunfire began to have its effect on the *Lion*, which slowed down. Beatty's subsequent flag signals for his other ships to take a new course, press the enemy, and attack the enemy rear, were misunderstood, causing them to concentrate on the *Blücher*, by then a flaming wreck. She fought to the bitter end, taking perhaps seven torpedoes and more tan 70 shells before going down. Of her complement of 1,026 men, 792 were lost. By the time Beatty shifted his flag to the *Princess Royal* the German battle cruisers had escaped. The *Seydlitz* sustained heavy damage; the *Derfflinger* slight damage. Although the *Lion* took 17 German shell hits, only 12 of her crew were wounded. Material damage was severe, however; repairs took four months. Two other British vessels were also hit, although with only light casualties and damage. The battle revealed deficiencies in British protective measures, and failure to correct these had an impact in the 1916 Battle of Jutland. The Royal Navy did, however, take strong steps to correct signalling procedures.

For the Germans, cordite fires in the *Seydlitz's* after-turrets led to changes in their procedures for handling ammunition, mainly by limiting the number of charges in opened cases at any one time. But *Derfflinger's* crew neglected these measures at Jutland and, as with *Seydlitz* at Dogger Bank, the ship suffered fires that put both of her after-turrets out of action. Also the battle produced severe criticism of Admiral Ingenohl for making no arrangement to support Hipper's squadron with battleships. This, coupled with the Falklands disaster and the loss of the battle cruiser *Yorck* to friendly mines, hurt Ingenohl's standing with the Kaiser, who replaced him with Admiral Hugo von Pohl on 2 February. Wilhelm II ordered Pohl not to risk his heavy ships, which had an impact on events the next year at Jutland.[61]

Unrestricted submarine warfare

In early 1915 the naval staff finally won the Kaiser over to unrestricted submarine warfare against Britain. The risk of this policy was that it might bring the United States into the war. President Woodrow Wilson had pointed out early on to Berlin that submarine warfare to keep supplies from reaching Britain limited the freedom of American trade on the high seas. Wilson also believed that it was immoral to sink a vessel without both warning and making provision for the safety of its passengers and crew.

On 4 February 1915, nevertheless, the German government declared the waters around Great Britain and Ireland, including the whole of the English Channel, to be a war zone. From 18 February every merchantman, including neutral vessels, in this zone would be subject to attack. The Germans justified this decision on the grounds of both self-preservation and a countermeasure against the British blockade. Indeed, unrestricted submarine warfare was no more a violation of international law than the British blockade.

To a query from Washington Berlin responded that if Britain lifted the prohibition on imports into Germany of food and raw matériel she would abandon her submarine blockade. While willing to lift the ban on foodstuffs in return for an end to the submarine attacks, London was not willing to lift the prohibition on raw materials. The British government announced on

1 March that Britain would intercept all trade with Germany, bringing vessels into British ports for search.

Germany began the U-boat campaign with an incredibly small force of only 29 boats.[62] It also carried great diplomatic risk, especially regarding the United States. During 1915 there were no fewer than six incidents involving vessels carrying passengers from neutral countries. On 19 February *U-16* sank the Norwegian tanker *Belridge* in the North Sea. On 1 May the *Gulflight*, the first US merchant ship torpedoed without warning, went down to *U-30* off Sicily with the loss of two lives. This paled, however, next to what happened a week later with the Cunard liner the *Lusitania*.

On 1 May the *Lusitania*, one of the two largest passenger liners in trans-Atlantic service, sailed from New York for Liverpool. The Admiralty knew from decoded German radio traffic that three U-boats were operating south of Ireland, but the *Lusitania*'s captain was given no warning of them; nor was he told that her escort, the cruiser *Juno*, had been withdrawn. On 7 May a torpedo from *U-20* detonated just forward of the *Lusitania*'s bridge as the ship passed about ten miles off the coast of southwest Ireland. A second explosion, almost certainly from a contraband cargo of small-arms ammunition, caused the liner to sink rapidly by the bow, drowning 1,201 of the 1,965 passengers on board. At least 124 of the dead were Americans.[63]

Defending her actions against resultant criticism, Berlin pointed out that passengers had been warned not to sail on the *Lusitania* into the war zone. Many Americans called for war with Germany, but Wilson set himself strongly against such a step.

Many in the German navy believed that unrestricted submarine warfare was the only effective means of fighting Britain, even if it meant US entry into the war. Most German political leaders, however, understood the necessity of avoiding war with the United States. Chancellor Bethmann-Hollweg tried to ease tensions between the two nations. On 5 June, therefore, Berlin ordered U-boat captains not to sink large passenger ships on sight. Nevertheless, on 19 August 1915, *U-24* sank the British passenger liner *Arabic*, killing 40 people including three Americans. This brought the temporary cancellation of Germany's unrestricted submarine warfare policy. Admiral Tirpitz challenged this decision, pointing out that while U-boats had sunk 748,000 tons of British shipping in 1915, Britain and her empire had launched more than 1.3 million tons. He believed that a vigorous campaign would bring sinkings to 600,000 tons a month and enable Germany to end the war in 1916.

The proponents of submarine warfare underestimated Britain's maritime strength, but their arguments finally won the Kaiser's approval. Unrestricted submarine warfare resumed on 23 February 1916, with the proviso that only armed freighters were to be sunk without warning. But on 14 March a

German submarine sank the French passenger ship *Sussex* off Boulogne. Although no Americans were lost, a sharp note from Washington brought a pledge from Berlin that no merchant ships would be sunk in the future without warning and making provision for the safety of those aboard. This ended unrestricted submarine warfare. Bethmann Hollweg supported the compromise solution that would not bring the United States into the war. This policy continued until early 1917.[64]

Air war

Air power also came into its own in 1915. Although German planes had dropped bombs on Paris during the 1914 Battle of the Marne, this achieved little beyond outraging Parisians when Notre Dame Cathedral was slightly damaged. Much more important were aerial reports of German military movements prior to the Battle of Mons and the sighting of Kluck's turn west of Paris that led to the First Battle of the Marne.

The most important aircraft of the First World War were two-seaters used for reconnaissance, aerial photography, and artillery observation. Tethered balloons were also used for these purposes, but aircraft proved far less vulnerable. Control of the air over the battlefield soon became vital, with most aerial combat occurring over or near the trench lines where the bulk of reconnaissance and spotting took place.

Both sides developed anti-aircraft guns to shoot down planes from the ground. The Germans knew anti-aircraft fire as "flak", an acronym for *flieger* (plane) *abwehr* (defence) *kanone* (cannon), and the British as "ack-ack". Anti-aircraft artillery steadily increased in effectiveness during the war thanks to advances in munitions, sound location, searchlights, and crew training.

But the best way to shoot down enemy aircraft was to arm one's own planes. Pilots and observers on both sides began carrying small arms and taking occasional shots at enemy aircraft. Not long afterward they also carried machine guns aloft. These were mounted either for an observer to fire or fixed in order that the pilot could aim the plane at a target. The machine gun became the key weapon of the air war. A biplane could mount a gun with a drum magazine on its upper wing in order to avoid the propeller arc. But aiming and reloading were difficult and when the gun jammed, as was often the case, clearing it by hand was both arduous and dangerous. More than one aviator fell from his cockpit in the process.

In April 1915 Frenchman Roland Garros, a stunt pilot before the war, mounted an automatic rifle on the hood of his monoplane and installed a primitive synchronizer gear designed by Raymond Saulnier that allowed bullets to pass safely through the plane's propeller. Because the device was imperfect, Garros also fitted the propeller with metal cuffs to deflect stray bullets that might hit the blades. Although crude, the process was effective and over the next several weeks Garros shot down several enemy planes before he was shot down by anti-aircraft fire during a bombing run on a German train. Dutch aircraft designer Anthony Fokker, working for the Germans, took it a step farther. He developed a truly effective cam-operated synchronizer that allowed bullets to miss the propeller altogether. He combined his synchronizer with the Spandau or Parabellum machine gun mounted on an Eindecker (monoplane).[65] In August 1915 there began an eight-month period known as the "Fokker Scourge", when the Germans dominated the skies over the Western Front before the Allies developed their own effective synchronizer gear.

Specialized aircraft also appeared. Two-seaters were the mainstay for observation purposes. There were also single-seater "scouts", "fighting scouts", or "fighters" as they came to be known. They were used not only to shoot down enemy aircraft in "dogfights" but also in ground attacks.

Pilots were an exclusive club but those who flew fighter aircraft were the prima donnas of the war. Contrary to popular myth, overall pilot fatalities were not out of line with the infantry on the ground, although loss rates for aces were higher.

Planes themselves underwent considerable change. Five generations of fighter aircraft appeared during the war. The last, appearing just before the end, were single-wing all-metal craft. By the summer of 1917 a series of outstanding Allied fighters, including the SE5 and Sopwith Camel, began to reach the front, giving the Allies a qualitative superiority that they held the rest of the war. Aircraft were consumed at a high rate; in 1918 the British estimated the life of a warplane at only six months. Fortunately for the Allies they were able to outproduce Germany. At the end of the war the French had a front-line strength of 3,700 aircraft, the British 2,600, and the Germans 2,500. One scholar has estimated total aircraft production by all powers during the war at 150,000 planes.[66]

By 1917 the Allies developed an integrated doctrine of air power, using fighters in connection with artillery fire to attack observation balloons and ground troops. This culminated in the 1918 St Mihiel offensive in which no fewer than 1,481 Allied airplanes took part. Under the command of American Colonel Billy Mitchell the Allied air forces flew trench-strafing, close air support, interdiction, and air superiority missions pioneered by the British. In the process Mitchell demonstrated the potential of air power for the future. He even tried to convince General John Pershing of the feasibility of parachuting an entire division behind enemy lines.

Bombers developed later than fighters. Early bombing was, more often than not, random. The British Royal Naval Air Service may have conducted the first effective "strategic" bombing raids of the war in September and October 1914, when planes carrying 20-pound bombs flew from Antwerp to strike Zeppelin sheds at Düsseldorf and destroyed one airship.[67]

The Germans used Zeppelins for both aerial reconnaissance and bombing missions. The lighter-than-air Zeppelin was in fact the first strategic bomber. Although more vulnerable than airplanes they had much greater bomb-carrying capacity. In 1914 Germany had some 20 of them supporting both its army and navy. On 6 August *L6* flew from Cologne to attack Liège, Belgium. Its bombs killed nine civilians before, holed by Belgian ground fire, it crashed near Bonn.

The Kaiser, initially refusing to permit air raids on London, then altered this stance. On 19–20 January 1915, Germany carried out it first aerial bombing raid on Britain, using Zeppelins. The largest raid was against London on 13 October. The material damage inflicted by Zeppelins was relatively modest. A total of 51 Zeppelin attacks (208 sorties[68]) during the war on the British Isles dropped 196 tons of bombs, killing 557 people and wounding 1,358. British sources estimated that the raids caused £1,500,000 in property damage.

By mid-1916 British defenders had gained the upper hand. Countermeasures included searchlight batteries, anti-aircraft guns, and aircraft machine guns firing incendiary bullets, to which the hydrogen-filled Zeppelins were particularly vulnerable. Zeppelin raids declined steadily to only four in 1918. Although the German Zeppelin campaign diverted British air defence resources from the Western Front (12 fighter squadrons of 110 aircraft and 2,200 men, plus anti-aircraft units with more than 17,000 additional personnel), its actual effect was minimal.

German navy use of Zeppelins for scouting was frequently negated by bad weather, as when dense mist prevented two Zeppelins at the 1916 naval Battle of Jutland from making any notable contribution. In all, the German Navy lost 53 of its 73 airships, while the army lost half of its fleet of 52. Weather, accidents, air raids on Zeppelin sheds, and improved defences made Zeppelin service even more hazardous than U-boat duty. Heavy Zeppelin losses led the German Army to abandon them entirely in June 1917, although the navy continued to employ them for observation and reconnaissance.[69]

Aircraft were not as vulnerable to anti-aircraft fire as Zeppelins. By early 1915 the first bombing directives had appeared, making the bombers an extension of artillery, able to strike well beyond the range of conventional guns. During the March 1915 Battle of Neuve Chapelle the British were the first to use bombers as an extension of the land campaign. Hoping to disrupt the flow of men and supplies to the fight in progress, the British sent bombers against railway installations.[70]

The planes used for these missions were former observation aircraft adapted for the purpose. The French were the first to form units of aircraft specifically dedicated to bombing missions.[71] Most early bombing was, however, extraordinarily inaccurate, and problems grew with increases in anti-aircraft guns and fighter aircraft.

The Germans developed the twin-engine G plane or *Grossflugzeug* (known as the Gotha, after one of its builders) and multi-engine *Riesenflugzeug* or "R" series bombers, some of which could carry up to a 2,200-pound bomb. The first Gotha/R raids began in May 1917. Most of these were at night with London as the target. In all the Germans mounted 435 bomber sorties over Great Britain. Although destruction by them during the war was limited, their attacks did kill 1,300 people, injure another 3,000, and inflict a fair amount of material damage. Virtually all the belligerent air forces engaged in strategic bombing and every capital, save Rome, was struck.[72]

The British had their twin-engine Handley-Page bomber. Similar to the Gotha in appearance, it had an endurance of eight hours and a bomb load of nearly 1,800 pounds. Despite this the British largely ignored it as a strategic bomber. By September 1917 there were just 18 of them in France, assigned to naval squadrons at Dunkirk. Not until June 1918 did the Independent Air Force (IAF) come into being. Commanded by General Hugh Trenchard, in September 1918 it had 120 aircraft, mainly Handley-Pages, for long-ranging bombing. In October 1918 Marshal Foch agreed to the creation of an Inter-Allied Air Force with Trenchard in command.

In May 1918 the British had flown a prototype of their Handley-Page V/1500. This four-engine bomber could carry 7,500 pounds of bombs and stay aloft for more than twelve hours. Three were fuelled and loaded for a raid on Berlin when the Armistice intervened. Had the war continued into 1919, the Allies would have launched massive bombing raids against Germany.[73]

Aircraft were also employed at sea, where they were especially useful for hunting submarines, locating enemy battle fleets, and adjusting naval gunfire.[74] The British even experimented with using them to launch torpedoes against ships. In 1915 they sent seaplanes armed with torpedoes against Turkish supply ships in the Dardanelles. Few naval officers, however, thought in terms of attacking warships in this fashion. Also, seaplanes were inferior in performance to land-based planes because their carriages had to be heavier to sustain the shock of landing aboard ships.

Aircraft carriers appeared, although none had full-length flight decks. Planes taking off from them were expected to land on shore or, in exceptional cases, in the water alongside, where they would float on air bags until they could be hoisted aboard. During the war only the Royal Navy used aircraft carriers in combat. Its *Ark Royal*, although she did not have a full flight deck, was the first ship commissioned in any navy that might be called an aircraft carrier. The first clear-deck carrier was the British *Argus*. Converted from a cruiser, she did not undergo sea trials until October 1918.[75] Aircraft carriers did not come into their full potential until the Second World War.

As 1915 drew to a close, both sides, despite enormous casualties, were far from exhausted. Each developed plans for renewed offensive actions on the Western Front. The Germans struck first, triggering the war's two biggest land battles. The new year would also see the largest sea battle of the war.

Chapter Four

1916: the cauldron

By the end of 1915 the British had 38 divisions in France. This fact and the enhanced quality and quantity of British munitions seemed to offer the Western Allies the possibility of ending the deadlock on the Western Front. At the very least, it offered some relief for the French, who had borne the brunt of the Allied military effort.

On 6–8 December Allied military leaders again met at Chantilly and agreed to develop a coordinated military strategy against the Central Powers. They approved Joffre's plan for simultaneous attacks on the Western, Italian, and Eastern Fronts. His Western Front plan involved a joint offensive north and south of the Somme River. Since this was where the two Allied armies met, Joffre believed that an attack there would maximize British participation. Although General Haig preferred to conduct his own offensive in the Ypres area, he agreed to Joffre's plan. By February 1916 the size of the attack had been set at 39 French and 30 British divisions. In order to give the British time to train new units and build up their supply of shells the offensive was set for late summer.[1]

Battle of Verdun

But the Germans struck first. General Falkenhayn knew the Central Powers could not afford to remain on the defensive. The Allies had superior resources in men and matériel and were increasing their numbers at a faster rate. At the same time the British naval blockade was creating shortages in Germany of both food and raw materials. OHL knew therefore that the German Army must strike a decisive blow in 1916. Austria-Hungary urged that the target be

Italy, but Falkenhayn vetoed that as well as an attack on Russia. Germany had already made substantial gains on the Eastern Front, and he believed the Russian army had been so mauled that it was unlikely to be a threat for some time. He hoped that internal pressures would drive both Russia and Italy from the war. In any case Falkenhayn considered the British Empire to be Germany's "arch enemy" and the Western Front its decisive theatre. Since Germany could not defeat Britain directly, he would strike France: "England's best sword".[2]

By the end of 1915 France was reeling. She had sustained 2,000,000 casualties, half of them dead. One more big push might finish her; at the least, a German attack would forestall any Allied Western Front offensive. Falkenhayn selected the fortress city of Verdun as the objective.[3]

Verdun, split by the Meuse River, lies 160 miles east of Paris. It had been a fort as early as Gallic times (its name means "powerful fortress"). In Roman times it had controlled transportation between Reims and Metz. France had acquired Verdun as a consequence of the Thirty Years' War (1618–48). After the 1871 loss of Alsace-Lorraine to Germany it became the cornerstone of new French defensive system. The French excavated four kilometres of passageways there capable of lodging 6,000 men and storing supplies.[4]

In the period immediately preceding the war the French downplayed fortifications in favour of the *attaque à outrance*, but the fortified Verdun–Belfort line, with a reputation as the world's most powerful, induced Schlieffen to favour a strike north through Belgium. The rapid reduction of the Belgian fortresses of Liège and Namur in 1914, however, seemed to prove the ineffectiveness of fortifications, and in 1915 the French had siphoned off men and armaments, especially 155 mm guns, from Verdun to other sectors.

In 1916 Verdun lay in the middle of a narrow salient projecting into German-controlled territory – its southern face was the counter-salient of St-Mihiel. The Verdun sector was heavily fortified but only lightly garrisoned. In early 1916 the French had only a single trench line some three miles beyond the outer forts along the Meuse Heights and only one reserve trench line. Not until the last week of January did Joffre begin to improve the Verdun defences, the result of prodding by Lieutenant Colonel Emile Driant, a brilliant soldier and National Assembly deputy then serving at Verdun, who bypassed the chain of command and reported the dire situation directly to his fellow parliamentarians. They reported it to Minister of War General Joseph Galliéni, who put pressure on Joffre.[5]

The salient lent itself to a converging German attack and it allowed concentrated artillery fire from three sides. Its woods and hills would screen troops and artillery, easily brought up via nearby railways and Metz. At the same time the French would find it difficult to resupply and reinforce Verdun. Only one road and a railroad line connected the fortress to the rest of France. The extreme narrowness of the salient would also make it difficult for the French to manœuvre, especially on the right flank with their backs to the Meuse. Taking Verdun would provide security for German railway communications south, less than 15 miles from the French lines. Falkenhayn knew that an Allied push there could render the whole German front untenable. The Germans also hoped that the capture of Verdun would have a serious effect on French morale, imperil their entire right wing, and threaten the Briey coal basin. Victory would also boost German morale, which had been shaken recently by the beginning of rationing within Germany. At the very least the Germans hoped to capture the east bank of the Meuse and hold the shortened front with fewer men.

Falkenhayn expected to catch the French by surprise. His attack would come on a narrow front from the north, supported by massive amounts of artillery. The code name for the operation was *Gericht* ("judgment"). For some time after the battle opened the French assumed that the Germans had chosen Verdun for a breakthrough similar to their own attempts of 1915, and there is still controversy over whether Falkenhayn intended to take Verdun. Certainly it was not his principal aim. Believing France would throw all remaining manpower into the defence of Verdun, he would use massive artillery fire to bleed her to death (*aufbluting*) in a battle of attrition. Following a heavy preliminary bombardment German infantry would secure a shallow penetration. The French were then expected to counterattack and would be slaughtered by massive artillery and machine-gun fire.

Falkenhayn entrusted the offensive to his Fifth Army, commanded by the Kaiser's son and heir Crown Prince Wilhelm. By 11 February, along a narrow front the Germans had assembled more than 850 guns, including some of the heaviest in the history of warfare, and 72 battalions of elite assault troops. The French had only 270 guns and 34 battalions of infantry in half-completed positions.

Bad weather, including snow, delayed events. The attack, originally scheduled for 12 February, was postponed, enabling the French to detect the German build-up and bring up reinforcements. Joffre and the French high command still largely discounted indications of a German attack; up until a few days before the attack Joffre was assuring Haig that the main blow would come on the Russian front. The French also failed to give proper attention to the sector because of their planned offensive along the Somme.[6]

The preliminary German bombardment finally opened at 7.15am on 21 February, raining 100,000 shells an hour on the French positions. The Germans then shifted their fire behind the French lines, and at about 4.00pm launched their ground attack on a six-mile front between Brabant and Ornes. The Crown Prince had wanted simultaneous attacks on both sides of the salient but, to minimize German losses, Falkenhayn initially ordered that the attack be confined to the left bank of the Meuse.[7]

The Germans planned to have their artillery do most of the work. Troops unable to advance were to halt and call for artillery support. Infantry were not to attempt frontal assaults of strong points; those that could not be reduced were to be bypassed and encircled. The Germans also had a new weapon, the flamethrower, to force defenders from their positions, and they were issued light mortars, grenades, barbed wire, and entrenching tools.[8]

The seven attacking German divisions met only two French divisions, much reduced by the preliminary bombardment, and easily took the outlying French defence zone. But in order to reach the main French forts the Germans had to capture the Bois des Caures, a small wooded area, held by two battalions of French chasseurs (light infantrymen) – 1,300 men commanded by Driant. Although the Germans concentrated all their strength there Driant reported to headquarters: "We shall hold against the Boche although their bombardment is infernal."[9] His men held for two critical days. Driant himself was killed, one of the first French heroes of the battle.

The initial assault had not gone as smoothly as the Germans had hoped. Not only had the French fought well, but the narrowness of the assault frontage worked against the Germans. Also the lack of a supporting attack west of the Meuse allowed French artillery to enfilade the Germans from across the river.

Still the Germans pushed forward. Brabant fell on 23 February and a French counterattack failed at the Bois des Caures. By the next day the defenders had lost half their 20,000 men and the Germans had taken the French reserve trench.

The Germans now faced Fort Douaumont. Located on high ground that commanded any approach, it was the linchpin of the Verdun defensive system. Reputedly impregnable, the fort was a quarter of a mile across and constructed of steel and concrete to be impervious even to the Germans' 420 mm "Big Berthas". It mounted one 155 mm and two 75s in retractable steel turrets, and its interior vaults could house a whole battalion of infantry. On 25 February the fort was manned by just 57 men – a fact unknown both to the Germans and to the French sector commander. Crack French units that were to occupy Douaumont did not receive orders to do so, and that day a handful of German soldiers took it without loss.[10] Its fall proved an almost fatal blunder for the French, as Douaumont dominated the remaining French defensive positions.

That same night French General Noël de Castelnau, sent by Joffre to assess

the situation, arrived at Verdun. He recommended that the entire Second
Army, then in reserve, be sent to Verdun. Castelnau also decided to maintain
the defence on the right bank of the Meuse with no withdrawal to the river,
a decision that committed the French Army to a costly holding action. On the
night of the 25th, Second Army General Henri Philippe Pétain took command at Verdun.[11]

Pétain set up his headquarters at Souilly, a village south of Verdun on
the Bar-le-Duc road. A general with a sense for defensive war who had the
respect and loyalty of his men, Pétain immediately rushed in reinforcements
and ordered that the remaining forts be fully manned. He developed an elastic
defensive scheme based on a "principal line of resistance" of the remaining
forts, to be held at all costs. In front of that extended an "advanced line of
resistance" designed to canalize German advances. A third line of redoubts in
the rear held reserves and reinforcements. Pétain also used artillery to good
advantage.

Pétain questioned both the strategic value of Verdun and the decision to
hold everywhere. In early March, when French President Raymond Poincaré
and General Joffre visited his headquarters, Pétain even suggested the possibility of withdrawal, whereupon Poincaré supposedly told him, "Don't
think of it, General. It would be parliamentary catastrophe."[12] As Falkenhayn
expected, Verdun became a matter of national honour for the French. The
same reason also kept the Germans from breaking off their attacks.

The French now faced a critical stituation. Although they had contained
German attempts at a breakthrough, assaults continued until 5 March. The
sole route into Verdun was the secondary road from Bar-le-Duc. Along what
became known as *la voie sacrée* (the sacred way), 66 French divisions – three-
quarters of the entire French Army – marched to the cauldron. "Ils ne
passeront pas" (they shall not pass), became the French rallying cry.

Falkenhayn now expanded the battle by extending it to both banks of
the Meuse River. On 6 March the Germans attacked the western face of
the salient, broadening the front by an additional 12 miles. Pétain, however,
had anticipated this and had reinforced there, with the result that the Germans
gained little more than a mile. On 8 March the Germans attacked on both
banks of the Meuse, but the French lines held.

The battle now became a true contest of attrition. Attacks and counterattacks raged throughout March. Casualities steadily mounted in savage
fighting back and forth across a ridge commanding the Meuse known omi-
nously as Mort-Homme (Dead Man). On 2 April the French lost the village
of Vaux, and its fort was threatened.

By rotating units in and out of the battle the French frustrated the German
plan to wear them down. They also organized an effective supply system along

the sacred way to sustain their eventual force at Verdun of 450,000 men and 140,000 animals. Despite German artillery fire, a steady stream of trucks (as many as 6,000 a day, or one every 14 seconds in each direction around the clock) brought in supplies and carried out wounded.

On 9 April the Germans launched their third main attack on both sides of the salient. Again the French held. Attacks and counterattacks continued (including an unsuccessful French effort to recapture Fort Douaumont on 22 May) until the German assault halted on 29 May. Generals Robert Nivelle and Charles Mangin ably assisted Pétain during the battle. Pétain was now such a national figure that Premier Aristide Briand suggested him for command of an army group. On 1 May Nivelle took command of French forces at Verdun.

At the beginning of June the Germans launched another attack against Thiaumont Farm and Fort Vaux, the smallest of the Verdun forts and the northeast bastion of its permanent fortifications. Vaux finally fell on 7 June. Once in possession of Douaumont and Vaux, the Germans could assault the last ridges on the right bank of the Meuse before Verdun: Froideterre, Thiaumont, and Souville. They assigned 19 regiments to the attack, of which 12 were on the 4-mile-long front line. The Germans positioned reserves close behind the line in order to take advantage of successes and provide continuity of effort in what would be the largest attack against Verdun.

On 23 June, after a two-day artillery preparation (including, for the first time, phosgene gas), the assault began. The Germans hoped to enter Verdun in two days. In bitter fighting Fleury and the fortifications of Thiaumont changed hands repeatedly. On 25 June the Germans committed their reserves. Pétain doubted that the French could hold and recommended abandonment of the eastern Meuse line. With a British drive along the Somme imminent, Joffre refused.

On 11 July the Crown Prince ordered 13 regiments to attack on practically the same front as the assault of 23 June. Although the Germans reached the superstructure of Fort Souville, less than 2.5 miles from Verdun and the closest they came to the city, by 20 July French counterattacks pushed them back.

The British Somme offensive forced the Germans to abandon their attack on Verdun. The Brusilov offensive also helped, for Falkenhayn heeded Conrad's urging and sent three divisions east. In the fall the French took the offensive. Nivelle utilized the creeping barrage (shifting fire forward 100 yards every four minutes, with the aim of suppressing German fire rather than destroying specific targets).[13] The French retook Douaumont on 24 October and Vaux on 2 November. On 15 December another French attack drove the Germans back more than three miles from Souville. By

August 1917 the French had recovered their front-line positions of February 1916.[14]

The Germans had not bled France to death or even taken Verdun. They had taken a few square miles of territory but at a terrible price. Estimates on casualties vary. The official French figure for losses in the battle for ten months of 1916 is 377,231 men. The Germans lost roughly 337,000. Taking into account fighting at Verdun before and after the 1916 battle, the French estimate for the battlefield is 420,000 dead and 800,000 gassed or wounded. Alistair Horne called Verdun "the worst battle in history".[15] Captain Augustin Couchin, later killed on the Somme, provided a personal touch in a letter of 14 April: "I came here with 175 men; I leave with 34, several of them half mad."[16]

The battle also profoundly affected German military strategy. They were unable to mount another such attack in the West until the spring of 1918, after the collapse of Russia. The battle also discredited Falkenhayn. The 29 August 1916 Romanian decision to enter the war against Germany was the last straw, as he declared it would not happen.[17] The Kaiser replaced him with Generals Paul von Hindenburg as chief of staff and Erich Ludendorff as quartermaster-general (assistant chief of staff). They believed the solution to the war lay in the East and promptly shifted the major German effort to that front.[18]

Although the Battle of Verdun was a victory of sorts for France it also had a significant adverse effect. War-weariness gripped the country and doubts arose about victory. For France Verdun symbolized heroism and fortitude, but also great suffering. It left behind a profound negative influence that lingered on long after the war. After Verdun, the French Army, perhaps even France, was never the same.

Joffre now came under severe criticism. His offensive strategy in 1915 had produced only failure and high casualties, his critics arguing that France would have done better to pursue a strictly defensive strategy until resources allowed a successful offensive. They also blamed Joffre for being caught by surprise at Verdun. In December 1916 French Premier Briand engineered Joffre's retirement, promoting him marshal of France and making him a technical advisor by way of compensation. Robert Nivelle replaced him as commander of French forces on the Western Front.

Battle of the Somme

The second great 1916 land battle on the Western Front, the Battle of the Somme, was closely tied to the fighting at Verdun. The battle there absorbed much of the French Army, making the joint Somme effort impossible and shifting the burden to the British. The purpose of the Somme attack also changed to that of relieving the German pressure on Verdun.[19]

In hindsight it is easy to criticize both the location and the plan for the Somme attack. Haig, who preferred the Ypres sector, had yielded to Joffre's decision to attack there. Joffre probably selected this juncture between the two armies as a means of assuring British cooperation. Certainly there were no obvious strategic objectives close behind the German lines.[20]

As finally developed, Haig's offensive occurred along 20 miles of front north of the Somme River, with General Sir Henry Rawlinson's British Fourth Army, formed in January 1916, making the main effort. South of the Somme General Marie Fayolle's French Sixth Army carried out a supporting attack, while in the north two divisions of General Sir Edmund Allenby's British Third Army mounted a diversionary attack. Haig sought to pierce the German lines and then widen the gap. General Sir Hubert Gough's three British infantry divisions and two Indian cavalry divisions would then rush through and swing to the northeast. Rawlinson wanted more modest goals – a limited "bite and hold" plan: a lengthy bombardment, limited infantry advance to readjust the line, consolidation, and then destruction of German counterattacks so as to inflict maximum casualties on the enemy. British resources were certainly inadequate for what Haig intended.[21]

In Haig's defence it should be noted that Joffre exhorted him to begin the offensive as soon as possible, and it was launched six weeks before Haig thought his men would be ready for battle. He also expected a larger French commitment to the battle and believed that Joffre deceived him on that score.[22]

Opposing the British, German General Fritz von Below's Second Army had six divisions on line, supported by five in close reserve. Although OHL expected an effort to relieve pressure on Verdun, Falkenhayn believed it would come in Alsace. Below, however, thought the attack would occur in his sector and put his men to work building an impressive defensive complex. They dug trenches into the hard chalk ground and excavated numerous deep bunkers. Some were 40 feet underground and largely impervious to shells. Along the whole line they had three, in some places four, defensive lines to an average depth of five miles.[23]

By June the BEF, with contingents from Australia, Canada, India, New Zealand, and South Africa, had over a million men organized into four armies of 58 divisions. With only 36 artillery batteries on 1 January 1915, the BEF had 191 batteries by 1 July 1916.[24]

Haig committed 18 divisions to the attack, 11 of which were from Kitchener's half-trained New Army. Most of these men were volunteers who had joined in large groups, in some cases from whole neighbourhoods, villages, associations or clubs. Such units often were designated "Pals Battalions". Their commanders hoped that what they lacked in experience would be made up in spirit. Because of their lack of training, the initial assault would be made in straight linear formations without complicated tactics or movements.[25]

To compensate for the infantry's lack of training, the British planned a massive artillery preparation. Rawlinson and other generals believed that this would eliminate the majority of first-line German defenders. After the shelling British Tommies would simply climb out of their trenches, dress up their formations, and walk (not run) with their 70lb packs across No Man's Land.

On 24 June the British began their preliminary barrage with 1,537 guns. Originally scheduled to last five days, the bombardment continued for seven when bad weather intervened. By the time the shelling had lifted, the British had fired 1,627,824 rounds. Mitigating the effect were a high number of duds and the fact that the British lacked guns heavy enough to destroy the new extensive German defensive works. The shelling also failed to destroy the German barbed wire – one of its principal aims. Patrols prior to the main attack reported that the wire was not only still intact in most places but was jumbled into even greater obstacles. Headquarters refused to believe the reports, attributing them to a reluctance to attack.[26]

At 7.20am the British detonated the first of three large and seven smaller mines dug under the German positions. The decision to blow this mine at 7.20am, a full ten minutes before the assault, was unwise, because it alerted the German infantry and their artillery immediately fired on every British trench in the area. At 7.28am the British blew the other mines, including the two with 24 tons of explosives each, the largest mines yet detonated on the Western Front.[27]

Exactly at 7.30am on 1 July the British halted artillery fire to allow resighting of their guns. The German guns were also silent and an eerie calm fell over the battlefield. The artillery fire then shifted from the forward German positions and almost 70,000 British troops in 84 battalions began to cross the 500–800 yards between the lines. Even though they were weighed down with unbelievable loads of ammunition, rations, personal gear, entrenching equipment, and even barbed wire, many of the troops saw the advance as a bit of a lark. They had been assured that after such a bombardment nothing would be left of the enemy, and that it would be an occupation rather than an assault. Lieutenant M. Asquith of the 1st Barnsley Pals told his men, "It's a walk-over." Another officer, a company commander and soon to be a fatality, gave each of his four platoons a ball to kick across No Man's Land, even kicking out the first one himself.[28]

107

As soon as the shelling shifted rearward the Germans left their deep bunkers and set up machine guns in the protective depressions of newly created shell craters. They then proceeded to slaughter the advancing British, who moved forward in long lines. Because Haig wanted to keep the momentum going in order to break through all the German lines, reserves went forward at the same time as the assault troops. Inevitably the attackers bunched up under fire. Some units did not even get past their own barbed wire before being mowed down. Others took their initial objectives but at high cost, some casualties resulting from British artillery firing on a fixed timetable.

As the day progressed Rawlinson continued to feed more men into the battle; by its end he had committed 143 battalions. At the end of what would be the bloodiest single day in British military history almost half of the men were casualties. The casualty rate for officers was a phenomenal 75 per cent. In all the British had sustained 57,470 casualties, 19,240 of whom were killed or died of their wounds. Historian Martin Middlebrook noted that in that one horrible day British casualties exceeded their combined total for three wars: the Crimean War, the Boer War, and the Korean War. German losses were only one-seventh those of the British, about 8,000.[29]

Almost none of the first day's objectives were attained, but senior British commanders located in the rear were slow to realize the magnitude of the catastrophe. The French on the extreme right, thanks in part to their heavier artillery, did make gains, but that was not the main attack. Only the British XIII Corps had some success; it took Montauban and crushed a subsequent German counterattack.

Haig's best course after the failure of the 1 July offensive was to reduce the scale of his diversionary attacks and transfer men to Flanders for a later offensive there.[30] Nevertheless, he continued the offensive, partly because Joffre stressed that it was vital to relieve pressure on Verdun. Haig, confident that sooner or later he could break through, decided to concentrate on his right where there had been some success. He reorganized his forces, establishing a new army. Later designated the Fifth, under Gough on the left, the army was astride the Ancre River. Haig also inserted fresh divisions and began replacing those with the heaviest losses.[31]

The next major British effort came in a daring night attack on 13–14 July with minimal losses. Attacking abreast, four British divisions took a 6,000-metre stretch of the Bazentin Ridge, the forward slope of which was the German second defensive line. The Germans quickly rushed in three divisions of their own. On 20 July the French and British mounted another attack with 17 divisions, the French taking a strong German position between Maurepas and the north bank of the Somme.

On 23 July the British tried to extend their advances farther north along Bazentin Ridge. Although bitter fighting raged back and forth, the sole British success came when two Australian divisions of the Anzac I Corps took Pozières. The Germans, meanwhile, continued to bring up reinforcements. Falkenhayn also reorganized Below's units south of the Somme into another army under General Max von Gallwitz.

On 4 September the French committed General Micheler's Tenth Army to the battle, extending the fighting 12 miles south of the Somme. The Allies then continued the assault on both sides of the river, north to the Ancre.[32]

Haig launched another major assault on 15 September with 12 divisions along a 10-mile front Combles to the Ancre. But rain had created muddy conditions and the offensive bogged down. To the south French forces achieved some success, advancing five to eight miles, but this had little influence on the main battle.[33]

First use of tanks

The most significant aspect of 15 September was the first use of tanks.[34] In 1915–1916 the French and British had independently developed armoured fighting machines. Neither coordinated with the other and this resulted in a profusion of machine types and no clear doctrine of tactical employment.

First Lord of the Admiralty Churchill had, in the autumn of 1914, allocated £70,000 of Admiralty funds for construction of "trench spanning cars". In January 1915 these had become "steam tractors with small armoured shelters and equipped with caterpillars". In February Churchill had formed a Landships Committee at the Admiralty. Before he resigned following the Gallipoli fiasco he convinced his successor, Arthur Balfour, not to drop the experiment.[35] The French called their new weapon a *char* (chariot). The British knew theirs as a "tank", the term used to disguise the contents of the large crates containing the vehicles when they were shipped to France.

The key figure in British tank development, Colonel E. B. Swinton, thought of tanks in ambitious terms. He believed that they could have a decisive impact on the battlefield. Rather than reveal the tanks prematurely, Swinton wanted to build a large number and then employ them without the warning of a preliminary bombardment. As he stated in his January 1916 "Notes on the Employment of Tanks":

Since the chance of success of an attack by tanks lies almost entirely in its novelty and in the element of surprise, it is obvious that no repetition of it will have the same opportunity of succeeding as the first unexpected effort. It follows, therefore, that these machines *should not be used in driblets* (for instance, as they may be produced), but the fact of their existence should be kept as secret as possible until the whole are ready to be launched, together with the infantry assault, in one great combined operation.[36]

Infantry would follow the tanks to exploit the breakthrough, with artillery performing counter-battery work against enemy guns. This concept seems reasonable today but was thought ridiculous at the time.

By the summer of 1915 both the British and French were producing large numbers of these machines. The British planned to build 150, the French 400. In the summer of 1916 Haig thought that even a few of them might be sufficient to tip the balance. Swinton opposed this but was overruled and replaced.

The Mark I tanks used in the Somme Offensive weighed fully loaded 28 tons each; they had a top speed close to 4 mph – over rough ground only 2 mph – a crew of eight men, and 0.5-inch armour. The "male" version had two 6-pounder naval guns in its sponsons and four Lewis machine guns. The "females" had six Lewis guns.[37]

Of the original 150 tanks, only 59 were in France when Haig made his decision to employ them; of these only 49 actually reached the battlefield. Plagued by mechanical problems, only 35 tanks got to their point of departure; 31 of these crossed the German trenches; only nine tanks surmounted all problems and pushed on ahead of the infantry.[38]

The tanks were far from impressive in their debut, in large part because they were too widely dispersed and not used according to a plan. Their crews were also not well-trained. Still, the few that did get into action had such a psychological impact that Haig immediately ordered 1,000 more.[39]

The French tank programme began later than the British. In December 1915 Colonel Jean Estienne, an artillery commander, wrote to Joffre suggesting that the French build caterpillar-type vehicles similar to the Holt tractors he observed in use by the British to service their artillery. After investigation Joffre ordered 400 of these from the Schneider works. In 1916 Estienne organized and commanded the "Artillérie d'Assault". His first general order of January 1917 called for tank assaults to be mounted in early morning and in fog, if possible. Attacks would be continuous with the tanks (capable of 2 mph for up to six hours) followed by carriers with fuel and supplies. Estienne also stressed the need for thorough coordination beforehand with infantry, artillery, and air forces. Estienne and his superiors regarded the new weapon as "portable artillery" supporting infantry.[40]

The French built many more tanks than the British (4,800 to 2,818) and used them for the first time in the April 1917 Nivelle Offensive. The Germans were not much interested in tanks, dismissing them on the basis of the 1916 British performance as unreliable and a waste of effort. They manufactured only 20. The development of German tank warfare was left to the next generation.[41]

On 16 September Field Marshal Paul von Hindenburg arrived on the Western Front to assume command of the German armies. He and Ludendorff did little to alter the situation on the Somme. But that same day Hindenburg gave orders to start construction of a rear defensive line known as the Siegfried, or Hindenburg, Line, to which the Germans withdrew in early 1917.

Haig attacked again on 25 September, this time north of the Ancre. Two days of vicious fighting produced only slight gains. By this time, autumn rains had settled in, turning the shell-torn ground of the Somme battlefield into a sea of mud. Although Haig favoured shutting the campaign down for the winter, Joffre insisted that the British keep up the pressure on the Germans, and fighting continued on a lower but still lethal scale. On 13 November the British won their last "victory" of the Somme campaign: a 7-division attack on either side of the Ancre following detonation of a mine under the German positions. The British advanced three-quarters of a mile and captured a fortified position at Beaumont-Hammel and 1,200 German prisoners. On 19 November a blizzard hit followed by more rain. The campaign was over.

Altogether the British had committed 55 divisions (including four Canadian, four Australian, and one New Zealand), the French 20, and the Germans 95. (It should be noted that German divisions tended to be slightly smaller than their French and British counterparts.) The losses were enormous, even higher than those at Verdun. In five months of fighting, British forces suffered nearly 420,000 casualties and the French 195,000. They had advanced a maximum of seven miles on a 20-mile front, none of which was key terrain. The German defenders had fought the Allies to a standstill, but they too paid a terrible price: as many as 650,000 casualties, and they could less afford them.

The Somme battles did help relieve the pressure on Verdun. The last German attack there came only ten days after the initial British infantry assault on the Somme. Tacticians on both sides advocating change were now taken more seriously, especially in the German army. Heavy losses, particularly among officers and NCOs, contributed to the German decision to pull back to the Hindenburg Line, a better prepared and shorter position that could be held more easily with fewer troops. From that position the Germans perfected their doctrine of the flexible defence-in-depth that would cause the Allies so much difficulty in 1917. The Battle of the Somme also had a heavy psychological cost for the British. Before the battle most British troops were patriotic and highly motivated volunteers. Although many remained idealistic afterward, it was no longer fashionable to express it openly.[42]

War at Sea: Battle of Jutland

While the Battle of Verdun raged but before the Somme began, the Battle of Jutland occurred at sea. Before the war admirals in both the Royal and Imperial Navies had anticipated a major naval battle, probably in the North Sea, that would decide the war and world mastery. The British expected another Trafalgar; the Germans referred to it as *Der Tag* (The Day).[43] Such an event almost came true on the afternoon of 31 May, when the British Grand Fleet and the German High Seas Fleet met off the western coast of the Jutland Peninsula near the outer entrance of the straits into the Baltic Sea called the Skagerrak (as the battle is known in Germany). It was the largest naval engagement of the war and one of the largest in world history.

In January 1916 Admiral Reinhard Scheer succeeded the ailing Admiral Hugo von Pohl in command of the High Seas Fleet. More aggressive than Pohl, Scheer favoured using the fleet in carefully prepared surprise attacks to reduce the Grand Fleet piecemeal. Once the odds had been shaved to a point where the Germans believed they might have a chance of winning, Scheer would orchestrate an all-out encounter. Jutland was an attempt to reduce the odds.

It was not Scheer's first effort. Earlier, in April, he had ordered the shelling of the English coastal towns of Lowestoft and Yarmouth to coincide with the Easter Sunday rising of Irish nationalists, abetted by Germany. At that time the Germans had allowed an inferior British force to get away.[44]

The Jutland operation was much larger, in part because of political pressure that the German navy not remain idle while the army was engaged in the bloodletting of Verdun. On 30 May, therefore, Scheer took the High Seas Fleet out on a sweep of the North Sea in hopes of luring a portion of the British Grand Fleet into action.

A scouting force of 40 fast vessels preceded the main German force by about 40 miles, beyond visual contact. Commanded by Admiral Franz von Hipper, it included five battle cruisers. Hipper's task was to lure a portion of the British Grand Fleet back into the main body of the High Seas Fleet where it could be destroyed.

The Germans, however, suffered from poor scouting and the belief that only they could spring a trap. Unknown to them, the entire Grand Fleet, alerted by heavy German signal traffic, was at sea. Admiral Sir John Jellicoe had 28 dreadnoughts, 9 battle cruisers, 34 cruisers, and 80 destroyers to fight Scheer's 16 dreadnoughts, 6 pre-dreadnoughts, 5 battle cruisers, 11 cruisers, and 63 destroyers.

As the German ships steamed north a British scouting force, about 70 miles from the main body of the Grand Fleet, rushed to meet them. It consisted of 52 ships including Admiral David Beatty's six battle cruisers and Admiral Hugh Evan-Thomas' squadron of four new fast dreadnoughts.

At about 2.30pm on 31 May, about a hundred miles off Jutland, the two opposing scouting forces made contact. Hipper then turned south to draw the British ships into Scheer's trap. Beatty, an aggressive commander, did as Hipper hoped, turning on a parallel course and signalling Evan-Thomas to follow. At about 3.45pm both sides opened fire at a range of about nine miles. Evan-Thomas' dreadnoughts, however, missed Beatty's signal and were slow to close. The result was a disaster for Beatty's battle cruisers, the inadequacies of which as ships of the line (at least in turret armour and magazine protection) were soon apparent. Beatty's flagship, the *Lion*, was badly damaged when she took a direct hit on one of her midships turrets. She was saved only by quick flooding of her midships magazines. The *Indefatigable*, hit by three German shells, blew up and immediately sank. Only two members of her 1,000-man crew were saved. Within 30 minutes another battle cruiser, the *Queen Mary*, also blew up. Beatty merely ordered his remaining ships to engage more closely. Up to this point the Germans had suffered no losses.

Beatty now played the lure himself. After sighting the High Seas Fleet, he reversed course to join Jellicoe, drawing Scheer after him. This "chase to the north" continued for over an hour, the two fleets, nearly 250 warships in all, closing at an aggregate speed of about 40 knots.

At about 6.00pm a third British battle cruiser, the *Invincible*, was struck by a German shell and blew up, breaking in half. Only six men survived out of a crew of more than 1,000. Observing the loss, Beatty is supposed to have remarked nonchalantly to his flag captain on the *Lion*, "Chatfield, there seems to be something wrong with our bloody ships today."[45]

At dusk, about 6.30pm, the Germans were proceeding north in line-ahead formation, confidently expecting soon to finish off the rest of Beatty's ships. Then out of the smoke and mist Jellicoe's main body suddenly appeared in one long line on the horizon. British shells immediately splashed among the leading German ships, hitting three. Jellicoe had "crossed the T" of the German line, allowing all his ships to fire, whereas only a limited number of German guns could return fire.

Although the Germans enjoyed certain advantages in long-range gunnery and fire control, their ships were clearly outclassed by the heavier guns of the more numerous British dreadnoughts. Sensing impending disaster and before Jellicoe could complete deployment of his forces, at 6.35 Scheer ordered a difficult high-speed 180-degree turn. The German warships disappeared back into the mist. Jellicoe, instead of pursuing, continued southward in an effort to cut the Germans off from their base. Twenty minutes later, Scheer executed another 180-degree turn in the hope of finding a better position, but British cruisers spotted his ships. Once again Jellicoe crossed the "T" of the German line. This time it appeared that the Germans might not escape, but Scheer reversed course yet again, ordering his destroyers to lay down a smoke screen and launch torpedoes.

There were two ways to deal with torpedo attacks at sea. One was to turn directly into their path, to present the smallest possible target. The other was to turn away and attempt to outrun them. Jellicoe decided on the latter. In October 1914 and again in April 1915 he had submitted this policy to the Admiralty, "If, for instance, the enemy battle fleet were to turn away from an advancing fleet, I should assume that the intention was to lead us over mines and submarines, and should decline to be so drawn." This had been approved by the Sea Lords and by Churchill as First Lord.[46] It could cost the British the opportunity for a decisive victory, but pressing the attack could also have brought disaster; as Churchill later put it, Jellicoe "was the only man on either side who could lose the war in an afternoon".[47]

Scheer used the cover of night to make good his retreat. Although there were numerous individual encounters, on 1 June the High Seas Fleet was back in its bases. In this only major encounter of the battle fleets during the war the British suffered higher casualties than the Germans, losing 14 vessels (3 battle cruisers, 3 cruisers, and 8 destroyers) to only 11 German ships (a battleship, a pre-dreadnought, 4 cruisers, and 5 destroyers). The disparity in tonnage losses was even greater: 111,980 for the British and 62,233 for the Germans. But Scheer's claim of victory was hollow. Within 24 hours, Jellicoe had 24 dreadnoughts available for action, whereas Scheer had only ten (as opposed to 37 and 21 respectively before the battle). The lone-term effects also favoured the British. Their blockade of Germany continued as before and the Germans avoided again risking their capital ships in a showdown battle. Increasingly they lay idle at anchor as the German Navy concentrated on the submarine war.[48]

Italian Front: Fifth Battle of the Isonzo

On the Southern, or Italian, Front an inconclusive slugfest continued. In March Cadorna launched another attack along the Isonzo River. This Fifth Battle of the Isonzo, 11–29 March, ended when the Austro-Hungarians attacked in the Trentino region at Asiago.[49]

Conrad had long tried to convince Falkenhayn to support an Austrian attack on Italy, but it conflicted with his own desire to strike the French at Verdun. Instead he wanted Austro-Hungarian divisions sent to the Western Front – lack of military cooperation was not restricted to the Allied side. Both Germany and Austria-Hungary proceeded independently, Falkenhayn attacking Verdun and Conrad attacking the Italians in the Trentino.[50]

Trentino (Asiago) Offensive

Conrad's plan, culminating in what became known as the Trentino, or Asiago, Offensive (15 May–17 June 1916), called for 15 divisions to push through the Alpine mountain passes of the Trentino, seize the northern Italian plain, and trap the two Italian armies on the Isonzo and Carnic fronts. Given the scale of the attack and the difficult terrain, it was hard for him to mask his intentions. Cadorna doubted that Conrad would risk a major operation in the Trentino, where the Austrians could be supplied by only two rail lines, and he believed any attack in the Trentino would be a feint. Even so, in late March and early April he shifted the equivalent of five divisions to reinforce First Army. After an unsatisfactory visit to the front he replaced First Army commander General Ugo Brusati with General Guglielmo Pecori-Giraldi.

The Austro-Hungarian attack began on 15 May. Archduke Eugene's Austrian Third Army under General Kövess and his Eleventh Army under General Dankl overran the Italian First Army, but they were unable to break out onto the Asiago Plateau. The difficult terrain created transportation and supply problems, while Cadorna utilized his superior lateral communications to good advantage.

By 2 June the threat was over, for the Russian Brusilov Offensive in Galicia (prompted in part by Rome's pleas) forced Austria-Hungary to shift men to the Eastern Front. Cadorna then retook some territory.[51] In the Trentino Offensive Austria-Hungary sustained 44,000 casualties (2,000 POWs); Italy lost more than 52,000 (40,000 of them POWs) and more than 400 guns.

Sixth through Ninth Battles of the Isonzo

Cadorna, noting that the Austrians had weakened the Isonzo front for the drive in the Trentino, again attacked the former. In this Sixth Battle of the Isonzo (6–17 August) the Italians took Gorizia but failed to achieve a break-through. The 1916 fighting on the Italian Front closed with three more battles along the Isonzo: the Seventh (14–20 September), the Eighth (10–12 October), and the Ninth (1–14 November).[52]

The Eastern Front

The war on the Eastern Front, calm from November 1915 to March 1916, also resumed in response to the struggle at Verdun. At the time the front lines ran some 500 miles from south of Riga on the Baltic Sea through the Pinsk marshes to the Romanian frontier. Three Russian army groups opposed the Central Powers: General Aleksei N. Kuropatkin in the north, General Aleksei Evert in the northwest, and General Nikolai Ivanov in the southwest.

Russia's most pressing need was to restore the fighting capacity of her army. After the dismissal of the Grand Duke Nicholas in August 1915, Tsar Nicholas II had assumed command. The tsar, however, had neither the military training nor an aptitude for command. Although he left management of the army to Stavka, his presence at military headquarters had a most unfortunate effect in Petrograd, where the reactionary Tsarina Alexandra and the monk Gregorii Rasputin now dominated matters.

Communication and coordination within the higher echelons of the Russian army was abysmal. Still, Russian Army Chief of Staff General Mikhail V. Alekseev, the *de facto* commander of the army, accomplished a great deal. He instituted training programmes and made up many equipment shortages. Production of rifles, for example, grew to 100,000 a month. At the same time Russia imported 1,200,000 rifles from abroad.[53] By the beginning of 1916, therefore, the Russian army had been largely rebuilt. The military reversals of 1915 had, however, negatively affected Russian public opinion, producing urban demonstrations and much criticism. The Allies realized that Russia needed time to recuperate.

Battle of Lake Naroch

As in August 1914 events in the West dictated action in the East. The calm was shattered when Paris appealed to Petrograd for action to draw off German forces from Verdun. The Russians loyally responded. On 18 March they launched a two-pronged attack from Evert's sector of the front in the Vilna–Lake Naroch area against General Hermann von Eichhorn's German Tenth Army. General V. V. Smirnov's Russian Second Army, with 5:1 superiority over the opposing German forces, made the major effort.

The Battle of Lake Naroch (18 March–14 April) began with a two-day preliminary bombardment, the longest thus far on the Eastern Front. Despite some initial Russian gains the offensive was halted by superior German artillery and the spring thaw.[54] The Russians suffered as many as 122,000 casualties (12,000 of them frostbite deaths); the Germans only 20,000.

Brusilov Offensive

The Austrian Trentino Offensive brought another appeal to the Russians, this time from Italy. On 14 April, at a meeting presided over by the tsar, army leaders debated renewing the offensive. Evert and Kuropatkin argued that Russian forces were too weak. But Aleksei Brusilov, who in March had replaced the incompetent Ivanov as commander of the Southwestern Front, and Inspector General of Artillery Sergei Mikhailovich, thought otherwise. Brusilov, who had distinguished himself during the Carpathian retreat and was probably the best senior Russian general of the war, urged simultaneous attacks at several points in order to confuse the Germans as to the location of the main thrust.[55]

Brusilov gained the support of those present, and Stavka adopted a plan whereby he would stage an attack in the direction of Kovel (Kowel), with supporting attacks aimed at Lemberg in Galicia and Czernowitz in the Bukovina. After the enemy shifted units south to block these, Evert would launch the main Russian drive toward Vilna. The plan ran afoul of Stavka's inability to coordinate complex manœuvres and Evert's disdain for offensive operations.

Brusilov's four Southwestern armies (40 infantry and 15 cavalry divisions) faced an Austro-Hungarian army group of 49.5 divisions (38.5 infantry – 2 of them German – and 11 cavalry) strongly entrenched in three fortified belts. It was good that he was a tireless worker as Brusilov had constantly to deal with innumerable problems, including lack of will in his subordinates and doubts from the top. Chief of Staff General Alekseev believed his plan was both too ambitious and diffuse. He wanted a concentration of forces at one point for a massive breakthrough, but Brusilov clung to a simultaneous dispersed attack along the 300-mile front to make it impossible for the enemy to shift resources.

The Russians sapped their front-line trenches forward to within 75 to 100 yards of the Austrian lines. They dug tunnels under the Austrian wire, stockpiled reserves of shells, and constructed huge dugouts to hold reserves. They also made accurate models of the Austrian defences and trained in them.

Brusilov held a manpower advantage of about 100,000 men (600,000 to 500,000) and 1,938 guns as opposed to 1,846; but only 168 of these were heavy guns, while his opponents had 545.[56] Brusilov used aerial photography to locate enemy guns and his artillery and infantry worked closely together. Another tactical innovation was positioning the bulk of his guns no farther than two kilometres from the front. Appeals from Stavka caused Brusilov to move the date of his attack forward to 4 June, even though Evert said he would not be ready to attack until 14 June.

Brusilov was largely successful in achieving surprise. On 4 June the Russians began a massive and accurate barrage that silenced many enemy guns. The next day Brusilov's infantry advanced. The Austrians had already been hard hit in their front-line positions by accurate Russian fire, and three of Brusilov's four armies broke through. Within the first day the two Russian flank armies advanced ten miles. By 6 June Brusilov had taken 41,000 prisoners (including many Czech units which defected *en masse*) and 77 guns; by 9 June the total had risen to more than 72,000 prisoners and 94 guns. Both the Austrian Fourth and Seventh Armies were routed.[57]

On 8 June the Russians took Lutsk; Austrian Archduke Frederick Josef, enjoying a birthday lunch there, barely escaped capture. By 23 June Brusilov's troops had taken some 204,000 prisoners and 219 guns. Austria-Hungary seemed near collapse, but Brusilov could not immediately follow up his victory. His own losses had been heavy, he had outrun his supply lines, and he had only one division in reserve. He could do no more. It now rested on General Evert with a million troops and two-thirds of the Russian artillery – a 3:1 superiority in men and guns – to attack the Germans in the north. This offensive was to have begun on 14 June, but Evert repeatedly claimed shortages. After Brusilov's attack had begun he again put the attack off until 3 July. Evert's inability or unwillingness to capitalize on Brusilov's achievement doomed Russian chances for success in 1916.[58]

The Germans were not so hesitant. On 8 June, during a meeting between the two in Berlin, General Falkenhayn insisted that Field Marshal Conrad transfer forces from the Italian Front to the East. And, again utilizing the excellent German railroads, Hindenburg sent reinforcements south.

On 16 June General Alexander von Linsingen's army group launched a counter-offensive southeast of Kowel, temporarily checking Brusilov but at the cost of 40,000 casualties (16–24 June). On 28 July Brusilov, slowed by ammunition shortages, resumed the offensive. His third assault, between 7 August and 20 September, brought the Russians into the Carpathian foothills. By 12 August his armies had taken a total of nearly 379,000 prisoners and 496 guns since 4 June.

During the next month, however, the offensive became bogged down, handicapped by the distances involved and supply problems. Linsingen then managed to stabilize the front well east of Russia's final objectives of Lemberg and Kowel, eventually forcing Brusilov to abandon the Bukovina and Galicia.

Brusilov later contended that had Evert attacked on schedule, Austria-Hungary would have been driven from the war. This conclusion seems valid. Without German reinforcements, Austria-Hungary would certainly have been defeated. Even so the Brusilov Offensive probably finished Austria-Hungary as a military power, and it contributed to Emperor Karl's removal of Conrad from command in February 1917. The offensive may also have saved the Italian army when Austrian units were transferred from the Trentino to the Russian Front. It also weakened the German attack at Verdun and helped bring the fall of Falkenhayn.[59]

Although the greatest Russian feat of arms of the entire war, the offensive's cost had been high: as many as 1,412,000 Russian casualties (212,000 of them POWs), against 750,000 Austro-Hungarian (380,000 of them POWs) and 18,000 Turkish casualties. More importantly, the Russian people saw it as just another military failure and it contributed to their revolution the next year.

Romania declares war

In 1916 the war widened to include Romania, which both sides had courted for two years. Located astride the Danube River, the most important transportation artery in the Balkans, Romania could deny or facilitate the flow of materials between Germany and Bulgaria and Turkey; its common border with Hungary was the Central Powers' only remaining uncommitted frontier. The Central Powers were therefore most anxious that Romania join them or at least remain neutral.

The Allies saw Romania similarly and exploited her irredentist claims against Austria-Hungary to bring her over to their side. Germany's failure at Verdun and that of Austria in the Asiago Offensive were factors in Romania's decision. But the most important influence was the initial success of the Brusilov Offensive. Romanian Premier Ian Brătianu and King Ferdinand I had long coveted the Hungarian province of Transylvania and knew that

Romania would never have it if it fell to the Russians. As a result they signed a secret treaty with the Allies promising Romania the Bánát of Temesvár, Transylvania, and the Bukovina. The Allies also pledged a simultaneous Russian advance in the Bukovina and Allied push from Salonika.[60]

On 27 August 1916, Romania declared war on the Dual Monarchy. The next day, seeking to capitalize on the situation before the Central Powers could shift resources to meet them, three Romanian armies (First, Second, and Fourth) crossed the Hungarian frontier at 18 different points. The Romanians kept their remaining army, the Third, in reserve near Bucharest, and left defence of their southern frontier to the Russians in the false hope that Bulgaria would not attack.

The Romanian Army of 620,000 men (440,000 effectives) was ill-trained and badly led. Only recently expanded in size, it suffered from severe shortages and outdated equipment. Ammunition and transport were especially in short supply, and Russian promises to make up shortages did not materialize.

Vienna had done little to prepare for a possible Romanian assault and the Romanians met initial success. In the first month they took about a quarter of Transylvania; indeed most of their difficulties resulted from their own logistical incompetence. Russian support was limited because of heavy casualties in the Brusilov Offensive. Many Russians, however, were bitter because they believed that Romania had waited until the Brusilov advance was spent before entering the war.

The Romanians were to be disappointed by their allies. The Russians sent only modest aid, given grudgingly. In mid-September some Russian divisions arrived in the Dobrudja to reinforce the Romanian Third Army and Brusilov reluctantly sent his Ninth Army into the Bukovina. The promised Salonika offensive also fizzled out. Although he commanded a significant force, General Sarrail feared a Greek attack in his rear if he moved north. Bulgarian troops soon halted his slow-developing drive and it had no impact on the Romanian fighting.

The Central Powers, meanwhile, moved quickly and immediately coordinated efforts for a multinational counteroffensive. Falkenhayn, removed as chief of staff following Romania's declaration of war, now received command of the German Ninth Army and was assigned the task of driving the Romanians back. In less than six weeks he mounted a brilliant three-pronged counterattack that by October had driven the Romanians back to their own frontier. At the same time General August von Mackensen led a mixed German, Bulgarian, and Turkish force against the Romanian Dobrudja at the mouth of the Danube into the Black Sea. After a counterattack by the Romanian Third Army across the Danube failed, Constanza,

Romania's primary Black Sea port, fell on 23 October. Halting there to regroup, Mackensen sent German units to reinforce Falkenhayn in Transylvania.

In the north, after blunting aggressive Romanian counterattacks in Transylvania, Falkenhayn struck again. By mid-November he had broken through the main Transylvanian passes and entered Romania's central Wallachian Plain. In an effort to trap Romanian forces between two pincers, Mackensen forced his way across the Danube. A gallant Romanian counter-attack on 1 December failed and Bucharest fell five days later. By the middle of the month the Central Powers held all the Dobrudja and Wallachia as well as a portion of southern Moldavia. Although the Romanians managed to delay the German advance long enough for the Russians to reinforce their southern border and for the British embassy to organize the sabotage of the Romanian oil wells, by any measure Romania's war effort was a disaster. Romania lost 350,000 men; the remainder of the army retreated into Moldavia, where it was somewhat shielded by the Russians.

The Central Powers now occupied Romania and Germany acquired the rich Romanian agricultural lands to add to her *Mitteleuropa* empire. The conquest of Romania decidedly improved the strategic situation for the Central Powers. It added to Russia's burden by lengthening her front by 250 miles without any advantage or reinforcement in compensation. Although the same could be said for the Central Powers, which had even fewer resources overall, they no longer faced the threat of possible enemy intervention on their southeastern flank and were able to hold their lines in the east with fewer troops than before. Romanians deeply resented the Treaty of Bucharest, and the country re-entered the war against the Central Powers on 10 November 1918.[61]

Balkan Front

Greece, meanwhile, had tried unsuccessfully to remain neutral. Her intense antipathy to Turkey and Bulgaria as well as continued Allied pressures, however, made this almost impossible. The Greek government gradually polarized into two camps. The first, centred around King Constantine, feared the Allies more than the Central Powers and preferred neutrality. The second, around ex-Premier Eleutherios Venizelos, favoured the Allies, holding that if the Central Powers won, Bulgaria and Turkey would claim Greek territory. As the war continued, the political division intensified.

Political and military interests led the Allies to follow a policy of coercion against Constantine. The Central Powers made no such moves, confident that they could easily contain any Allied move north. Indeed, they held the Allies in check at Salonika with only second-line troops until October 1918.

In May 1916, when a Bulgarian–German force occupied Fort Rupel in Greek Macedonia, Britain and France concluded that Greece was secretly in league with the Central Powers. Actually, since the Allies already occupied some Greek territory, Constantine had merely allowed the Central Powers the same prerogative. In June, however, Britain and France responded by bringing economic pressure to bear on Greece. They imposed a blockade of her ports and sent Athens an ultimatum demanding the demobilization of her army and the formation of a new government. Constantine responded by placing the Greek Army on a peacetime footing and by scheduling new elections.

The Western Allies, meanwhile, had transferred the refurbished Serbian Army of some 118,000 men from Corfu to Salonika, where in late June it went into action. Some Russian troops who had been fighting in France and an Italian force also arrived at Salonika in July and August. By that date Sarrail commanded about 250,000 men.

The Allies now began an advance against Bulgarian troops, precipitating the Battle of Doiran which lasted from 2 to 21 August. Bulgarian and German troops then counterattacked and pushed the Allies back, taking Seres on 19 August. Drama and Kavalla fell on 18 September, the Fourth Greek Army surrendering without resistance.

At the end of August a pro-Allied movement led by Venizelos and fostered by Sarrail established itself at Salonika and, on 29 September Venizelos set up a provisional government in Crete. He then went to Salonika where, on 23 November, his provisional government declared war on Bulgaria and Germany.

The Allies, angered by the Greek surrender of Kavalla, now brought heavy pressure to bear. They demanded that Greece surrender her fleet, to which Athens agreed on 11 October. Their next demands, that Athens dismiss diplomatic representatives of the Central Powers and surrender war matériel, however, were rejected. On 29 November, therefore, the British and French sent landing parties ashore at Piraeus. These met Greek resistance and withdrew on 1 December. A week later the Allies declared Greece under blockade and on the 19th they recognized Venizelos's provisional government.

On 5 October Sarrail began another Allied offensive in Macedonia. After taking Monastir he pushed on to Lake Okhrid and linked up with an Italian force that had driven the Austrians north. There was no advance, however, and in the winter of 1916–17 the Balkan Front was quiet. The Central Powers opted simply for containment, pleased to see Allied forces tied down in a minor theatre. The fighting in 1916 in Macedonia claimed about 77,000 Allied casualties (including 22,000 British troops with malaria, who were evacuated); some 60,000 Bulgarians and Germans were also lost.[62]

The year ended as it had begun, in stalemate. Despite their numerical superiority and overwhelming naval advantage, the Allies had merely succeeded in containing the Germans on the Western Front. In 1917, however, they planned to take the offensive.

Chapter Five

1917: the turning point

The year 1917 started out badly for the Allies: the German U-boat campaign seemed on the brink of success. France and Britain suffered appalling losses in offensives on the Western Front leading to mutinies in the French Army, and the Central Powers smashed the Italians at Caporetto. But two events overshadowed all others: the entry of the United States into the conflict and the military collapse of Russia.

Political changes in Britain at the end of 1916 influenced Allied military decisions in the new year. On 4 December Herbert Asquith resigned as prime minister.[1] His successor David Lloyd George, who saw more clearly than any other British policymaker the link between strategy and national morale, despised Haig and Chief of the Imperial General Staff General Sir William Robertson for the great wastages of the Western Front. He dared not sack them because they enjoyed the support of his Conservative colleagues and of the King. But he did what he could to reduce Haig's freedom of action and to push for relatively cheap peripheral operations.[2]

At the end of 1916, pleased by a substantial increase in their strength, Allied leaders agreed to continue the Western Front as the critical sector of war. They planned large-scale attacks there to be supported by Russian and Italian offensives. General Robert Nivelle's French Army spring offensive was the centrepiece of this effort.

During fighting at Verdun Nivelle had introduced new assault tactics and "deception" bombardment in which artillery fire was begun, halted to encourage the Germans to reveal artillery positions, and then renewed. Once enemy guns were silenced, assault units attacked objectives behind a "creeping" barrage. Nivelle's success at Verdun, especially the recapture of Forts Vaux and Douaumont, brought his elevation to supreme command.[3]

Nivelle projected energy and optimism. Handsome and charming, he was

entirely confident that his tactics would succeed on a wider scale. He over-
hauled plans for simultaneous French and British thrusts that would have
continued the war of attrition and shifted the effort to the Aisne front. In a
14 January 1917 paper, he declared: "We shall break the German front when
we wish, on condition that we do not attack the strongest point and that we
execute the operation by surprise and abrupt attack, in twenty-four or forty-
eight hours."[4] But Nivelle's formula of massive frontal assaults against well-
fortified defensive positions was essentially the same that had been tried and
failed over the preceding two years.

Although fluent in English, Nivelle did not get along well with Haig,
promoted to field marshal on 1 January. Nivelle convinced Lloyd George that
the war might be won decisively without significant new British outlay, but
Lloyd George warmed to Nivelle in part because he trusted him more than
Haig. Lloyd George agreed to send Haig six additional divisions on the
understanding that by 1 April the British would take over 20 additional miles
of trenches. The British would then have 62 divisions in France.

Allied talks at Calais on 26–27 February, ostensibly about rail transportation
problems in the British sector, centred on the British–French command
relationship. Lloyd George insisted that Haig place his forces under Nivelle's
operational command, much to the anger of Haig and Robertson, who
enlisted the support of King George V and the War Cabinet. Haig acceded to
this arrangement, but only for the spring offensive and with assurance that the
BEF would keep its separate identity.[5]

Operation ALBERICH

Preparations delayed Nivelle's offensive into early April. The Germans, meanwhile, were made aware of his intentions because of Nivelle's public postur-
ing, aerial reconnaissance, spies, and a trench raid that captured a set of
operational plans. The Germans responded by assuming a defensive posture
on the Western, Eastern, and Italian Fronts.[6]

In a brilliantly executed operation, the Germans actually shortened their
front in the West. OHL had initiated planning for this step the previous
September. The new, heavily fortified defensive line was located some 20
miles behind existing Western Front positions. Called by the Germans the
Siegfried Stellung (Siegfried Line) after Wagner's hero, the Allies knew it as the
Hindenburg Line after the German Army commander.

Colonel Fritz von Lossberg, a genius in defensive warfare, developed the
plan. The most important section of the line, and first to be completed, ran

from Arras to Soissons and eliminated the Noyon salient held by Crown Prince Rupprecht's army group. This shortened the German line by 25 miles and freed 14 divisions for redeployment in the East.

The new system employed tactical innovations learned in fighting at Verdun and on the Eastern Front. One new approach was to locate front lines on the reverse slope of hills rather than on the forward slope as was customary. This kept infantry hidden from enemy artillery spotters. Crests of hills would be held only by light forces with machine guns to provide warning of an enemy attack. Attacking infantry would be silhouetted when reaching the crest and present a more favourable target to the defenders.

Another idea was the elastic defence, or defence in depth, whereby the enemy forces would have to penetrate a series of defensive lines 6,000–8,000 yards deep until they were exhausted. This great depth would also force the attacker to reposition his artillery; before this could occur, designated coun-terattack divisions would launch vigorous attacks.

A key feature of the system was the wide latitude given local commanders in deciding when to withdraw and when to counterattack. The German Army routinely placed far greater faith in the judgment of junior commanders on the spot than did other armies.

The Siegfried Line also incorporated reinforced concrete bunkers, tunnels, electric lighting, and concrete machine-gun positions. Ludendorff withdrew to the Siegfried Line reluctantly, fearing the morale impact of yielding territory on the army and home front. But this was offset by greatly improved living conditions for troops and the prospect of freeing divisions for the East. H–L believed Russia was on the verge of collapse and withdrawing to the Siegfried Line would enable Germany to deliver a knock-out blow.

The withdrawal, named Operation ALBERICH after the malicious dwarf of the *Niebelung* saga, began on 16 March and ended on 5 April. The Germans removed everything of any use and left behind a wasteland, destroying houses and bridges, uprooting railroad tracks, poisoning wells, even felling trees. Booby traps lay everywhere. Crown Prince Rupprecht opposed these ex-treme measures but H–L overruled him. While they left children and old people behind, the Germans evacuated 125,000 French civilians to work elsewhere. The Allies did not realize what was happening until too late and not a single German soldier was lost in the move.[7]

Although the withdrawal should have given the Allies pause, momentum drove the offensive forward. Nivelle persisted despite knowledge that the Germans had undoubtedly captured detailed plans for the offensive during a trench raid on 4 April. On the 6th in the presence of President Raymond Poincaré during a conference at Compiègne, Premier Alexandre Ribot and Minister of War Paul Painlevé revealed that General Micheler, whose recently created French Reserve Army Group was to make the assault, was pessimistic about its chances. Nivelle's threat to resign, however, brought criticism to an end.[8]

Battle of Arras

On 9 April the British began a diversionary attack along a 14-mile front known as the Battle of Arras (April 9–15), to draw off German reserves from the Aisne. Haig's plan called for General Henry S. Horne's British First Army and General Allenby's British Third Army to attack positions held by General Baron Ludwig von Falkenhausen's German Sixth Army. If these were successful, Haig would insert General Hubert Gough's British Fifth Army and exploit any breakthrough with cavalry. More than 2,800 guns supported the attack. Haig also had 48 tanks, but he distributed them along the entire line rather than using them *en masse*.

Vimy Ridge was a key British objective. This high ground north of Arras and the River Scarpe dominated the Douai plain to the east, and Haig considered its capture vital to protect the left flank of his main attack. Twice in 1915 the French had assaulted it, and the British were embarrassed by the May 1916 German success in retaking some ground there. Haig insisted that Nivelle include Vimy Ridge as a British objective.

Horne assigned the task to the four divisions of General Sir Julian Byng's well-trained Canadian Corps. Byng planned his assault meticulously. Haig insisted on a four-day preliminary bombardment, which grew to five, to cut the German wire and impose maximum strain on the defenders. Ammunition was more plentiful, identification of targets through flash-spotting and sound-ranging more effective, and a new "106" instantaneous fuse on high-explosive rounds assisted in cutting barbed wire without cratering the ground.[9] The bombardment included the heaviest concentration of gas thus far in the war in order to kill large numbers of horses and prevent German transport of shells to the front.

The Canadian infantry jumped off at 5.30 on the morning of 9 April, preceded by a well-timed creeping barrage. By nightfall they had taken most of the ridge, 4,000 prisoners, and 54 guns. The next day the Canadians took the ridge's highest point, Hill 145. Vimy Ridge was secured at a cost of 7,700 Canadian casualties. It was one of the notable feats of arms of the entire war and certainly the high point for Canadian troops. It showed the British had learned much from the Somme disaster, and it also brought tactical changes in machine-gun deployment. Until that point machine-gun fire had been regarded as primarily defensive, but the Canadians had used 150 Vickers machine guns to lay down offensive barrages.[10]

German Sixth Army commander General von Falkenhausen contributed to the Allied success by not having adopted the new three-tiered defensive system along his entire front and by electing to keep his reserve divisions too far back to be able to intervene quickly. Vimy Ridge was the only major Allied success of the battle.[11]

Although the attackers penetrated enemy lines by nearly four miles they did not break through, and to the south Gough's army made little progress. Some Australian units penetrated to the Hindenburg Line on 11 April but had to withdraw for lack of reinforcements and artillery support. Bad weather also worked against the British. The Germans were able to patch their lines. Von Lossberg was brought in as Sixth Army's chief of staff to reorganize the defences, and no reserves were drawn from the Aisne sector.

On 23 April Haig resumed the offensive, but this assault by nine divisions of the Third and Fourth Armies on a nine-mile front served merely to divert German attention from the French.[12] Total British losses in the Arras Offensive through 26 May were some 159,000 men; German losses ran to about 180,000 (21,000 POWs) and 252 guns.

Nivelle Offensive

At 6.00 am on 16 April Nivelle began his offensive (the Second Battle of the Aisne and Third Battle of Champagne). General Micheler's 1.2 million-man Reserve Army Group attacked along a 40-mile section of front between Soissons and Reims, his objective the wooded ridges paralleling the front known as the Chemin des Dames. The brunt of the attack would be borne by General Charles Mangin's Sixth Army and General Olivier Mazel's Fifth Army.

A 14-day bombardment by 5,544 guns preceded the attack, although much of its effect was wasted against the lightly held German forward defensive zone. Mazel's Fifth Army also had 128 Schneider tanks, the first French use of these machines in the war. The 15-ton Schneider mounted a 75 mm gun and two machine guns and had a crew of six men. It could move at 5 mph but had a maximum trench spanning capability of only 70 inches, a major shortcoming.[13]

The 16 April–9 May Nivelle Offensive produced only minimal gains, in large part because the Germans were well-prepared. Ludendorff had reinforced General Max von Boehn's Seventh Army with General Fritz von

Below's First Army. Front-line positions that would absorb most of the French artillery fire were only lightly held and machine-gun strong points were reinforced. Counterattack divisions were positioned to respond quickly to any attacks. Just prior to the assault, moreover, German fighters swept the skies free of French air observation and their accurate artillery fire destroyed a number of French tanks on their way forward.

The French *poilus*, most of whom were serving under newly appointed officers, attacked with enthusiasm. Within several hours they had taken most of the German first-line trenches; their artillery, however, failed to silence the enemy guns or destroy the numerous enemy machine-gun positions. The "creeping" or "rolling" barrage was also too rapid for the infantry to keep up, particularly in broken and wooded terrain and, as a result, German artillery and machine-gun fire took a heavy toll.

The greatest French success was on the left, where Mangin's Sixth Army forced the Germans back some six miles. Pétain launched a subsidiary attack in Champagne by General Anthoine's Fourth Army, which seized some ground. In three days of fighting the French took 20,000 prisoners and 147 guns. But continued attacks brought little additional gain.

Nivelle had promised to call off the offensive immediately if it was unsuccessful, but it continued. On 21 April Nivelle brought up Denis Duchêne's Tenth Army, inserting it between Fifth and Sixth Armies, but he reduced his goal to easing the threat to Reims and securing the Chemin des Dames. Additional French attacks on 4 and 5 May brought limited gains along the ridge before attacks ended on the 9th.[14] In its entirety the offensive claimed 187,000 French casualties; the Germans lost 163,000 men (including 29,000 POWs) and 252 guns.

French Army mutinies

The Nivelle Offensive produced results that compared favourably to Joffre's earlier one, but Nivelle had promised both a breakthrough and victory; and since expectations were so high, morale suffered and this time the French soldiers mutinied. President Poincaré ordered Chief of the General Staff Pétain to end the mutinies, and on 15 May Pétain replaced Nivelle as commander-in-chief. Foch became Chief of the General Staff.

The French Army mutinies had begun on 17 April when 17 men of the 108th Infantry Regiment abandoned their posts before an attack. Ultimately the mutiny seriously affected 46 of 112 divisions. Pétain adopted a common-sense approach, visiting disaffected units and personally talking to their men. He recognized the legitimacy of complaints over poor food, inadequate medical services, and insufficient leave, but he reminded the soldiers that the Germans were still in France.

Within a matter of weeks Pétain's eloquent appeals had restored morale and regained the soldiers' confidence. Of some 35,000 "strikers", as the men called themselves, 2,873 were court-martialled and received sentences, many of which were suspended. A total of 629 death sentences were handed down, of which only 43 were actually carried out.[15]

Pétain instituted reforms in pay and leave, and he promised no future attacks unless there was real hope of success. To a great extent Pétain went over to the defensive: "I am waiting for the Americans and tanks", he repeatedly said.[16] He also pledged to the soldiers that any future attacks would be supported by maximum use of artillery.

Fortunately for the Allies, French censors prevented word of the mutinies from spreading beyond the military. The Germans did not learn of them until too late. On 19 July 1917, when they launched a tentative offensive by four divisions to test the will of the French to continue fighting, the Germans encountered the 77th Division, one of those affected by the mutiny. The 77th counterattacked and drove the Germans back to their original lines. And an attack at Verdun on 20 August by eight divisions to bolster morale, to show the British that the French Army was still active, and to keep the Germans off balance, captured more than 10,000 German prisoners and the heights overlooking Verdun from the north. It demonstrated conclusively that the army's ability to conduct offensive actions had been restored.[17]

The mutinies and events in Russia played into the hands of defeatists in France, and by the fall of 1917 there were serious doubts about France's ability to continue in the war. In November 1917 the shaky Painlevé government fell, leaving President Poincaré with the possibilities of a government headed by Joseph Caillaux that might try for an immediate peace or one under nationalist Georges Clemenceau. Poincaré chose Clemenceau and, in historian Gordon Wright's words, the nation "entered upon a kind of civilian dictatorship . . .".[18] France would fight on.

The United States enters the war

In April, meanwhile, the United States had entered the war. In August 1914 President Woodrow Wilson had firmly proclaimed US neutrality, calling on Americans to be neutral in "thought" as well as action. Washington, however, insisted on the US right to trade with all the belligerents; but since the Entente controlled the seas, the United States traded only with it and the Germans charged that this was hardly neutral. Certainly this created strong US financial interest in an Entente victory and helped influence the American decision to join the Allies.

American relations with the warring powers vacillated. The German invasion of Belgium along with subsequent atrocity stories increased American public support for the Entente. But British seizure of US merchant vessels bound for Germany as well as its tampering with the mails outraged American public opinion to the extent that Wilson asked for and received Congressional authority to levy an embargo against Britain.[19]

Notes from Washington and Berlin flew back and forth across the Atlantic with Berlin pointing out that the British blockade, which denied food to the German people, was contrary to international law. Certainly the blockade severely diminished Germany's capacity to wage war. Both food and fertilizers were scarce and, when the summer 1916 potato crop failed, the winter of 1916–17 became known as the "Turnip Winter". Germans were indignant that the United States, while protesting vehemently over German submarine warfare, was not as adamant about British interference with neutral trade. Berlin was also bitter over US munitions sales to Britain.

In what may have been the most fateful decision of the war, therefore, the German leadership decided to resume unrestricted submarine warfare. Without this Russia would still have collapsed and Germany would have had to deal with only France and Britain on the Western Front in 1918, conceivably giving her victory that spring. OHL, however, was not focusing on what the United States might do when it made the decision. As historian Holger Herwig has noted, "Incredibly, the United States was dismissed as either an economic or military factor."[20]

By the end of 1916, despite the handicap that they provide for the safety of merchant vessels' crews, German U-boats were sinking about 300,000 tons of Allied shipping a month. Well ahead of 1915 totals, such success formed the rationale for deciding to institute unrestricted submarine warfare, when submarines would no longer have to attack on the surface where they were vulnerable to Allied armed merchant ships and decoy armed Q-ships.[21]

OHL expected even greater results from unrestricted submarine warfare. Since Britain had to import well over half its food and raw materials, OHL anticipated that an all-out submarine offensive would soon bring her to her knees. If Britain dropped out of the war France would have to follow suit, and the war would be won. German military leaders accepted the probability that resumption of unrestricted submarine warfare would bring the United States into the war, but by the time America had built up her forces the war would be over.

On 31 January the German foreign ministry announced to the world that Germany would resume unrestricted submarine warfare the next day. Although this was the key factor in the US declaration of war, other influences were also at work, including the infamous "Zimmermann Telegram". This January 1917 communication from German State Secretary for Foreign Affairs Arthur Zimmermann to German ambassador to Mexico von Eckhardt called on him to approach the Mexican Government about joining the war on Germany's side should the US enter the war. He also sought Mexican assistance in shifting Japanese support to the side of the Central Powers. In return Germany would provide financial assistance and, following a German victory, return to Mexico lands lost to the United States in 1848.[22]

Zimmermann hoped to embroil the United States in war with Mexico and Japan. This would prevent the US from playing a role in Europe, end the flow of American arms to the Entente, and force Russia to fight a two-front war against Germany and Japan. Zimmermann's confidence was based on the already tense relationship between the United States and Mexico that had brought 12,000 troops under General John J. Pershing into northern Mexico.[23] When Pershing's troops proved unable to capture guerrilla leader Pancho Villa, Berlin equated present military ineptitude with future military capacity.

The British intercepted the Zimmermann telegram, decoded it, and forwarded its contents to Washington. The resulting uproar forced Wilson to revise his foreign policy and call on Congress to authorize the arming of merchant ships. When Robert La Follette led ten senators in a filibuster, on 28 February Wilson released the telegram to the press. Although a few Americans, including some senators, denounced it as a hoax, all doubts were removed when Zimmermann foolishly admitted its authenticity. The telegram had the effect of making much of the United States, especially its western states, strongly pro–intervention.

Another factor influencing US entry into the war was the revelation of German sabotage activities, the most notorious of which was the destruction of the New Jersey Black Tom munitions plant with a loss of $22 million. Two German military attachés stationed in the United States, one of them Franz von Papen, were implicated in these activities.[24]

German torpedoes soon claimed American lives. On 26 February eight Americans died when the British steamship *Laconia* was sunk without warning. On 12 March Wilson issued an executive order arming American merchant ships. Within the week three homeward-bound US merchantment were sunk with further loss of lives. On 2 April, with American resentment against Germany swelling, President Wilson asked Congress for a declaration of war. This was passed by large majorities in each house and, on 6 April, Wilson announced that a state of war existed between the United States and Germany.

The most immediate impact of the US entry was financial; it became the chief supplier of Allied credit. The United States could also provide great assistance in food and matériel. For example, US annual steel production was 93,400,000 tons, three times that of Germany and Austria-Hungary combined.[25] US entry into the war was also a great morale boost to the Entente at a time when it was reeling and a corresponding depressant for the Central Powers.[26]

The United States quickly seized 109 German vessels interned in its ports, including the 54,000-ton *Vaterland* (promptly renamed the *Leviathan*), and began an ambitious shipbuilding programme. The US Navy was the world's fifth largest and its ships were immediately available. Substantial naval assets were sent to Europe and by July, 34 US destroyers were operating under British command out of Queenstown in escort and anti-submarine duties. A US battleship division also went to Scapa Flow, although it did not see action during the war, and 120 subchasers were dispatched to European waters.[27]

Getting the small US Army ready for war was another matter, however. In early April it numbered just 133,000 regulars and 67,000 National Guardsmen. President Wilson appointed General Pershing – who had the advantages of recent field command experience, political connections, and knowledge of French – to command the American Expeditionary Force (AEF).[28] Training camps for new volunteers were quickly established, but if the United States was to have any impact in the land war it would have to be prolonged. By 1 December 1917, only four US divisions had reached France.[29]

The United States ultimately raised a 4,000,000-man army and a navy of 800,000 men. Although American manpower proved critical in the Allied victory, for the most part US forces used French equipment. This was because it took time to gear up such military production and available shipping was crammed with food, supplies, and men. By the armistice not one US-manufactured plane or tank had gone into action against the enemy in France; of 3,500 artillery pieces the US Army used in Europe, only 500 were of American manufacture; and of 9 million shells expended only 200,000 came from the United States.[30]

Wilson refused to be bound by agreements between the Allied powers regarding future partition of enemy territory. He insisted that the United

States was not a formal "ally" but an "associate" in the same war. While the United States did later (7 December 1917) declare war on Austria-Hungary, it never did so against either Bulgaria or Turkey.[31]

War at sea: Germany's submarine campaign

Given the stakes involved it seems incredible that OHL gambled Germany's future on a perilously small submarine force. Germany began unrestricted submarine warfare with just 104 boats, including three at Constantinople.[32] Only about a third of these would be on station at any one time; a third would be *en route* or returning and the remaining third undergoing maintenance. Also, the number of German submarines did not grow appreciably during the rest of the war.

In February 1917, the first month of unrestricted submarine warfare, the Germans sank about 540,000 tons of Allied shipping. In the three months from April to June 1917 they sent to the bottom another 2 million tons of merchant shipping. In April alone the tally was 350 ships of 849,000 tons, a monthly figure never attained by the more powerful German U-boats of the Second World War and well beyond what German planners calculated would be necessary to win the war. The U-boats were sinking ships faster than the Allies could build them. At one point in 1917 Britain had only six weeks of food reserves remaining. As Winston Churchill put it, "The U-boat was rapidly undermining not only the life of the British islands, but the foundation of the Allies' strength; and the danger of their collapse in 1918 began to loom black and imminent."[33] If this rate of sinkings continued, Britain would indeed be driven from the war.

To defeat the U-boats the Allies committed the resources necessary. Allied technology played an important role: better and more lethal depth charges (submarines of the First World War could dive only to 250 feet) and improvements in hydrophone technology to listen for submarine propellers. Also in June 1917 the Allied Submarine Detection Investigation Committee instituted a new technique whereby a patrol vessel sent out a beam of sound through the water; when it struck an object it was reflected back as an echo. This came to be known as ASDIC, later SONAR.[34]

But the key element in defeating the submarine menace was the convoy system. Admiral Jellicoe and other senior British commanders initially rejected it because the Royal Navy lacked sufficient numbers of destroyers to carry out both fleet and escort duties. The Admiralty had its attention focused on fleet actions – especially the anticipated "Big Thing" in the North Sea and, as a result, continued to build battleships and cruisers rather than destroyers and subchasers. Convoys were instituted in May 1917 on the insistence of Prime Minister Lloyd George and US Admiral William S. Sims, then in London representing the US government. American destroyers soon took over about a third of the escort work.

Convoys consisted of large numbers of merchant vessels travelling together. Although German submarines still registered kills, the proportion of ships sunk to those sailing was only a small fraction of what it had been when merchant ships travelled singly.

As the convoy system expanded the U-boats were contained. At the end of October 1917 the Admiralty announced that, of 99 convoys to Britain totalling 1,500 ships, only 24 had been lost. Losses to submarines from January to November 1918 were only 600,000 tons more than the April-June 1917 total. Submarine losses also rose. Altogether German submarines sank more than 11 million tons of shipping during the war. The German Navy may have made a crucial mistake in not attacking military shipping. Not one ship carrying US troops to Europe was lost in the crossing.[35]

Other naval actions

Surface warfare in 1917 was limited to individual ships or squadrons. Early in the year the Germans carried out three destroyer raids in the English Channel. The first of these, on the night of 25/26 February, was uneventful. In the second raid, on the night of 17/18 March, the Germans sank two British destroyers and a small merchant vessel at no loss to themselves. The third, on the night of 20/21 April, was disrupted by Royal Navy Commander E. R. G. R. Evans, whose destroyer, the *Broke*, sank two German destroyers. In May and June the British responded by bombarding German destroyer and submarine bases at Ostend and Zeebrugge. While these raids caused some damage, they did not seriously affect German U-boat operations.[36]

Naval actions also took place in the Mediterranean. In order to confine the large Austro-Hungarian surface fleet in the Adriatic away from Mediterranean supply routes, the Allies constructed a net barrier or barrage in the 45-mile wide Straits of Otranto at the heel of the Italian boot. It ran from Brindisi and Otranto in Italy across the straits to Italian-controlled Vlorë on the Albanian coast. On 15 May Austro-Hungarian Navy Captain Miklós Horthy von Nagybána led a squadron out on a raid against the drifter line maintaining the barrage. In the largest naval action of the war in the Adriatic, Horthy's ships sank 14 small Allied drifters, then escaped relatively unscathed from superior British, French, and Italian warships.[37]

On 15 July British destroyers mounted a raid on German coastal shipping. Off the Dutch coast they sank two German merchant vessels and captured four others, disrupting German trade with Rotterdam. On 17 November a British battle cruiser squadron attacked German minesweepers in Heligoland Bight, but the German vessels escaped. The war at sea in 1917 closed with a successful German raid in December against British shipping with Scandinavia. This forced Admiral Beatty (commander of the Grand Fleet after Jutland) to detach a battleship squadron to protect future Scandinavian convoys.[38]

German Chancellor Bethman-Hollweg's independence of mind, his sympathy with demands by the Left for parliamentary reform, and his increasing pessimism regarding the war all led to his resignation in July. Forced by H-L and Crown Prince Wilhelm, this marked the end of any pretence of civilian government in Germany. Georg Michaelis, H-L's minion, became the new chancellor.[39]

British offensive in Flanders

Fighting on the Western Front, meanwhile, resumed in the summer. Given the French Army mutinies and Pétain's penchant for the defence, the initiative passed to the British. Hoping to buy time until the Americans could arrive in strength and to relieve pressure on the French, in June Haig launched an offensive in Flanders.

Haig hoped to break through the German lines in the Ypres salient between the North Sea and the Lys River, liberate Belgium, outflank the German defensive system from the north, and cut German communications with their bases on the lower Rhine. The Royal Navy supported the plan in the mistaken assumption that Germany had submarine bases in Belgium. Jellicoe had informed the War Cabinet that, without their destruction, the Royal Navy might not be able to continue the war into 1918.[40]

Haig also believed that he had a limited window of opportunity. Following what one historian has called "perhaps the most crucial British strategic debate of the war" the War Cabinet endorsed Haig's plan. Lloyd George favoured sending resources to the Italian Front where the Italians might do the dying, or to the Middle East.[41] While the prime minister chose not to challenge him directly, it was clear to Haig that if he failed to utilize the considerable assets then available they would be diverted to other theatres.

British Army morale was then high and effective strength greater than at any time since the 1916 Battle of the Somme. Haig assigned the main effort of the attack to Gough's Fifth Army; it would strike northeastward from Ypres toward Ghent. To its left would be General Henry Rawlinson's Fourth Army; to its right, General Herbert Plumer's Second Army. General François Anthoine's elite French First Army was sent north to participate in a secondary role. Haig, however, shelved the plan to land two divisions of Rawlinson's Fourth Army on the Belgian coast at the mouth of the Yser River.

Battle of Messines Ridge

Before an offensive could be launched from the Ypres salient Messines Ridge had to be taken. Only six by eight miles in size and at most 250 feet high, it dominated the southern part of the salient. Haig assigned the task of taking the ridge to General Plumer.

The meticulous Plumer, regarded by his men with deep affection, built up road and rail communications, ordered constant patrolling, developed careful programmes for barrage and counter-battery artillery attack, and stepped up aerial observation. A major element in his plan was mining. As early as 1915 the British had begun digging shallow tunnels under Messines Ridge. Plumer expanded this to include 19 deep tunnels from 60 to 90 feet underground. The British dug five miles of tunnels, some of which were over half a mile long, and filled them with over a million pounds of explosives.[42]

On 21 May 1917, the British began an intensive 17-day artillery bombardment by 2,266 guns and fired some 3.5 million shells. At the same time 300 Royal Flying Corps aircraft won air superiority over the point of attack.

At 3.10 am on 7 June the British exploded the mines beneath Messines Ridge. The blasts, which could be heard as far away as London, produced craters up to 70 feet deep and 300 feet across and wiped out the German positions. The British followed this with a massive barrage and an assault by nine divisions, including Australian and New Zealand troops and 72 Mark IV tanks. The attackers also employed a new weapon, the Livens projector. Designed by Captain W. H. Livens, Royal Engineers, it was used to hurl canisters of asphyxiating gases into the German lines. By late afternoon the attackers had secured the eastern sides of the ridge and straightened the Ypres salient, a great boost to British morale.[43] The fighting between 1 and 12 June claimed some 25,000 British casualties (including 11,000 Anzacs); the Germans lost approximately 23,000 men (7,000 prisoners) and 154 guns.

Third Battle of Ypres (Passchendaele)

As had been the case at Vimy Ridge, there was no immediate exploitation of a successful initial attack. Fully seven weeks elapsed before Haig followed up the success at Messines. This was in part because he gave Gough responsibility for the offensive, and his Fifth Army had to be relocated to the area held by Plumer. While he admired Plumer's methodical approach, Haig wanted Gough, his youngest army commander and fellow cavalryman, in command. Haig was also in no particular hurry. Buoyed by favourable situation estimates from his chief intelligence officer, General John Charteris, who believed that the Germans were near collapse and could not quickly transfer reserves from the Eastern Front, he was confident of decisive results in 1917.[44]

On 30 May Fifth Army, now 17 divisions, took over the Ypres salient. Plumer's Second Army to its right, with 12 divisions, had only a secondary role. In the sector Haig had 3,000 guns, more than a third of them heavy pieces. Fifth Army also had three brigades (136 tanks) of the newly established Royal Tank Corps, and two divisions of Anthoine's French First Army would carry out a supporting attack.

The area Haig selected for Gough's assault was a poor one. Since the Germans held the high ground they were able to observe British preparations. They had also established an elastic defence-in-depth system in the sector, with a zigzag series of strong points and thick-walled mutually-supporting concrete pillboxes in place of the old rigid defensive line. Forward positions were lightly manned, with the bulk of the defenders in reserve poised for quick counterattacks. The Germans had also brought up reinforcements.[45] Despite these preparations, one historian places the principal blame for what followed squarely on Haig: "As at the Somme, the BEF was embarking upon a major offensive with a defective plan and with ambiguous objectives."[46]

What followed is known as the Third Battle of Ypres or the Passchendaele Campaign of 31 July–10 November 1917.[47] On 17 July the British began a 14-day preliminary bombardment, in which they fired 4,283,550 shells – their heaviest total of the war.[48] On 31 July, 12 divisions of infantry went over the top on an 11-mile front. Inclement weather was already a factor. The heaviest rains in decades, along with the preliminary shelling, destroyed dikes protecting the otherwise swampy terrain.

Although Fifth Army in the north advanced about two miles, little was achieved in the vital central Passchendaele Ridge sector. The destruction of the dikes and the rains produced an impassable morass in which tanks were useless. On 2 August the attack was suspended. Gough expressed reservations about continuing it, but Charteris convinced Haig that enemy forces would break in another attempt.

The second British push came on 16 August. A smaller version of the first, it was even less successful. Once again the left flank made the most progress. This time haphazard staff work compounded the problems of bad weather and mud. Passage to the front line was by slippery plank roads and duckboard tracks that were prime targets for German gunners. At the end of August Haig did what he should have done at first; he gave the main effort to Plumer, extending Second Army's front northward to include terrain previously controlled by Fifth Army. On 21 August Pétain carried out the first in a series of limited operations at Verdun. The weather at Ypres also changed; September was dry.

On 20 September, after his usual careful planning Plumer launched a series of limited attacks on narrow fronts. Advances were supported by heavy artillery barrages and half of the 1,300 British artillery pieces (one for every five yards of front) were heavy guns. Special assault groups, fighting as self-contained units, outflanked enemy strongpoints. Shallow rushes never outranged artillery support and divisions were limited to 1,000-yard frontages, often with two of three brigades in support and reserve. This allowed attacking troops to remain fresh enough to withstand inevitable German counterattacks.

In October the rains returned. Royal Engineers laid plank roads and duckboards across the mud to bring shells forward, but progress was both slow and slight, and the mud prevented many tanks from reaching their objectives.

The Germans retaliated by using mustard gas for the first time, and by using their planes to strafe British infantry, the first massive use of air support for ground troops. Plumer's tactics forced the Germans to revert to their previous tactic of defending forward areas, although this led to heavy casualties from British artillery fire.

When bad weather partially lifted, a combined attack by the two British armies resulted in gains, although German counterattacks produced heavy British casualties. A costly third attack on 4 October just managed to pre-empt a major German counterattack and coincided with the return of rain. Plumer and Gough wanted to halt the attack at this point, but Haig refused to give up.

The last attacks occurred between 26 October and 6 November. The British took both Passchendaele Ridge and village. Two brigades of Lieutenant General Sir Arthur Currie's Canadian Corps secured the latter, now no more than a brick smear in the mud, on 6 November. Haig then ordered his men to take up defensive positions. The assaults on Passchendaele Ridge and village gave name to the whole offensive, which became a lasting symbol of the futility and butchery of war on the Western Front.[49] While the British had deepened the Ypres salient by some five miles, this came at the horrible cost of 245,000 men (14,000 POWs) and more than 50 tanks. More than 90,000 of the British casualties were listed as missing in action; 42,000 were never found – many of them simply disappeared into the mud.[50] The French cost was 8,500 men; German losses were about 230,000 men (37,000 POWs) and 86 guns.

The losses in the Third Battle of Ypres brought Haig severe criticism. Most historians maintain that he underestimated German strength and believed in the possibility of a breakthrough long after most of those present had given up hope of achieving it. His defenders insist that British strength was weakened when Lloyd George shifted five divisions to the Italian Front following the Austrian breakthrough at Caporetto. Certainly Passchendaele deepened distrust between Lloyd George and Haig and Robertson, and it further encouraged the prime minister in his efforts to withhold British forces from Haig or divert then from the Western Front. The heavy British casualties left no reserves to exploit the later success at Cambrai, they also impacted British effectiveness in the German March 1918 offensive.[51] As Correlli Barnett has noted, perhaps the most important consequence of Passchendaele lay in the 1920s and 1930s "when the image of futile slaughter printed on the public mind by the writers and poets was to cause a wave of pacifist feeling in Britain that helped to prevent timely rearmament against Hitler's Germany".[52] The only advantage from the battle was that it allowed the French Army time to recover.

Battle of Cambrai

Undaunted, Haig persevered. Within a few weeks he initiated the Battle of Cambrai (20 November–5 December).[53] On the British side it involved 19 divisions and three tank brigades of General Julian Byng's Third Army. The Germans initially had six divisions of General Georg von der Marwitz's Second Army; later they would have 20 divisions engaged.

The British, from the first use of tanks in 1916, deployed them in small packets. At Cambrai they had more than 400 tanks under their own commander, General Hugh Elles. These included 376 of the latest Mark IV model, a slightly more powerful version of the 1916 Mark I. To the crews its chief difference from the Mark I was that it would usually keep out the new German armour-piercing bullet, whereas its predecessor would not. For the first time, tanks were a key element in the British plan and this time they were used en masse.[54]

Haig aimed his main attack at German-held Cambrai, about 35 miles south of Lille. This area had the advantages of firm, dry ground (essential for tanks), sufficient cover to assemble a large attacking force in secrecy, and a thinly held enemy line. The German defences consisted of a series of outposts in front of three well-constructed lines: the main Hindenburg Line and two secondary lines located about one and four miles farther back. A 13-mile long tunnel, 35 feet below ground, allowed German reserves to wait and rest in safety.[55]

Colonel J. F. C. Fuller developed the initial attack plan, envisioning it as the first in a series of tank raids leading to a decisive battle in 1918.[56] Haig and Byng expanded it into a full-blown offensive designed to smash a six-mile wide gap in the German lines, to capture Bourlon Ridge four miles west of Cambrai, and then to launch five cavalry divisions through the gap between the Canal du Nord and the Canal de l'Escaut to disrupt the German rear. The plan was overly ambitious for First World War conditions. Its success depended on complete surprise and the securing of Bourlon Ridge before the Germans could deploy their reserves. The British used low-flying aircraft to mask the noise of the tanks' arrival. They also brought up 600 additional artillery pieces to provide supporting fire without, however, benefit of registration.

The assault by nine tank battalions (374 tanks) followed by five infantry divisions began at 6.20 am on the dry but foggy morning of 20 November. Instead of a long and counterproductive preliminary bombardment, the 1,003 British guns laid down a short but intense barrage on the enemy front line, then shifted their fire rearward to disrupt the movement of enemy reserves and blind enemy direct-fire artillery with smoke. The tanks led the attack, each transporting at its front a large fascine (a bundle of brushwood). They were closely followed by the infantry, advancing in small groups in open order rather than in the usual extended line assault formation.

The tanks worked in teams of three with each having a well-defined task. The first would crush a gap in the wire; without crossing the enemy trench, it would turn left to work down the near side of the front trench and sweep it with machine-gun fire. The second would use its fascine to cross the trench (often as much as 13 feet wide) before turning left to work down the far side. The third then would move to the support trench, drop its fascine to cross it and also turn left. With their fascines, each team of tanks would be able to cross three obstacles. The British infantry would then mop up survivors, secure the captured trenches against counterattack, and prepare for the next move forward by the tanks.[57]

On the first day the attack went largely according to plan. Most German infantry simply fled. At Masnières, however, the Germans blew a bridge while a tank was crossing the canal there, forcing the infantry to fight without tank support and impeding its progress. The chief obstacle was at

Flesquières, where a British infantry division came under withering German fire. More than a dozen tanks were knocked out in succession by guns firing from behind well-sited and camouflaged concrete bunkers. If the infantry had been able to operate with the tanks, these might have been destroyed. On this first day of the Age of Armoured Warfare, one lesson was clear: in order to be successful, tanks, infantry, and artillery had to work together as teams.

By nightfall the British had penetrated the Hindenburg Line up to five miles. In Britain church bells rang out, but the celebration was premature. The Germans held at Bourlon Ridge, and Bavarian Crown Prince Rupprecht rushed up reserves to plug the gap. Because of heavy losses at Passchendaele earlier, the British lacked sufficient infantry reserves to counter them. They also did not have tank reserves; too many had been in the first two waves and were either knocked out by German field guns or, more often, suffered mechanical breakdowns. In the first day 65 tanks were lost to enemy action, 71 broke down, and 43 got stuck. The great tank armada no longer existed. The next day when the British resumed their attack, cooperative action between tanks and infantry was largely over and the battle reverted to the typical First World War pattern.[58]

Although they gained a foothold, the British never completely captured Bourlon Ridge. In the week that followed virtually no more gains were made. Reinforced to 20 divisions, the Germans mounted a counterattack beginning on 29 November. Utilizing their new infiltration techniques, they again made effective use of ground-attack aircraft.

On 3 December Haig ordered a partial withdrawal. When the battle finally ended two days later the Germans not only had retaken 75 per cent of the territory lost on the first day but, in the extreme south had even made inroads into the original British positions. In the battle the British lost about 44,000 men (9,000 POWs), 166 guns, and 300 tanks; German casualties were more than 41,000 men (11,000 POWs) and 142 guns.[59]

The Battle of Cambrai, nonetheless, restored surprise as an attack element on the Western Front. It also showed that the tank and infiltration tactics could restore battlefield fluidity, a hallmark of fighting on the Western Front in 1918.

Italian Front

Events in Italy, meanwhile, nearly brought disaster for the Allies in 1917. At the beginning of the year Italian Army Chief of Staff General Luigi Cadorna feared the Germans would send troops to support the Austrians on his front. General Nivelle sent General Foch to reassure Cadorna and they arranged for Britain and France to shift troops to Italy if needed.[60]

Tenth and eleventh battles of the Isonzo

Despite his pledge to attack simultaneously with the British at Arras and the French in Champagne, Cadorna did not mount his own offensive until 12 May. This, the Tenth Battle of the Isonzo (12 May–8 June), produced only slight gains with 157,000 Italian casualties. The Austrians lost 75,000 men.

The Eleventh Battle of the Isonzo (18 August to 15 September) saw Cadorna mount an assault with 52 divisions and 5,000 guns. General Luigi Capello's heavily reinforced Italian Second Army struck north of Gorizia on the left, while the Duke of Aosta's Italian Third Army attacked between Gorizia and Trieste on the right. Although Austrian Field Marshal Svetozar Borojević von Bojna's Fifth Army easily halted the southern thrust, to the north Capello's Second Army captured the strategically important Bainsizza Plateau. But exhausted and having outrun their supply lines, the Italians were forced to halt. With his own forces near collapse, new Austro-Hungarian chief of staff General Arz von Straussenburg appealed to Germany for assistance.[61]

Twelfth battle of the Isonzo (Caporetto)

Berlin's response led to the Twelfth (and final) Battle of the Isonzo, better known as the Battle of Caporetto (24 October–12 November 1917).[62] Convinced that Italy's recent successes required German aid to drive that country from the war, Ludendorff took the lead in creating a new army, the Fourteenth. Seven of its 15 divisions were German as was most of its artillery. German General Otto von Below commanded. The Central Powers massed 35 divisions (28 Austrian and seven German) against 41 Italian. Borojević von Bojna had overall charge but Below and his chief of staff Krafft von Delmensingen planned and led the offensive.

The Central Powers planned to use surprise and new tactics to offset their numerical disadvantage. The Germans first used these (what Western military analysts came to call "Hutier" tactics, named after German General Oscar von Hutier) on the Eastern Front in September 1917 at Riga.[63]

While France and Britain sought to overcome military stalemate through new machines, the Germans endeavoured to do the same through new battlefield tactics. They studied both their own and Allied methods on the Western Front, especially Russian tactics in the 1916 Brusilov Offensive. Brusilov's innovations, such as dispensing with prolonged preliminary bombardments, sprang from necessity (that is, a shortage of ammunition). German changes were made by design.

Hutier tactics included massing fully briefed and highly trained assault forces at the last moment. Secrecy was attained by covert night movements and concealment by day. Artillery registration was performed by single guns firing over a period of several days. The long preliminary bombardment disappeared in favour of short, intense barrages firing a mix of high explosive, gas, and smoke shells to mask enemy strong points. Bombardments were designed to cause maximum confusion and to disrupt enemy communication and artillery.

The short bombardment was followed immediately by an attack spearheaded by specially trained infantry units. Armed with large numbers of rapid-fire weapons, they bypassed rather than reduced enemy strong points, leaving them to be taken later by follow-up forces. The assault troops, supported by light artillery, flowed into enemy weak points and sought to punch corridors deep to the rear rather than trying to advance along a whole front. Such tactics isolated enemy front-line units, disrupted communications, and allowed attackers to reach the enemy rear areas before significant reserves could arrive.[64]

The Central Powers also augmented their air assets on the Italian Front, giving them area aerial superiority and preventing enemy aerial intelligence-gathering. They were also aided by bad weather. Despite German precautions, Cadorna knew something was afoot. Several days before the attack deserters warned of an imminent major assault. But Cadorna dismissed the possibility of a large-scale offensive on the Isonzo front. Believing its terrain was too rugged, he expected the attack to come in the Trentino instead. This seemed confirmed by an enemy diversionary thrust there on 27 October.

Cadorna positioned his reserves behind his Third Army, rather than along the Isonzo. He did order a defence in depth along the entire line with only light forces to hold forward positions; but Second Army Commander Luigi Capello, who was ill, did not carry out the order. Capello had his worst troops in the area of greatest danger and spent his time planning a counteroffensive to hit the attacker's flanks.

Below's Fourteenth Army led the assault, supported by the Austro-Hungarian Tenth Army on its right and the Austrian Fifth Army on its left. Although the attackers were at an overall numerical disadvantage, Below's strength at the point of attack was much greater than that of his adversary. The Central Powers also had 4,126 guns. The barrage of 24 October, which included gas and smoke shells, was intense, short in duration, and deep. It opened at 2.00am on a 25-mile front and ended just six hours later. The infantry then moved forward and by the end of the first day had advanced up to 12 miles. Crucial gaps in the Italian lines raised concerns that Third Army's flanks to the south as well as those of Fourth and First Armies to the north and west might be turned if the attackers reached the Tagliamento. This river also guarded Cadorna's headquarters at Udine. With the key stronghold of Montemaggiore lost and his line disintegrating Cadorna ordered a retreat to the Tagliamento. He intended to hold that line until positions on the Piave River could be prepared. While this decision was the best one under the circumstances, it also conceded the Austro-German forces a major tactical victory by forcing a retreat to close the gap that the collapse of Second Army had opened between the Italian Fourth and Third armies.

By the evening of 31 October the Italians were over the Tagliamento. There they repulsed enemy efforts to cross until the night of 2/3 November, when falling water levels allowed elements of an Austrian division to ford at Cornino. On 4 November Cadorna ordered all bridges on the Tagliamento destroyed and a withdrawal behind the wide Piave, the bridges of which were destroyed on the 9th, the same day that Armando Diaz replaced Cadorna as Italy's supreme commander.

With only 33 divisions, 3,986 guns, and six airfields left behind the Piave, the Italians faced 55 enemy divisions. But the Central Powers had outrun their supply lines and artillery support. Now General Diaz had a much shorter front to defend and his troops were entrenched behind a river line in the south and anchored on the Asiago Plateau and Monte Grappa in the north. The Italians were in a good strategic position for the first time in the war, facing troops worn down from a 50-mile pursuit.

Further efforts by German and Austro-Hungarian forces between 11 and 18 December to force the Piave line and flank it by overwhelming the Italian Fourth Army at Monte Grappa failed. On Christmas Day Borojević suspended the offensive. By salvaging a situation that seemed lost, the Italians believed that they had reclaimed their honour. Bolstering their morale was the arrival in early November of five British and six French divisions commanded by General Plumer.[65]

The Battle of Caporetto was a débâcle for Italy. Her army sustained 320,000 casualties (265,000 taken prisoner) and lost 3,152 guns, 1,732 mortars, 3,000 machine guns, 2,000 submachine guns, and more than 300,000 rifles. In marked contrast, Austro-German losses were only about 20,000 men. Caporetto is the only battle fought in Italy during the Great War that has survived in popular memory. Italian historian Mario Caracciolo believes that Italy's allies played up the disaster to disguise their own poor performance in 1917. But the Italians themselves have kept the debate about Caporetto alive because it came as a rude shock and triggered a search for scapegoats.[66]

Many Italians attributed the débâcle to left-wing and papal defeatism, political corruption, and military incompetence. Others blamed workers from Turin who had been sent to the front as a punishment for spreading defeatist attitudes, while still others castigated Cadorna and Capello for depressing morale with their rigid personalities and their harsh discipline. The army did resort to summary execution to punish mutinous units and to make examples of those who fled to the rear during the retreat. These, however, reinforced the popular impression of chaos and panic in which incompetent and blood-thirsty generals punished the troops for their own failures.

Perhaps surprisingly the Italian Army recovered quickly. By the summer of 1918 Diaz had 7,000 guns along the Piave, including 1,100 provided by France and Britain. He also had 50 Italian and four Allied divisions to repulse Borojević's last major offensive; and in October the Italians virtually annihilated the Austrians at Vittorio Veneto, on the first anniversary of Caporetto. Another important result of the battle was the Allied conference at Rapallo that took place on 5 November 1917. It led to the decision to institute a Supreme War Council, the first real Allied effort to achieve unity of command.[67]

March 1917 Revolution in Russia

Although Italy survived its greatest threat and continued in the war, Russia did not. At the end of 1916 the Allies simply did not understand the extent of Russian weakness. (Events leading up to the March 1917 revolution are described in Chapter 8.) What happened in Russia was attributable, more than anything else, to the failed leadership of Tsar Nicholas II. Political ineptitude, economic dysfunction, and general war-weariness combined to topple the tsarist regime.

On 16 March 1917, a Provisional Government was organized. It consisted entirely of moderate to conservative Duma leaders, with the sole exception of Aleksandr F. Kerensky, a Socialist Duma deputy, who became minister of justice. The Allied governments were at first delighted with the news, convinced that the March Revolution would stimulate the Russian people to even greater sacrifice. To ensure that end, however, they made loans to Russia contingent on her continued participation in the war.

The leaders of the Provisional Government needed no such urging. The country's tremendous sacrifices and war aims drove them forward. They also believed the war would focus attention on external affairs and away from more pressing domestic problems. This decision proved a fatal blunder for the Provisional Government. More than anything else, it brought the Bolsheviks to power in Russia. The Provisional Government, which came to be dominated by Kerensky, lurched from one crisis to another and lasted from mid-March to early November 1917. Shadowing it was the Petrograd Soviet (council). Soviets sprang up all over Russia, emulating those of the Russian Revolution of 1905. They were dominated by the Socialist parties.[68]

The new government initiated reforms ranging from the restoration of Finnish autonomy to freedom of expression and political amnesty. The Russian people were swept up in a sense of unlimited freedom; the crime rate soared and factories closed. Army discipline collapsed and soldiers deserted in increasing numbers. The Provisional Government sought the cooperation of all parties and agreement to a political truce. Initially the leaders of the small militant Bolshevik socialist party agreed. But among exiles returning to Russia was Vladimir I. Lenin. On 16 April, the evening of his return, he proclaimed "The April Theses" that outlined the Bolshevik programme and called for a complete break with the Provisional Government and an end to what he called the "predatory" war. In late May Leon Trotsky arrived from the United States; later he joined Lenin in the Bolshevik leadership.

Considering the overall situation the Provisional Government was perhaps fortunate to last as long as it did. In late April 1917, after Foreign Minister Milyukov publicly announced that Russia would continue in the war, there were angry demonstrations in Petrograd. The government promptly fell and, in the new coalition, Kerensky became minister of war.[69]

Kerensky (Second Brusilov) Offensive

Kerensky staked all on a great summer offensive. A charismatic leader and a gifted orator, he personally visited the front to explain to the troops the need for an offensive. His plan called for local attacks to hold the Germans in the north while the major attack once again fell on the weaker Austro-Hungarians in Galicia.[70]

In spring 1917 the Eastern Front was static. The opposing armies maintained positions on a line running from Riga in the north, west of Minsk and down the eastern slope of the Carpathian Mountains to the Black Sea halfway between Costanţa and Odessa. The Germans were in no hurry to attack. Fully aware that Russia was in turmoil, they had not only assisted Lenin's return to Russia but had also spent vast sums to destabilize the new government and help bring the Bolsheviks to power because they were the only Russian party that opposed the war.[71]

The Central Powers still had about 80 divisions in the East. The southern armies were mostly Austro-Hungarian: the Austrian Second Army was north of Lemberg. General Count Felix von Bothmer's "Südarmee" of four German, three Austrian, and one Turkish division was opposite Brzezany and south of Lemberg. General Tersztyánszky's Third Army was north of the Dniester River, while the Seventh Army was just south of Kalusz. After Hindenburg's elevation to supreme command Field Marshal Prince Leopold of Bavaria assumed nominal command of all German armies in the East, but General Max Hoffmann was *de facto* commander.[72]

Relations between Germany and Austria-Hungary had become tense. Emperor Franz Josef died in November 1916 and Archduke Karl succeeded him. The new Emperor had little enthusiasm for the war and in fact wanted to extract the Dual Monarchy from it, an attitude of which Berlin was well aware. Although nothing came of this, in early 1917 Karl and Foreign Minister Ottokar Czernin conducted secret negotiations with the Allies through Prince Sixtus of Bourbon-Parma.

At the end of May Kerensky appointed the aggressive and capable Aleksei A. Brusilov to command the Russian Army. Brusilov fully supported a renewed drive in Galicia. His attacking force consisted of 45 divisions in three armies: Erdelli's Eleventh Army in the north, Beikovitch's Seventh Army in the centre of the front, and Lavr Kornilov's Eighth Army south of the Dniester River. Brusilov's immediate objective was the oil fields near Drohobycz but his ultimate goal was Lemberg.[73]

Russia's last great effort of the war, known both as the Kerensky and the Second Brusilov Offensive, opened on 1 July on a 100-mile front. Initially the poorly equipped Russian forces, including a vanguard of Finnish and Polish troops, made significant headway. General Kornilov's Russian Eighth Army made especially good progress, driving back the Austrian Third Army, reaching Kalusz, and threatening the oil field at Drohobycz. On the northern flank the Russian Eleventh Army forced the Austrian Second Army back to Zlochow, and Seventh Army pushed the Südarmee back nearly 30 miles.

Many Austrian troops simply threw down their arms and fled. The Russians took thousands of prisoners and considerable stocks of war supplies. But Brusilov lacked reserves. The Russians rapidly outran their supply lines and their drive petered out. Russian discipline also broke down as German reinforcements, profiting from the advantage of interior lines and a developed railroad net, stiffened the resistance.

Since April, in fact, the Germans had anticipated a Russian offensive. Deserters had betrayed the enemy plans and Hoffmann had already drawn up his own counteroffensive. Once the Russian drive had been blunted he set in motion his riposte, augmented by six German divisions sent from the Western Front by rail. Hoffmann placed these in the area between Zoboroth and the Sereth River with the intention of striking toward Tarnopol. The German assault, launched on a 12-mile front on the right flank, began on 19 July.[74] It was preceded by an intense bombardment planned by master German artillerist Lieutenant Colonel Georg Bruchmüller.[75]

The demoralized Russian formations disintegrated and the Central Powers advanced nine miles the first day alone. Tarnopol fell on 25 July, triggering withdrawals along the entire front. Czernowitz fell on 3 August; by early August the Russians had evacuated both Galicia and the Bukovina. The entire southwestern front simply collapsed. Discipline ended as Russian soldiers shot their officers and refused to fight. The gains of 1916 were wiped out and there was no Russian army south of the Pripet Marches.

The German offensive halted on the border of Galicia because of insufficient resources. Additional gains were contingent on advances to the south, but neither Archduke Josef's Austro-Hungarian forces south of Czernowitz nor Field Marshal August von Mackensen's army group in Romania made significant progress. Hoffmann was pleased with the results. Ludendorff was not as happy; Romania and Russia had yet to be driven from the war, a precondition for any massive 1918 Western Front offensive.[76]

News of the Russian military disaster coincided with the "July Days" in Petrograd when Bolsheviks and other radicals attempted to seize control of the government. The Provisional Government responded by jailing most of the Bolshevik leaders; Lenin managed to avoid arrest and went into hiding in Finland. As unrest and demoralization spread Kerensky became head of the Provisional Government.

In early autumn pro-monarchist elements attempted to undo the March Revolution. In August Kerensky had replaced a totally exhausted Brusilov with General Lavr Kornilov. Military discipline had all but evaporated and many hoped that Kornilov could right the situation. He demanded a free hand and an end to political discussion groups formed to spread democratization in the army. Of humble origins, Kornilov had come up through the ranks and was widely respected. He and Kerensky, two men of equally strong will, soon clashed. Kornilov attempted a coup d'état supported by most of the army's officers, the middle class, and the Allied governments.[77]

German Riga Offensive

The coup attempt was made possible by the fall of Riga. In early August Ludendorff had called on Hoffmann to mount an offensive across the Dvina River to seize the fortress city of Riga. It was a key Russian position along the Baltic coast and its fall would open the way to Petrograd. If the Germans could capture it now the Russians might finally seek an armistice.[78] on 1 September, following a massive but short artillery bombardment planned by Colonel Bruchmüller and involving a mix of high explosive and gas shells from 170 German artillery batteries, General Oskar von Hutier's German Eighth Army attacked Riga, held by General Vladislav N. K. Klembovski's Russian Twelfth Army.

During the attack Hutier initiated for the first time on a large scale the new assault techniques repeated six weeks later at Caporetto. While a holding attack on the west bank of the Dvina River threatened the city Hutier sent three divisions across the river on pontoon bridges to the north to close around the fortress. Although Riga fell just two days later, success came so quickly that the Germans were unable to exploit it. Anticipating the assault Klembovski had, on 20 August, begun to withdraw his army from its bridge-head southeast of the Dvina. That same day he began to withdraw supplies from Riga as well. When the Germans attacked, the Russians simply abandoned Riga and streamed eastward. The Germans took only 9,000 Russian prisoners and casualties were minimal on both sides.[79]

At the same time the Germans carried out small amphibious landings on Oesel, Moon, and Dagoe Islands in the Gulf of Finland as well as a landing on the mainland. This operation, which involved 19 capital ships, employed an infantry division and a cycle-equipped infantry brigade. Concluded on 20 October, the operation was not essential to Hutier's attack and had been implemented mostly to provide a role for the nearly idle High Seas Fleet.[80]

Bolshevik Revolution

The Baltic coast was now completely exposed and Petrograd undefended. Kornilov demanded that Kerensky transfer authority to him to deal with the crisis, but Kerensky dismissed Kornilov instead. Kornilov then ordered his troops to march on the capital. Panic erupted both within the Provisional Government and Petrograd Soviet at the thought of a Kornilov dictatorship.

Kerensky was soon destroyed by the war he had sought to ride to political advantage. Betrayed by the army and underestimating the Bolshevik threat, he turned for help to the extreme left and armed Leon Trosky's Red Guard of soldiers, sailors, and workers sympathetic to the Bolsheviks. The Bolsheviks would later use these very weapons to seize power. Ironically this move was unnecessary as revolutionary workers and Bolshevik propagandists halted the trains before they could reach Petrograd and persuaded Kornilov's tired and hungry soldiers to go home. On 12 September Kornilov was arrested. (Later he escaped and fought the Reds in the Civil War.) Although the right-wing attempt to seize power had been halted, Kerensky was at the mercy of the radical left.[81]

Conditions in Russia continued to deteriorate, especially in the cities. Food shortages and the collapse of the ruble kept Petrograd volatile. In late September, buoyed by an infusion of German funds that allowed workers to be paid, the Bolsheviks advanced their slogans of "peace, bread, and land" and "all power to the Soviets". Lenin realized more than any other Russian political leader the extent of war-weariness in Russia and the desire for peace at virtually any price.

In early October Trotsky was elected chairman of the Petrograd Soviet. The government coalition meanwhile collapsed. It was not until 6 October that Kerensky was able to form a new government with a socialist majority. To fend off the Bolshevik surge, on 27 September he declared Russia a republic and initiated arrangements for a constitutional assembly.

It was far too late for such measures, however. Lenin returned to the capital and the Bolshevik Party leadership voted secretly to attempt a coup. A political bureau (politburo) was set up in which Lenin continued as the political leader, while Trotsky coordinated military operations. The attempt was planned for the night of 6/7 November, coinciding with a meeting of a Congress of Soviets (local socialist councils that had sprung up all over Russia) in Petrograd. A force of revolutionary soldiers, sailors, and Red Guards occupied strategic positions in the city and arrested members of the Provisional Government. Kerensky escaped, having failed to win military support, and fled abroad. On the evening of 7 November the last remnants of the opposition, having taken up positions in the Winter Palace, surrendered to the Bolsheviks. With Trotsky presiding, Lenin marched into the hall of the new

Congress of Soviets and announced the new government. The Communist era in Russia had begun.[82]

War-weariness gripped most of the warring states. Certainly events in Russia helped encourage or spread unrest elsewhere, most notably in Austria-Hungary and Germany.

Balkan Front

There was little activity on the Balkan Front in 1917. At the beginning of the year, French General Maurice Sarrail had on paper 600,000 men but malaria and other diseases actually reduced his force to only 100,000 fit for duty. Differences between the British and French as well as the Serbians' distrust of both exacerbated command problems. Sarrail was also reluctant to advance because of German air superiority and because Greek King Constantine continued to treat with the Central Powers. The Germans derisively referred to the Salonika force as "the greatest internment camp in the world".[83] The Allies made several inconclusive advances early in 1917. During 11–17 March Allied assaults failed at Monastir and at Lake Prespa (Djoran); they were also unsuccessful in the Battle of the Vardar that lasted from 5 to 19 May.

In March 1917 Aristide Briand, premier of France since November 1915, fell from power. His replacement Alexander Ribot was determined to bring Greece into the war on the Allied side. On 11 June new French envoy Charles Jonnart presented King Constantine with an ultimatum that he abdicate and renounce his throne on behalf of the crown prince. Concurrent with this demand, Allied troops moved into Thessaly and a French force occupied the Isthmus of Corinth. Constantine complied the next day and was succeeded by his second son Alexander who, on 26 June, appointed Eleutherios Venizelos as premier. On 27 June Greece declared war on the Central Powers. Sarrail failed, however, to take advantage of the situation, and on 10 December French Premier Georges Clemenceau replaced him by the competent Marie Louis Adolphe Guillaumat as commander of the Allied Armies of the East at Salonika. For the time being Guillaumat was occupied with restoring the morale of Allied troops and training the Greek Army.[84]

At the end of 1917 the Allies were still without unity of command, a glaring failure fully revealed by their failed offensives on the Western Front. Two massive and uncoordinated offensives there had cost half a million casualties. Germany appeared to have the upper hand. If OHL could shift sufficient manpower and guns from the East to the West quickly enough, they might be able to break the stalemate there before American resources could be brought to bear.

Chapter Six

1918: the end

As 1918 began the Allies found themselves in a less than satisfactory situation. On the seas their surface fleets were dominant and the German submarine threat had been contained, but on land, except in the Middle East, the Allied offensives had failed. Italy was close to collapse and Russia had all but been driven from the war. This latter was balanced by the entry of the United States. She was mobilizing her considerable resources to supply large quantities of finished goods, supplies, and foodstuffs. But the American Army was only slowly arriving in France and needed extensive training. For the Entente US troops were vital, and in the winter of 1917–18 a "race to France" began.

The Central Powers were reeling. The Allied blockade was slowly strangling Germany, and Bulgaria, Turkey, and even Austria-Hungary were wavering in their allegiance with popular unrest spreading as a result of the uncertainty. If Germany was to win the war it would have to be in 1918 and she would have to bear the brunt of the effort.

Russia leaves the war

Germany's hope of winning the war in the West before US resources could alter the balance hinged on peace on the Eastern Front. Here the Bolsheviks took the lead. The day after they had come to power, Lenin suggested an immediate armistice on all fronts to be followed by peace talks. The Western Allies rejected this out of hand – the Bolsheviks, much to the embarrassment of the Entente, had begun publishing terms of its secret partition treaties.[1]

Predictably the Central Powers reacted differently to the Russian overture. Hindenburg and Ludendorff had long concluded that the only way Germany could win the war was to defeat Russia and then shift forces to the West for an all-out offensive before American troops could influence the outcome. Berlin therefore responded positively to the Russian proposal.

On 3 December 1917, the two sides opened talks behind German lines at the Polish city of Brest-Litovsk, and on the 17th an armistice went into effect on the Eastern Front. On December 22 the first peace conference of the war followed, also at Brest-Litovsk, although meaningful talks there did not begin until 9 January.[2]

Commissar Leon Trotsky, who headed the Russian delegation, adopted a defiant attitude. His strategy was to delay until an expected German revolution drove that country from the war. The Russians also naively expected the Germans to negotiate on the basis of no annexations or indemnities. But General Hoffmann soon disabused Trotsky of this when he presented the harsh German demands. The German General Staff had formulated these and they shocked even the German negotiator, career diplomat Richard von Kühlmann.

Over a brief Christmas recess Trotsky returned to Petrograd and urged that Russia pursue a policy of "no war, no peace". This was unacceptable to the Germans, although the conferees did agree to extend the armistice until 12 February. Two days before its expiration Trotsky proclaimed that the Russians simply considered the war at an end. An astounded Hoffmann responded by signing a separate peace with Ukraine and informing the Russians on 16 February that the German Army would resume offensive operations in two days. On the 18th, German troops crossed the Dvina River to capture the city of Pskov. Trotsky returned to Petrograd for urgent consultations.

Most of the Russian Bolshevik leadership preferred continuing the war but having destroyed the army in their rise to power they were in no position to fight. The German Army, meanwhile, rolled forward in the easiest offensive of the war. It took all of Lenin's argumentative skills to convince the Bolshevik leadership to agree to peace.[3] He did so by telling them that the treaty would not last. Germany, he said, was on the brink of revolution. The most important thing was to consolidate Bolshevik power in Russia, without which there would be no hope for world revolution. Lost territory could be recovered later. Indeed, historian John Wheeler-Bennett concluded, "The Peace of Brest-Litovsk will preserve Bolshevism."[4]

The German advance continued even after the Russians had returned to the negotiating table. The Germans got all the way to Narva, within 100 miles of Petrograd, precipitating transfer of the government to Moscow.[5]

Treaty of Brest-Litovsk

On 3 March, 1918, the Bolsheviks signed the Treaty of Brest-Litovsk. (Trotsky, replaced as Commissar of Foreign Affairs by Georgi Chicherin, refused to attend the ceremony.) Under the treaty's terms Russia lost Poland, Courland, and Lithuania, leaving Germany and Austria-Hungary to determine their future status. Russia had to evacuate Livonia, Estonia, Finland, and the Åland Islands. She was also forced to evacuate Ukraine and recognize the treaty between the Ukrainian People's Republic and the Central Powers. She had to surrender the districts of Ardahan, Kars, and Batum to Turkey; and she had to agree to cease all Bolshevik propaganda. Finally Russia agreed to pay Germany an indemnity that the Russians estimated at from 4 to 5 billion gold roubles. In all, Russia lost a third of her population, 56 million people; she also lost 73 per cent of her iron and 89 per cent of her coal production. Wheeler-Bennett notes that Brest-Litovsk "for a peace of humiliation is without precedent in modern history".[6]

If there had been any doubts as to the future of the surrendered territories these were laid to rest when they were immediately brought under the Central Powers' control. In April German troops landed in Finland, the Kaiser offering its throne to his brother-in-law Prince Karl of Hesse. That same month German and Austro-Hungarian troops occupied Ukraine, vital for its grain production, and established a military dictatorship there under General Pavlo Skoropadski. The Kaiser also accepted the "invitation" of the Estonians to be their king, and in July Lithuania offered its throne to Prince Wilhelm of Urach, a younger member of the ruling family in Württemberg.[7]

The Treaty of Brest-Litovsk was momentous. It virtually pushed Russia back to its pre-Petrine frontiers. Russia lost nearly 1.3 million square miles of territory. This included approximately a third of Russia's arable land, three-quarters of her coal and iron, a third of her factories, and a quarter of her railroads.[8] In view of German protestations over the 1919 Treaty of Versailles it is worth remembering that Brest-Litovsk was much harsher on the defeated power. The Reichstag accepted the treaty overwhelmingly, even though it ran counter to its own July 1917 Peace Resolution that had called for peace on the basis of no territorial annexations (enacted when Germany seemed to be losing). The Majority Socialists criticized its "annexationist mentality" but did no more than abstain from the vote. Only the small Independent Socialist Party was opposed.[9] For the Allies the treaty did help to forge a unity of purpose, hitherto lacking.[10]

Treaty of Bucharest

The Central Powers completed their eastern triumph when, on 7 May, isolated Romania was forced to sign the equally punitive Treaty of Bucharest. She ceded the Dobrudja to Bulgaria, the Carpathian passes to Hungary, and a 90-year lease on her oil wells and mineral rights to Germany.[11]

Wilson's Fourteen Points

In part to counteract what had happened in the East the Western Allies now sought to win the propaganda battle. On 3 January 1918, Prime Minister Lloyd George announced British war aims and two days later President Wilson followed suit. The two men were in general agreement regarding the shape of the settlement but Wilson's Fourteen Points attracted the most attention; later they played an important role in the 1919 peace settlement. These called for:[12]

1. "Open covenants of peace, openly arrived at."
2. Absolute freedom of the seas, in peace as well as in war.
3. Removal of economic barriers between nations.
4. Reductions in armaments, "to the lowest point consistent with domestic safety".
5. An "impartial adjustment of all colonial claims", taking into account the interests of the people involved.
6. Evacuation of all Russian territory.
7. Evacuation of Belgium and restoration of her full sovereignty.
8. Evacuation of France and the restoration to her of Alsace-Lorraine.
9. Readjustment of Italy's frontiers along "clearly recognizable lines of nationality".
10. Autonomy for the peoples of Austria-Hungary.
11. Evacuation and restoration of Romania, Serbia, and Montenegro, with Serbia to have "secure access" to the sea.

12. Sovereignty for the Turkish portions of the Ottoman Empire, autonomy for the non-Turkish populations, and freedom of passage through the Straits.
13. An independent Poland with "free and secure access" to the sea.
14. The establishment of a "general association of nations" (the future League of Nations).

Wilson's proposals failed to bring a favourable response from the Central Powers; buoyed by the collapse of Russia and the near defeat of Italy they saw no need for compromise. On 24 January 1918, German Chancellor Count George von Hertling and Austrian Foreign Minister Count Ottokar Czernin replied. Czernin summed up the official position of the Central Powers when he said that the Allies were labouring under the mistaken belief that they were the victors. In any case, the men actually running the war for the Central Powers, Hindenburg and Ludendorff, were playing not for compromise but for a victorious peace, a *Siegfrieden*. OHL's war aims into the spring of 1918 included retention of Belgium, Luxembourg, and (the most important of her western goals) the French Longwy-Briey basin and its iron reserves. France and the Netherlands would become German economic satellites. Much of eastern Europe would be annexed outright and the rest converted into economic appendages. OHL also had extensive colonial demands in Africa and some in Asia. All this would have given Germany world hegemony. As Fritz Fischer has observed: "The weight of the German Reich in matters of commercial policy would unquestionably have put Germany in an impreg nable position of world economic power. The economic agreements were, moreover, to be safeguarded by military treaties."[13]

Ludendorff Offensive

OHL knew it had to act quickly. As early as 11 November 1917, Ludendorff had pointed out that Germany would have only a fleeting opportunity on the Western Front. He called for the transfer there of troops and guns from the East for one major offensive before America could redress the balance. It would be in the British sector.[14]

Ludendorff did not transfer West as many men as he might have. Historian J. W. Wheeler-Bennett has noted, "To enforce the peace and to bolster up the fantasies of the Supreme Command, no less than a million soldiers had to be retained in the East in 1918." A large proportion of these were older men, as most under 35 years old had been sent to the West; but if even half of this number had been sent West they could have gone to quiet sectors of the front and released younger men for the offensive. Ultimately more troops were sent West so that by October General Hoffmann had only half a million men under his command in the East. Had the half million men been available in the West in April 1918, Wheeler-Bennett believes it "might very well have turned the scale in favour of Germany".[15]

Ludendorff's plan was broad. Specific proposals came from General Hermann von Kuhl, Crown Prince Rupprecht's chief of staff; Colonel Friedrich von der Schulenburg, Crown Prince Wilhelm's chief of staff; and Lieutenant Colonel Georg Wetzell, chief of the Operations Section of OHL. Ludendorff put off the final decision until 21 January 1918, when he decided on a compromise. By March, 47 special attack divisions and more than 6,000 guns had been secretly deployed to a section of the front held by 28 trench divisions.[16]

The spring 1918 German drive is usually known as the Ludendorff Offensive. It envisioned a series of attacks designed to push the British army back on the Channel, isolating it from the French Army. Ludendorff sought to take advantage of the differing Allied defensive priorities: to the British it was defence of the Channel ports for resupply and access to Britain; for the French it was the defence of Paris. Once the two armies had been pried apart and the British pinned back, Ludendorff planned to hurl the bulk of his forces against the British. If they could be defeated, surely France would then give up. The defeat of the French Army, he believed, would merely bring a withdrawal to the interior of the country.[17]

The first German drive, code-named MICHAEL (after Germany's patron saint), was directed at the hinge where the British and French armies came together and lasted from 21 March to 5 April. For MICHAEL the Germans enjoyed substantial advantages in men and matériel. By the start of the offensive Ludendorff had amassed in the West 207 divisions against only 173 Allied (this included 4.5 US divisions, which at 27,000 men each, are here calculated at nine divisions). The attack itself involved 74 German divisions supported by 6,473 guns and 730 aircraft. With only 34 infantry divisions (and three cavalry) defending this point of the line, at places the British were outnumbered four to one. The defenders had 2,804 guns, 579 aircraft, and 217 tanks.

The Allies knew that the Germans would soon attack. The Supreme War Council had wanted a 30-division reserve that could be committed after the German attack, but Pétain and Haig both objected. Haig reasoned that the French would be far more willing to take units from him than to assist him (a presumption subsequently borne out), and he had few reserves to spare because London was reluctant to send him reinforcements. It now appears that it was Robertson and the War Office rather than Lloyd George who kept the reserves in Britain, in part because of Haig's assurances that he could hold out for 18 days without reinforcements.[18] In the end Haig and Pétain planned their own defensive battles, each with only limited arrangements for reinforcement of the other.

The Germans utilized the infiltration tactics already proven at Riga, Caporetto, and Cambrai. These relied heavily on decentralization of authority and two different types of divisions: the standard *Stellungsdivisionen* (trench) and new *Angriffsdivisionen*. The latter were the elite *Stosstrupen* ("shock troops"). Their *Sturmbataillone* (assault battalions) contained the healthiest and most motivated men. They were preferably young bachelors because of expected high casualty rates. Highly trained, they received the finest equipment and better rations.

The attack, to be launched in early morning darkness hopefully with ground fog, would begin with a short, massive artillery bombardment. This was immediately followed by infiltration-style assaults employing combined-arms platoons of about 50 men each armed with light machine guns and the 9 mm submachine gun to sweep enemy trenches. Pioneers cut paths through enemy wire; the assault troops also had light, direct-fire artillery. Attackers bypassed enemy strong points, leaving them for follow-on elements. No limits were set on divisional advances; these were determined by forward attack elements. Assault formations were followed by support elements with light trench mortars, flamethrowers, and heavier direct-fire artillery that could reduce all but the heaviest strongpoints. Reserve elements came next. They consisted of conventional troops who freed advance elements to continue the attack.

Artillery played a key role. Lieutenant Colonel Georg Bruchmüller had developed a system of responsive and flexible artillery support that he coordinated throughout the 1918 offensives. Artillery was massed secretly before the offensive, even the night before, in order to catch the enemy by surprise. There was no registration firing prior to the attack and the initial short, intense bombardment consisted mainly of smoke and gas shells to create maximum confusion and blind enemy gunners. Forward observers with the leading infantry elements controlled subsequent artillery fire, using Very pistols or flares to signal commands.

The Germans made virtually no use of tanks; their industry was unable to manufacture them in sufficient quantities. They did employ some captured British tanks in special formations but these did not influence the outcome of the spring battles. Aircraft were, however, integrated into the German assault. They were to secure command of the air over the battlefield and locate enemy guns and troop reinforcements. Heavier aircraft carried out bombing missions to disrupt enemy communications, while lighter planes assisted advancing elements with strafing runs against ground targets. Pilots communicated with the troops by ground panels or by radio.[19]

OHL also instituted an elaborate deception plan. All German commanders were led to believe the attack would be made in their own sectors. This heightened enthusiasm and confused the enemy. OHL also purposely allowed Allied air reconnaissance over areas where deceptive activities were occurring and sought to deny access where actual attack preparations were made. Intensified shelling and hints of an impending attack in the Verdun sector in mid-March convinced Pétain that the attack to the north was merely a feint.[20]

The Germans were well aware that the bulk of British forces were employed on the vulnerable northern end of the line. Two months earlier the British had extended their front southward by taking over 28 miles of French trenches, despite the fact that their strength was slightly less than that of 1917. Gough's Fifth Army troops discovered that the French had largely neglected the sector's defences, where the brunt of the German attack, was to fall. Haig also seems to have underestimated the threat there when he kept the bulk of his reserves in Flanders.

Although the Allies had come to recognize the value of an elastic defence in depth, deployments were incomplete and many commanders reduced first-line trench strength but neglected to build the requisite machine-gun strongpoints. In Gough's sector the forward defensive zone was too densely held. Haig had no reserves but he hoped that in a crisis Pétain would send troops, although the January agreement called for him to send only six divisions within four days of Haig's request.[21]

MICHAEL

The Germans opened MICHAEL, now flatteringly dubbed the *Kaiserschlacht* (Emperor's Battle) and also known as the Second Battle of the Somme, at 4.40am on 21 March. Bruchmüller's 6,473-gun preliminary bombardment lasted only five hours but fired 1.2 million shells. Heavy fog and the plentiful use of gas and smoke shells greatly inhibited Allied visibility.[22] The 74 German divisions attacked along the 50-mile front from La Fère to Arras, held in the north by Byng's Third Army (14 divisions) and south by Gough's Fifth Army (12 infantry and three cavalry divisions).

The attack easily forced back the heavily outnumbered Fifth Army. On the second day the British lost contact with French forces to their right and Gough ordered a retirement beyond the Somme. Hutier's Eighteenth Army had been successful but, to the north the Second and Seventeenth Armies encountered the better prepared defences of Byng's Third Army. Ludendorff still might have achieved decisive victory had he concentrated on taking the vital railroad junction of Amiens; but on the 23rd, believing the British were beaten, he gave his three attacking armies divergent axes of advance.[23]

On the 23rd also the Germans began shelling Paris with long-range heavy artillery at up to a 76-mile range. There were seven "Paris guns", each consisting of a 210 mm tube about 120 feet long inserted in a 15-inch battleship gun. They wore out after only 40–50 rounds and were rebored upward. The initial 210 mm projectile weighed 264 lb but each successive one was slightly larger because of bore enlargement. Between 23 March and 9 August the Germans fired some 400 rounds without impressive result: 256 people killed and another 620 injured.[24]

As Paris came under artillery fire the British were locked in desperate struggle. Although continuing to withdraw – Baupaume fell on the 24th and Albert on the 26th – British lines did not break. The Germans had now outrun their supply lines, which had to traverse terrain torn up in the earlier fighting and in the 1916 withdrawal to the Hindenburg Line. This also inhibited the bringing up of artillery. The attackers had also sustained heavy casualties and lacked immediate reserves to exploit breakthroughs, and they suffered from British aircraft attacks against troops in the open.

MICHAEL did bring a change in Allied command structure. While not affecting that battle it did have profound implications for the war's outcome. Allied leaders knew that one reason for the initial German success was lack of cooperation between the British and French commanders. On 23 March Haig and Pétain had met to discuss the situation. Pétain promised to send sufficient troops to prevent a rupture between the two armies, but the next day, citing his orders "to cover Paris at all costs", he refused. Pétain believed that the major German thrust would still come in Champagne toward Paris and that the British had been beaten and would now fall back on the Channel ports.[25]

In these desperate circumstances Allied leaders finally adopted a unified command structure. On the 26th they met at Doullens to entrust overall command on the Western Front to General Ferdinand Foch. On 3 April Foch became commander-in-chief of all Allied armies on the Western Front, including the Americans.

It was inevitable that a French general would be selected as France had the largest manpower commitment, but Foch's name was the only one proposed. Clemenceau later wrote, "The main point was that Foch had displayed qualities of the highest kind in desperate circumstances which, above every-thing, called for miracles of resistance."[26] Foch proved a capable commander and his positive attitude was an immediate morale boost. Although he and Clemenceau were soon in bitter argument, to his credit Clemenceau backed Foch to the end of the war. Without these two men the war outcome might have been quite different.[27]

MICHAEL was a great tactical success for Ludendorff. The German Army had recaptured much of the ground it had abandoned in 1916. It had also created a 10-mile wide gap in the Allied lines. But Foch moved up reserves and the Germans lacked the resources to exploit the opportunity. More importantly, MICHAEL scared the Allies to the point that they were able to overcome their pride and institute a uniform command structure. With his offensive on the Somme stalled Ludendorff sought to regain the initiative by launching another attack. On 25 March he sent out new orders reversing those of two days earlier. These shifted the emphasis of the offensive back to the centre and right where his Second and Seventeenth Armies had been held up. Code-named MARS, the new operation had Arras as its objective and began on 28 March. The stronger British positions there held. At the end of the month Ludendorff shifted emphasis to take Amiens, but by now the German troops were exhausted. Clear weather also allowed Allied aircraft to savage the attackers. On 5 April Ludendorff suspended the offensive.[28]

By that date the British had been pushed back up to 40 miles. Gough was unfairly singled out as the scapegoat for the British withdrawal and removed from command. Rawlinson replaced him and on 2 April the Fifth Army was renamed the Fourth.[29] The British suffered approximately 178,000 casualties (72,000 POWs) and lost more than 1,100 guns, 200 tanks, and about 400 aircraft. The French, with 20 divisions engaged, sustained around 77,000 casualties (approximately 15,000 captured). But the push had also been costly to the Germans, particularly to the elite Storm Troops. They had lost 239,000 men and now needed more men to hold a longer line.

By now the Allies fully realized their perilous situation. The British gov-ernment passed a conscription act that included all males between the ages of 18 and 55, and within a month London had sent to the continent its military reserve of 355,000 men. American numbers were also growing. By March 1918 some 325,000 US troops were in France and efforts were made to expedite the process. From May through July more than 675,000 arrived. By the end of the war the US Army had grown to 4 million men, over half of whom were in France. Ultimately 1.3 million of them reached the firing line.[30]

GEORGETTE

After a short regroupment Ludendorff launched his second blow to the north in Flanders. A smaller version of the original GEORGE, it was codenamed GEORGETTE. The German Fourth and Sixth Armies attacked just south of Ypres on both sides of the east–west running Lys River, which gave its name to the battle lasting from 9 to 21 April. The two German armies had 2,208 artillery pieces; the British First Army opposing them only 511. Ludendorff also assembled 492 aircraft for the offensive.[31]

Ludendorff hoped that a second attack, this time on the British left wing, would break the BEF or at least cripple it sufficiently to allow him to shift back to the south and finish the job. His sole aim was the destruction of the British forces, but his commitment of large resources meant his forces would be vulnerable to an Allied counterattack. Also, more than half the assault troops were "trench" rather than "attack" divisions.[32]

The attack of 9 April by the Sixth Army fell in a sector near Neuve Chapelle held by the 2nd Portuguese division, one of two fighting in France under British control since 1916. This division was of poor quality and had been held in the line longer than normal. The Portuguese broke immediately and left a six-mile-wide gap in the line. The next day the German Fourth Army, attacking to the north, drove the British off Messines Ridge and forced them to evacuate Armentières between the converging German thrusts.[33]

Haig's plea to Foch for reinforcements failed. Foch, gathering a seven-division reserve behind the British positions, declared the battle already over and French troops did not arrive until the 19th. On 11 April Haig issued a desperate order: "There is no other course open to us but to fight it out. Every position must be held to the last man: there must be no retirement. With our backs to the wall and believing in the justice of our cause, each one of us must fight on to the end."[34]

Although the British were forced back 15 to 20 miles in places their lines did not break. More important than Haig's appeal was the arrival of three divisions: two British and one Australian. And on the 14th Foch became General-in-Chief with more power to move French forces from a reluctant Pétain. By the 19th the French had taken over a nine-mile sector of front previously held by Second Army. This came too late, however, to enable Plumer to hold and he reluctantly ordered Second Army to withdraw from Passchendaele Ridge to a more secure line just east of Ypres. On 24 April the Germans again struck toward Amiens from Villers Bretonneux. The battle was notable in that the Germans employed 13 A7V tanks, advancing them in three groups in thick mist. The centre group of six German tanks exchanged fire at 200 yards range with three British Mark IV tanks and drove off the two "females". But the German tanks were themselves damaged by cannon fire from the "male" Mark IV and driven back. Later one of the German tanks in the southernmost group knocked out a British light Whippet tank, one of a group of seven brought up to counterattack German infantry. This first tank-to-tank battle in history underscored the need for tanks to have an anti-tank capability. That night Rawlinson launched a counterattack and drove the Germans back.[35]

Ludendorff had to regroup and on 29 April called off the offensive. Allied losses in the battle were more than 146,000 men (two-thirds of them British) and at least 573 guns. German losses were about 109,000 men.

By early May Ludendorff had succeeded in replacing approximately 70 per cent of his losses with men returned from hospitals and boys of the 1920 class. He still had a numerical advantage over the Allies on the Western Front – 206 divisions against 160 – but he no longer had the fine troops of the start of MICHAEL and there were many reports of lapses in discipline.[36]

British raids on Ostend and Zeebrugge

On 23 April, St George's Day, the Royal Navy launched raids against the Belgian ports of Ostend and Zeebrugge, transit points for German submarines and torpedo craft operating from Bruges against shipping in the English Channel. The submarine menace had been largely contained and this was mainly a Royal Navy effort to show solidarity with the army and boost morale. The operation, under Dover Patrol commander Admiral Roger Keyes, involved 165 vessels in an effort to sink three blockships in the entrance of the Zeebrugge–Bruges canal and two others at the entrance to Ostend harbour.

After several postponements, the operation finally went off on the night of the 23rd. It achieved only mixed success. At Zeebrugge the British did succeed in severing the mole from the shore by blowing up a submarine to cut the viaduct and they managed to sink two of the blockships in the canal.

The Ostend operation was not successful. Thanks to a shift of marker buoys by the Germans, the blockships were scuttled in the wrong place. Keyes tried again on the night of 10/11 May but managed to block only about one-third of the waterway. The Admiralty cancelled a third attempt. The whole operation cost the British 615 casualties and a destroyer and two motor launches sunk, all to block the canal at Zeebrugge for only a short time.[37]

BLÜCHER *(Third Battle of the Aisne)*

As Ludendorff readied a third drive on land, US Army divisions were at last in the line. The British and French had wanted to use the Americans as replacements. Pershing, with the support of President Wilson and Secretary of War Newton Baker, insisted on an independent American army holding a sector of the front. Given the emergency, on 28 March Pershing agreed to place his divisions under Foch's command to be used where needed. On 28 April the US 1st Infantry Division took up active fighting positions in Picardy.[38]

Ludendorff's new drive, again aimed at the juncture between the British and French armies, was to be the final decisive blow to drive the British back against the Channel and from the war. Before that offensive was launched, however, Ludendorff planned diversionary attacks against the French Army on the Chemin des Dames front. He believed that French reinforcements had twice save the British (this was not how the British saw it); the diversionary attacks were to hold the French in place. Afterward Ludendorff expected to return in order to finish off the British.[39]

Ludendorff's third drive, known as Operation BLÜCHER or the Third Battle of the Aisne, began on 27 May and lasted until 3 June. The Germans secretly positioned the 30 divisions of General von Boehn's Seventh Army in the Chemin des Dames sector, giving Crown Prince Wilhelm's Army Group a total of 41 divisions. Again the Germans relied heavily on artillery; their 5,263 guns faced only 1,422 British and French guns. The ratio of 3.7 : 1 is the highest the Germans achieved on the Western Front during the war.[40]

The Germans were also aided by the fact that French Sixth Army commander General Denis Auguste Duchêne, who had charge of the Aisne sector, ignored Pétain's call for an elastic defence. In order to retain the high ground of the Chemin des Dames, which had been won at such high cost, Duchêne placed most of his 16 divisions (including five British) forward in trenches along the crest of the 25-mile front.[41] An elastic defence would have had only outposts there, with the bulk of forces positioned behind the Aisne. The British divisions had been sent to a quiet sector of the front line to recuperate from the earlier offensives; three of them were in the front line when the German blow fell.

The 27 May massive 160-minute "battering ram" preliminary Bruchmüller bombardment shattered the French defenders in their forward positions. The German Seventh Army easily broke through the French lines and secured the bridges over the Aisne and undefended terrain behind it to the Vesle River. Within two days Seventh Army had taken Soissons and by the end of the month was in the Marne River valley, the natural route to Paris some fifty miles away.[42]

Ludendorff had not learned from his previous offensives, however. An opportunist rather than a strategist, he continued the attack too long, lulled by the surprising ease of the 40-mile advance toward Paris. But the Germans had again outrun their supply lines, while the French had managed to withdraw in good order. The Allies, fighting on interior lines, were able to make excellent use of railroad lines to bring up supplies and reinforcements, including US Army divisions. On 28 May the US 1st Division recaptured Cantigny and the Americans also helped blunt the subsequent German advance at Château Thierry and Belleau Wood.[43] The Germans had once again made a tremendous advance and been unable to exploit it. They were in a deep salient that was difficult to supply and hold. Also in their three offensives they had sustained more than 600,000 casualties, and these could not be replaced.

GNEISENAU

Ludendorff's next goal was to link the salient north along the Somme with the other to the south on the Marne and shorten the line. His fourth drive, known as GNEISENAU and mounted by Hutier's Eighteenth Army, began on 9 June on a 22-mile front between Montdidier and Noyon.

Foch anticipated Ludendorff's move. In any case German preparations were more open and deserters gave away its timing. This enabled the French to open counter-battery fire 15 minutes before the German barrage was to start and to inflict heavy damage on artillery and infantry in their assault positions. Again the Germans made a spectacular gain on the first day – six miles – but, assisted by the Americans, the French halted the German advance. On 11 June General Mangin counterattacked the German right flank and Hutier's drive ended.[44] Losses in the Noyon/Montdidier fighting from 9 to 14 June came to 35,000 French (15,000 POWs) and 30,000 Germans. The month-long delay that followed proved invaluable for the Allies who brought more US troops into the line.

Italian Front

As the fighting on the Western Front temporarily died down Austro-Hungarian forces were making their final push against the Italians along the

Piave River. Italian Army Chief of Staff General Armando Diaz learned the exact timing of the Austrian attack (3.00am on 15 June) and ordered artillery to fire on the Austrian staging areas, inflicting heavy losses. Nonetheless the Austrian attack, modelled on the Germans' Western Front offensive, met with some success. Although the Austro-Hungarians got 100,000 men across the Piave, a flood on the 17th swept away the majority of the bridges that had provided Austrian logistical support. On the 18th Diaz, making good use of excellent lateral communications, counterattacked. Within a week the Italians had recovered all the territory south of the river.[45] Instead of knocking Italy out of the war the battle cost Austria-Hungary 150,000 casualties (25,000 captured). The Italians lost 85,000 (30,000 POWs) and the British and French 2,500. It was the Dual Monarchy's last great effort of the war.

Champagne–Marne Offensive (Second Battle of the Marne)

In the West Ludendorff did what he could to re-equip and reinforce his troops and at dawn on 15 July launched his fifth offensive. Known to history as the Champagne–Marne Offensive or the Second Battle of the Marne, it raged until the 17th. Parisians could plainly hear the distant thunder of the heavy guns. Ludendorff committed 50 divisions of Crown Prince Wilhelm's army group east and west of Reims with the goal of capturing the city and the vital railroad running from Paris to Nancy. Seventh Army then moved up the Marne while Third Army struck south toward Chalons-sur-Marne.

Ludendorff hoped he could then return to Flanders and finish off the British. But there was no guarantee that the Germans would not continue up the Marne valley to Paris, and the fear that now gripped the French capital was reminiscent of the summer of 1914. Leaders on both sides believed that if the Germans took Reims they would have won the war.

Increasing numbers of German deserters betrayed most of the plan including its timing. This enabled Foch to order counter-battery fire against the German assembly areas during the night of 14/15 July. Although a number of men of the German Seventh Army crossed the Marne between Château Thierry and Dormans they got little farther. East of Reims General Gouraud's Fourth Army, applying the principles of elastic defence, stopped the German First and Third Armies. In three days the farthest German advance was barely six miles.

The strategic initiative now passed to the Allies. Even as the battle for Reims had raged, Foch husbanded a small reserve of 20 divisions – two American and 18 French – and 350 tanks. On 18 July Foch launched a counteroffensive with Mangin's Tenth Army and Degoutte's Sixth Army to its right. The US 1st Infantry and 2nd Infantry Divisions spearheaded the Tenth's attack, which fell on the right side of the Reims salient five miles south of German-held Soissons. Although casualties were heavy for the Allies (the 1st Infantry Division sustained 7,200 casualties that day and the 2nd Infantry Division nearly 5,000), the attack succeeded brilliantly. The 1st Infantry Division captured 3,800 prisoners and 70 guns from the seven German divisions it encountered; the 2nd Infantry Division took 3,000 prisoners and 75 guns. In all, the Allies took 12,000 prisoners and 250 guns from 11 German divisions. The threat to Paris was now ended and from this point on the Allies advanced and the Germans retreated. On 20 July Ludendorff called off his planned Flanders drive to concentrate on holding the area to the south, but he rejected Lossberg's sound advice that the army retire to the Hindenburg Line.[46]

Amiens Offensive

A week later Allied commanders met in Paris, where Foch, promoted by Clemenceau to marshal of France on 6 August, informed them of his plans for a series of attacks from Flanders to the Marne that would allow the Germans no respite. The first of these was known as the Amiens Offensive (8 August– 4 September) and aimed at reducing the second German salient south of the Somme. Foch entrusted it to Haig, whose ideas dominated the remainder of the 1918 campaign.[47]

Haig's Allied army group consisted of the Fourth British Army (Rawlinson) and the First French Army (Debeney). Fourth Army had been significantly enlarged to 14 infantry and three cavalry divisions of British, Canadian, and Australian troops and two US regiments. It also had 2,070 artillery pieces (684 of them heavy), 430 tanks (including a number of new 8 mph Mark A Whippet tanks that acted as cavalry), 12 armoured cars, and 800 aircraft. The French First Army had seven divisions, 1,066 guns (826 heavy), 90 tanks, and 1,104 aircraft. Opposing them was Marwitz's German Second Army of 14 divisions (four of which were in reserve), 749 guns (289 heavy) and 365 aircraft.[48]

The Allies made every effort to ensure secrecy and employ combined-arms concepts.[49] Early on the morning of 8 August, protected by heavy ground fog, the tanks rumbled forward. Simultaneously, Allied artillery opened up in heavy barrage and the infantry "went over the top". The main blow, delivered by the Canadians and Australians, came south of the Somme. The day really belonged to the tanks; only north of the river, where the British had few tanks, was there significant German resistance. By the end of the first day, and at little cost to themselves, the British had advanced up to six miles along a 12-mile front. They had also inflicted nearly 28,000 casualties (almost 16,000 POWs) and taken 400 guns. Ludendorff wrote in his memoirs that "August the 8th was a black day for the German Army in the history of this war."[50] This was not for the ground lost but the large number of Germans who surrendered after at most token resistance. The three-day total was some 75,000 German casualties (30,000 POWs) and 500 guns with Allied losses of approximately 45,000 men. By 9 September the Allies had retaken all the territory lost to the Germans in the spring 1918 offensives. The Amiens Offensive revealed the collapse of German fighting ability following the spring offensives and paralleling war-weariness at home. Indeed, as Ludendorff himself noted, German replacement troops were greeted with shouts from retiring troops of "Blacklegs!", "Strike-breakers!", and "You're prolonging the war!"[51]

St Mihiel Offensive

Now that the German threat to Paris had evaporated, Pershing received permission for an independent US Army action. For over a year Pershing had hoped for the chance to pinch out the St Mihiel salient that jutted into Allied lines south of Verdun and threatened the Paris–Nancy railroad line. It was also the entrance to the important Briey basin that supplied Germany with much of its iron ore. After sometimes acrimonious debate Foch finally agreed.[52]

The Germans, who recognized the need for a shorter line, were already withdrawing from the salient when on 12 September the US First Army with four French divisions attacked. The Americans struck from both the north and south as the French Colonial Corps pushed in from the west. They reduced the salient in just two days, capturing 15,000 Germans and 250 guns at a cost of 7,000 casualties and then halted.

Pershing had wanted the St Mihiel Offensive to be the beginning of a drive all the way to Metz. But with the Amiens Offensive going well, on 30 August Foch had ordered Pershing to limit his assault to reaching the base of the salient and then to shift his forces west to attack north of the Marne. Pershing was bitterly disappointed, and Foch's rejection of his plan was probably a mistake. The Americans believed, with some justification, that it would have yielded greater gains than Haig's attack toward Cambrai, the basis of Foch's subsequent plan.[53]

Meuse–Argonne Offensive

Foch's strategy was essentially one great pushing action all the way from Ypres to Verdun. On 26 September the French and Americans launched what became known as the Meuse–Argonne Offensive, which continued until the end of the war. The US First Army and the French Fourth Army drove the Germans back steadily. By 11 November the Germans had suffered more than 100,000 casualties (26,000 POWs) and lost 846 guns.

Battle of Vittorio-Veneto

Italy, which had remained largely quiescent after her June victory on the Piave, was also induced to resume the offensive. General Diaz, whom Foch had severely criticized for not acting, cited the lack of reserves. He now received French, British, American, and Czech reinforcements. Also by late summer it was clear that Austria-Hungary was breaking apart from military defeat, economic chaos, and Wilson's promise of the self-determination of peoples. Also prompting action was Rome's desire to be in a strong negotiating position at any peace conference. Diaz had available 57 infantry and four cavalry divisions, 7,720 guns, and 600 aircraft against 60.5 Austro-Hungarian divisions supported by 6,145 guns, and 564 aircraft.

The Battle of Vittorio-Veneto (24 October–4 November) began with stiff Austro-Hungarian resistance but ended in a rout. Many units deserted *en masse*. Some 30,000 Austro-Hungarian troops were killed or wounded but an incredible 427,000 were captured along with 5,000 guns. Allied losses were approximately 41,000 (of which 38,000 were Italian). Vienna asked for an armistice on 30 October. It was signed on 3 November and fighting on the Italian Front halted the next day.[54]

Balkan Front: Bulgaria leaves the war

Bulgaria was, however, the first Central Power to break. French General Louis Guillaumat, who had reorganized and trained Allied forces in the Balkans, convinced Paris and London of the need for an offensive. Although Guillaumat was recalled to France in July to assume command of troops defending Paris, his successor, the brilliant Louis-Félix François Franchet d'Espérey, was in full accord with an offensive strategy. Nominally he had at his disposal 700,000 men in 29 divisions, but the actual number available for duty was probably less than half that figure. Franchet d'Espèrey's goal was to sever communications between Germany/Austria-Hungary and Turkey.

On 15 September a multinational Allied force of Italians, Serbs, French, British, Greeks, and some Czechs attacked. The Allies pushed some 400,000 Bulgarian defenders (most German troops had been withdrawn) all the way from Albania to the Struma River. In the Battle of the Vardar (also known as the Battles of Dobropolje or Monastir-Doiran), 15–24 September, the Allies made impressive gains, especially in the centre of the front where the Serbs and French advanced 40 miles in less than a week. On 29 September French cavalry took Skopje.

The Bulgarian government, which had been sounding out the Allies since June, appealed for an armistice, which was concluded on 30 September at Salonika. Bulgaria agreed to demobilize its army and place all military equipment under Allied control, evacuate all Greek and Serb territory it still occupied, and place its transportation system and territory at Allied disposal. On 4 October Tsar Ferdinand abdicated and was succeeded by his son Boris.

Franchet de Espèrey also sent a force into Thrace with the goal of opening the Straits into the Black Sea, and other Allied troops transited Bulgaria. Belgrade fell on 1 November and on the 10th the Allies crossed the Danube. Franchet d'Espèrey had liberated the Balkans and was preparing to move on Budapest and Dresden when the war ended. His victories removed any possibility of the Germans using this territory for negotiating purposes. Allied troops also crossed into Romania, and on 10 November that country re-entered the war on the Allied side. Turkey had collapsed in October.[55]

Germany's collapse

Even Ludendorff knew the war was lost. On 29 September he asked for a new government to begin immediate negotiations for an armistice. On it would fall the odium of defeat and the shame of treating with the Allies. As he put it:

> I have asked His Majesty to bring those people into the government who are largely responsible that things have turned out as they have. We shall therefore see these gentlemen enter the ministries, and they must now make the peace which has to be made. They must now eat the soup they have ladled out to us.[56]

It was an astonishing statement from one who had been in complete control of German policy for the previous two years.

On 3 October Prince Max of Baden, dubbed "Max Pax", was installed as chancellor of a new, liberal German government; he sent President Wilson a note requesting peace on the basis of the Fourteen Points. On 26 October both Hindenburg and Ludendorff offered the Kaiser their resignations. He accepted only that of Ludendorff.[57]

General Wilhelm Groener succeeded Ludendorff as first quartermaster general. On 28 October a mutiny broke out in the High Seas Fleet at Kiel on word that the admirals planned a last-ditch foray at sea. By early November it had spread to other German seaports where councils of workers and soldiers on the Russian model had been formed.

Armistice

In these circumstances Allied leaders at Paris discussed the options of an armistice or continuing the offensive until Germany surrendered. An armistice would merely halt the fighting with the understanding that peace negotiations would follow. The British government supported it as did many French. Foch was disappointed; he and President Raymond Poincaré wanted total victory. Foch believed that two additional weeks of fighting would force a German surrender. General war-weariness worked in favour of an armistice; but some British and French leaders also sought it because prolonging the war might strengthen American influence over the peace settlement. Indeed, if the war had continued into 1919, Pershing would have commanded an army larger than either the French or British forces.

While President Wilson supported an armistice, his commander in the field did not. Meeting with other Allied commanders on 25 October, Pershing spoke in favour of continuing the war until Germany surrendered unconditionally.[58] But Pershing was overruled and, on the morning of 8 November, Foch received the German armistice delegation in the former royal hunting preserve of Compiègne.

To spare the German Army the onus of defeat, Hindenburg insisted that a civilian head the German delegation and Chancellor Max named Catholic Centre Party leader Mathias Erzberger. The German delegation was astonishingly low-level. It included former ambassador to Bulgaria Count Alfred von Oberndorff, Major General Detlev von Winterfeldt, two captains from the Army command at Spa, and Navy Captain Ernst Vanselow. When he bid farewell to Erzberger at Spa, Hindenburg embraced him with the words, "Go with God's blessing and try to secure what you can for our Fatherland."[59]

During the preliminaries in his special train at Compiègne Foch made the Germans as uncomfortable as possible. He then instructed General Maxime Weygand to read the armistice terms one by one, interrupted only by another officer who read them in German. The Germans were given 72 hours to accept the terms on threat of resumption of the war. After several days of negotiations and frantic telegrams back and forth to Berlin the parties reached agreement. The Germans signed the armistice at 5.00am on 11 November. Word was then flashed to the world that the armistice would go into effect at 11.00am that same day.

The agreement provided that the Germans would within two weeks evacuate all captured territory as well as Alsace and Lorraine. Within four weeks German troops were to be gone from the left (west) bank of the Rhine River and its right bank to a depth of 30 kilometres. Allied troops would occupy that territory and control crossing points over the Rhine at Cologne, Coblenz, and Mainz. The true nature of the arrangement was revealed when Germany was forced to turn over sufficient equipment to ensure she would be unable to resume the war. This included the bulk of her surface navy (10 battleships, 6 battle cruisers, 8 light cruisers, and 50 destroyers) and all submarines; 5,000 artillery pieces; 25,000 machine guns; and 1,700 aircraft. Germany would also have to surrender 5,000 locomotives, and 150,000 railway cars, along with 5,000 trucks. She would have to make reparation for war damages, and all Allied prisoners of war were to be returned immediately without reciprocity. The most controversial provision was the continuation of the naval blockade, which had exacted such a high price on German civilians, until a peace agreement was signed although London did promise to allow such provisioning of the German people as it deemed necessary.[60]

The Allied failure to insist on German surrender undoubtedly saved lives but had momentous consequences. The fact that Germany had been spared invasion during the war and the German armies were marched home in good order with drums beating and battle flags flying led many in Germany to believe the lie that began to circulate about "a stab in the back". Many, perhaps most, Germans believed their armies had not been defeated in the field but had been betrayed by corrupt politicians, Jews, war profiteers, or disaffection on the home front. Later this provided considerable grist for Hitler's hate mill, especially when leading German generals testified that the stab-in-the-back myth was fact. This led President Franklin Roosevelt during the Second World War to insist on "unconditional surrender".

The war was at last over. At 11.00am on the 11th day of the 11th month of 1918, the guns fell silent. Men on both sides came out of the trenches and cheered. At Pasewalk hospital near Stettin Lance Corporal Adolf Hitler, temporarily blinded by a British gas attack, threw himself on his bunk and wept for the first time since his mother's death.[61]

Cost of the war

The First World War differed from the Franco-German War in that victory was almost indistinguishable from defeat. No power won the war. Human costs alone had been staggering. More than 68 million men had been mobilized; of these at least 10 million had died (8 million from combat and the remainder from disease and malnutrition). Another 21 million men were wounded and nearly 8 million had been taken prisoner or declared missing, and at least 6.6 million civilians perished.

But the war amounted to much more than a vast military holocaust. It toppled all of continental Europe's dynastic empires: the German, Austro-Hungarian, Turkish, and Russian. The First World War occupies central place in the rise to power in Germany of Adolf Hitler; and it is hard to imagine the Bolsheviks coming to power in Russia without it.[62] The war also used up the capital and treasure accumulated over centuries. Its direct costs have been estimated at $180 billion and its indirect costs at another $150 billion.[63]

The war reshuffled the balance of power and made the United States the leading creditor nation and world financial capital. It greatly stimulated unrest in the colonial areas of the world, paradoxically advancing both Zionism and Arab nationalism. Wilson's statements about "self-determination of peoples" and "fighting to make the world safe for democracy" found ready acceptance overseas. The First World War was quite simply the most important single event of the twentieth century.

Chapter Seven

Other theatres of war

In the First World War fighting was not limited to Europe. The conflict is known as a world war because it was fought all over the globe and drew so many nations into the conflict, although activity on other fronts, at least in terms of men and resources committed, paled in comparison to that in Europe. Ironically it was the fighting in the Middle East, Africa, and Asia that more nearly approximated what the European commanders had originally anticipated – a war of rapid mobility and sudden changes of fortune.

Numbers of troops involved were relatively small but stakes were high. In many cases the prizes were vast territories rich in natural resources. Peripheral warfare discussed here includes the Caucasus Front, Africa, Asia, and the Middle East.

Caucasus Front

The Caucasus Front, while often covered as part of the fighting in Europe, was in fact isolated from it. While it involved chiefly Turkey and Russia its main victims were the Armenians. Persia (modern Iran) was only marginally involved. She lacked the military power to enforce her neutrality, and during the war both sides freely violated her territory. Russian forces occupied important Persian towns in the north while the British did the same along the Persian Gulf Coast.[1]

To the Western Allies Caucasia, which formed the border between Turkey and Russia, was a secondary theatre. The Russians, however, feared a Turkish invasion there because in the second half of the nineteenth century Russia had taken from Turkey the fort of Kars and the port of Batum, whose recovery was a principal Turkish war aim.

In 1914 the Turkish Army numbered 36 divisions, but during the war Turkey raised an additional 70. Most Turkish divisions were light, about 9,000 men and 36 artillery pieces each. The army did have some experience in modern war from fighting in the Balkans and North Africa; but morale was low because of irregular pay, and many soldiers were poorly trained and physically unfit. Most officers were incompetent.[2]

The Turks were also handicapped by inadequate logistical support and an appallingly poor transportation system. The railroad system consisted of one standard-gauge line from Constantinople to Baghdad, with narrow gauge tracks continuing on Gaza. The main road had significant gaps through the Taurus and Adana Mountains and one of 240 miles from Ras-al-Ain to Samarrah. After detraining at Ras-al-Ain troops bound for the Caucasus Front had to march another 250 miles. Head of the German military mission to Turkey General Otto Liman von Sanders did what he could to improve the Turkish military, and by the end of 1914 he had placed Germans in many positions of authority.[3]

Ignoring weather, mountainous terrain, and the limitations they imposed on supply, Turkish Minister of War Enver Pasha launched a winter offensive in Caucasia. He hoped to catch the Russians off guard, isolate their 100,000 troops, then move against southern Georgia and stimulate uprisings among Moslems in south Russia. Enver's plan called for XI Corps to harass Russian forces at Kars and draw them toward Erzerum, while his IX and X Corps enveloped the Russian right as I Corps attacked through Ardahan to cut Russian communications. But inept leadership, desertion, and frostbite reduced Enver's forces to only 80,000 men before the offensive began.[4]

On 17 December 1914, the Third Army invaded Caucasia from Armenia and caught the Russians in the process of withdrawing many of their best units for other fronts. The Russians, however, had an able field commander in General Nikolai Yudenich, chief of staff in the Caucasus. Rejecting Caucasus Army commander General Myshlaevsky's suggestions that he withdraw, Yudenich defended Sarikamish. The 29 December–2 January battle ended in a major Russian victory. The Turks lost 30,000 men in the battle and only about 18,000 men reached Erzerum. On 8 January the Turks took Tabriz but the Russians recaptured that important Persian town on 30 January and the whole Turkish offensive ground to a halt. Both sides had new commanders; Enver yielded field command to General Abdul Kerim and returned to Constantinople, while Yudenich was promoted lieutenant general and commander of the Russian Caucasus Army.[5]

In April 1915 the Turks fell on the Armenians, who had the great misfortune of being located in eastern Turkey bordering Caucasia. Armenia had become Christian in the fourth century, but in 1405 it had been divided between the Ottoman Empire and Persia. In the eighteenth century Russia had annexed the northern section of the Armenian Plateau, which meant there were both Russian and Turkish Armenias.

During the decades preceding the First World War there were Armenian revolts and Turkish repressions, but when the war began Armenian leaders assured the Turks of their loyalty. Turkish requisitions and harsh treatment of Armenians in the Turkish Army led many Armenians to hope for a Russian victory and an independent or at least unified, Armenia. In early 1915 volunteers formed battalions to fight on the Russian side, and on 20 April, following Turkish reprisals, the Armenians rose in revolt at Van and held that fortress until the Russians arrived on 19 May.

After the Van uprising Constantinople embarked on repression. In retaliation for the revolt and alleged partisan attacks on Turkish forces the government ordered the deportation of a large number of Armenians to Syria and Mesopotamia. In June and July 1915 the Turks deported over 1.5 million Armenians, more than half of whom died. Unfortunately for the Armenians their suffering was not at an end. One estimate places the number who were killed or died in camps in Syria and Mesopotamia between 1915 and 1922 at more than 1.4 million people.[6]

In the summer of 1915 Yudenich took the offensive. Believing he faced only three or four Turkish divisions he ordered General Organovski to attack northwest of Lake Van. But there were actually eight Turkish divisions in the area on 10 July when the Russian attack began, and within a week Abdul Kerim had moved up reinforcements. The Russians finally withdrew to Malazgirt, but the Turks, who outnumbered the Russians 5:1, surrounded and defeated the Russian force. Enver then ordered Abdul Kerim to pursue the remainder of the Russian corps, which was withdrawing north. Sensing an opportunity, Yudenich sent General N. N. Baratov and 22,000 men, most of them mounted Cossacks, to sever the Turks' line of communication as they moved north from Malazgirt. As the Turkish column stretched over some 20 miles, the task was relatively easy, but the Russians were unable to envelop the entire Turkish force. In the Battle of Kara Killisse (Karakilise or Karakose) the Turks lost 10,000 killed and wounded. The Russians also captured 6,000 Turks, a number of guns, and large stocks of provisions.

Although he had won a considerable victory Yudenich lacked the means to exploit it. Also, after months of fighting, on 3 August the Russians were forced to abandon Van, which the Turks reoccupied. On 2 September 1915,

Grand Duke Nicholas Nikolaevich arrived in the Caucasus region as Viceroy. He retained Yudenich as military commander and the Russians prepared for an offensive. German agents were active in Persia from early 1915, and that November Nicholas sent forces into northern Persia to remove a pro-German government in Hamadan. This completed Russian military operations for 1915.[7]

Caucasia caused the Russians considerable trouble in 1916, especially as the Allied evacuation of the Gallipoli peninsula at the beginning of the year freed up 22 Turkish divisions. General Falkenhayn refused an offer of 20 of them for the Western Front, recommending that they be redeployed within the Ottoman Empire. Enver deployed two to Mesopotamia, two to the Greek frontier, ten to coast-watching in Turkey, and the remainder to the Caucasus Front.

Yudenich believed that the Turks could not redeploy troops to the Caucasus before the end of March. On 11 January 1916, he surprised the Turkish Third Army with a broad advance on Erzerum from Kars. On the 18th the Russians were victorious at Köprukoy, but Yudenich was unable to envelop Abdul Kerim's Third Army. The Turks withdrew but Kerim lost 25,000 men, many of them to frostbite, in the retreat to Erzerum. The Russians had no siege artillery and Yudenich ordered his men to storm the city. In a three-day battle (13–16 February) the Russians broke through the ring of Turkish defensive forts and captured Erzerum. On the 19th the Russians captured Mush; on 1 March, Kamak; and on 2 March, Bitlis. They also seized a number of Turkish supply depots in the Erzerum area.

At the same time Yudenich launched a secondary offensive along the Black Sea coast in the form of an amphibious landing in the Turkish rear supported by naval gunfire from ships of the Black Sea Fleet. On 18 April General Lyakov, commanding two sea-lifted brigades, entered the port of Trebizond (Trabzon), which became a staging point for Russian logistical support.

Enver sought to regain the initiative. His Third Army, now under Vehip Pasha, engaged the Russians along the Black Sea littoral, while a new Second Army under Ahmet Izzim Pasha, formed of Gallipoli veterans, moved on Bitlis, outflanking the main Russian force and threatening its rear. As usual Turkish communications and transport were appalling; troops sent by rail to Ankara had to march for a month to get within striking distance of the Russians, and the offensive began before all were in position.

On 29 May Vehip struck west of Erzerum, but his attack soon faltered. The Russians were receiving reinforcements through Trebizond, and Enver ordered Vehip's Third Army to retake it in June. Vehip approached the port over the Pontic Alps but was unable to dislodge the Russians.

Yudenich counterattacked and on 2 July split the Turkish Third Army at the communications centre of Erzingjan (Erzincan), forcing the Turks to retreat. In this fighting the Turks sustained 34,000 casualties, about half of them POWs. The Third Turkish Army was ineffective the rest of the year.

On 2 August the Second Army belatedly began its offensive. Mustapha Kemal, hero of the Gallipoli Campaign and now a corps commander, scored the campaign's only success when on 15 August he took Mus and Bitlis. But Yudenich retook both on 24 August, whereupon both sides retired into winter quarters.[8]

In Persia fighting in 1916 involved only relatively small-sized forces. General Baratov advanced on Kermanshah with 20,000 men and 38 guns to draw Turkish forces from Mesopotamia. On 12 March he was at Karind and announced his intention to move against Baghdad. On 29 April, the day he set out, Kut fell to the Turks, enabling Halil Pasha to shift resources to Baghdad. On 1 June Baratov attacked Khanikin but was repulsed and withdrew to Karind. Halil then went on the offensive, forcing the Russians to give up all their gains, including Kermanshah.

In southern Persia, meanwhile, the British reinforced against a possible Turkish invasion. In March General Sir Percy Sykes arrived at Bunder and began to organize the South Persia Rifles, which ultimately grew to about 11,000 men. That autumn Sykes, with a mixed British, Arab, and Indian force, moved as far north as Isfahan, where the Russians were already in occupation, and Shiraz.[9]

At the beginning of 1917 the situation in the Caucasus favoured the Russians, who then held large parts of Turkish Armenia, Georgia, and Azerbaijan and had formed a Transcaucasian alliance with these peoples. The March Revolution in Russia ended this favourable position. Yudenich replaced Grand Duke Nicholas as civil and military commander of the Caucasus Front, but he was soon recalled to Petrograd. Discipline in the Russian Army broke down and Russian officers were no longer in control. Turkish troops on the Caucasus Front were then shifted elsewhere and the area was quiet for the remainder of the war.

The March 1918 Treaty of Brest-Litovsk gave Turkey control of the Caucasus. Its terms forced Russia to evacuate Anatolia and cede to Turkey the districts of Ardahan, Kars and Batum. A number of former tsarist officers refused to accept this arrangement and created a military force in the south that set up contacts with the Don and Kuban Cossacks.[10]

Persia, evacuated by the Russians and Turks after the fall of Baghdad, was by mid-1917 in a state of near anarchy. In January 1918 a small British force under General Lionel Dumsterville arrived. Its mission was to strengthen Georgia and Armenia against the Turks and establish alliances to prevent a possible German advance from Ukraine. Threatened by Bolshevik forces at

Baku, however, Dumsterville was forced to fall back on Hamadan. The British continued to reinforce Dumsterville and sent another unit to north-eastern Persia. Commanded by General Sir Wilfrid Malleson, its task was to block a possible Bolshevik attempt on India from that direction. At the end of the war the situation in Persia was still fluid.[11]

The Middle East: Palestine and Syria

The Middle East was for the British a critical theatre of war because control of the Suez Canal and the oil fields of the Persian Gulf was vital. To help secure the canal, on 5 November 1914, London announced the annexation of Cyprus and, on 16 December, a protectorate over Egypt, where the British had been in occupation since 1882. The British also strengthened their forces in Egypt against a possible Ottoman attack but remained on the defensive until 1916.

To the Turks the Suez Canal was an important military and economic objective. In January 1915 Turkish Minister of Marine and Governor of Syria Djemal Pasha, who hoped that the Egyptians would join the Turks in a holy war against the British, led 22,000 men in a ten-day march across the Sinai Peninsula from Beersheba. German General Friedrich Kress von Kressenstein actually commanded the force. The men literally had to drag field artillery, boats, and bridging equipment across the desert.

Fortunately for British commander in Egypt General Sir John Maxwell aerial reconnaissance gave warning of the Turkish approach. The Turks reached the canal on 2 February and, heavily outnumbered, attempted to cross. The British had 70,000 troops defending the canal, including five half-trained Indian divisions, but the Turks got several pontoon rafts across before being driven back that night and the next day. Maxwell then sent his own troops across the canal, forcing the Turks to retreat at a cost of up to 2,000 casualties; the Allies lost only 32. This was the only Turkish assault of the war against the Suez Canal but it caused the British to keep men in Egypt who were needed at Gallipoli.[12]

The next year was decisive on the Egypt–Palestine Front. In April 1916 the British, French, and Russian governments agreed on the partition of Asiatic Turkey. In the Arab portions of the Ottoman Empire the British were to have influence in Mesopotamia (Iraq) and in Syria at the ports of Haifa and Acre. The French were to receive a sphere consisting of the coastal strip of Syria (the Lebanon), the Adana Vilayet, Cilicia, and southern Kurdistan, with Kharput. Palestine would be under international administration. Russia was awarded

Armenia and part of Kurdistan and part of eastern Anatolia westward from Trebizond to a point to be determined later.

British–French claims to the non-Turkish portions of the Ottoman Empire were made more specific in the 9 May 1916, Sykes–Picot Agreement. It provided that the remainder of Arabia would be divided into British and French zones of influence, though all of it would be organized into an Arab state or federation of states. In April 1917 Italy adhered to the agreement and received recognition of its claims in Adalia and Smyrna.[13]

In March 1916 General Sir Archibald Murray assumed command of the newly constituted Egyptian Expeditionary Force (EEF). The evacuation of Gallipoli freed British resources and enabled them to push their Suez Canal defences eastward into the Sinai Desert. This ambitious undertaking provided a belt of protection for the canal and its shipping from Turkish artillery fire. Murray also used aircraft to bomb Turkish water stocks in one of the earliest uses of strategic air warfare. Concurrently the Senussi tribes in western Egypt rose in rebellion, but the British ended this in mid-March.[14]

In April Murray received permission from London for an advance eastward to El Arish on the far side of the Sinai Desert. He justified this by pointing out that El Arish could be supplied from the Mediterranean Sea, and by taking it he could outflank any Turkish attack and be able to hold his positions with one less division. Over the next ten months Murray staged a methodical advance in which he carefully arranged for adequate logistical support. Utilizing for the most part Egyptian labour, Murray constructed roads, airfields, a 12-inch water pipeline, and even a standard-gauge railway line 140 miles across the desert to Palestine.[15]

In June 1916 prolonged Franco-British negotiations with Arab chieftains in the Hejaz resulted in the so-called "Arab Revolt". This centred on the Holy City of Mecca, where the Grand Sharif and Amir Hussein Ibn Ali raised the standard of revolt and expelled the Turks. The Arabs then moved north against Medina. Using hit-and-run guerrilla tactics – suggested by a young British Army liaison officer to Hussein, T. E. Lawrence (later known as Lawrence of Arabia) – especially against the railway to Medina, they forced the Turks to disperse their resources.[16]

In the 3 August Battle of Rumanai Murray's EEF defeated 15,000 Turks thrusting across the Sinai under German General Kress von Kressenstein. The EEF inflicted 5,000 casualties on the attackers for only 1,100 of their own, and thereafter held the initiative. The EEF took El Arish without a fight on 21 December. Murray's mounted arm, the Desert Column, flanked Magdhaba and Rafa, the last Turkish strongholds in the Sinai, and the British then stood before Gaza on the Mediterranean Sea.

Political considerations now intervened. On 7 December Lloyd George replaced Asquith as British prime minister. The Somme Offensive had heightened Lloyd George's well-known distaste for the bloodbath of the Western Front. A shrewd politician, he sensed that a land victory was necessary to keep public opinion behind the war effort. Palestine presented that opportunity, and London now informed Murray that while his primary mission was to defend Egypt he was to advance beyond El Arish.[17]

Denied the two additional divisions he requested, Murray faced Turkish positions extending 25 miles from the coastline through Gaza along natural ridges to Tel-es-Sheria and thence to biblical Beersheba. Gaza commanded the coast road as well as roads eastward into Palestine. To the south Beersheba controlled wells critical to any force attempting to flank the Turkish line through the desert.

Murray twice attempted to take Gaza and twice failed. The First Battle of Gaza, 26–27 March 1917, began at night. The Desert Column penetrated Gaza's eastern perimeter and nearly encircled the town, but the cavalry, unaware of the infantry's progress, withdrew to water their horses and Kressenstein's Turkish troops forced an EEF retreat.

Murray misrepresented the battle as a victory and exaggerated Turkish casualities. The Imperial General Staff, therefore, ordered him to try again. The Second Battle of Gaza, 17–19 April 1917, resembled a miniature battle on the Western Front. The War Office had even sent out eight Mark 1 heavy tanks for a frontal assault. Instead of trenches and barbed wire the British troops encountered reinforced redoubts and cactus hedges. They were repulsed and Murray, whose force had suffered only 644 casualities, was relieved of command.[18]

London wanted to continue the offensive. Lloyd George saw attacks here as preferable to the heavier-cost battles of the Western Front, and there was need to relieve possible pressure on Mesopotamia from a large Turkish force assembled at Baghdad. London now sent out from Salonika the two divisions it would not give Murray earlier, along with three aircraft squadrons. In June General Edmund Allenby, former commander of Third Army in France, replaced Murray in Palestine. Lloyd George informed Allenby that he wanted Jerusalem "as a Christmas present for the British people". Allenby moved his headquarters near the front line and reformed the EEF into three corps, the XX, XXI, and the Desert Mounted, a cavalry detachment.[19]

At the same time Berlin sent General Falkenhayn to Turkey to command Yilderim ("Lightning"), composed of a Turkish army group and the German Asia Corps. Mustapha Kemal commanded the new Seventh Army of III and XV Corps that had been operating against Russia and Romania. When he discovered Falkenhayn was running everything, Mustapha Kemal resigned; Fevzi Pasha replaced him. The German Asia Corps, an elite formation of 6,500 men (three battalions of infantry, three troops of cavalry, three machine-gun companies, three trench mortar sections, three artillery batteries, one anti-aircraft battery, and four aircraft squadrons), was the largest German force in Turkey during the war. Assembled at Aleppo to go on to Baghdad, Yilderim was now redirected to Palestine.

Over the next weeks the Royal Flying Corps secured control of the skies over the Gaza–Beersheba Line. Having prevented Turkish reconnaissance, Allenby's intelligence officers "leaked" information indicating British preparations to assault Gaza. Instead, Allenby deployed forces to Beersheba, which was held by only 5,000 Turks in a single trench line. Here in the most famous cavalry charge of the entire war on 31 October the Australian Light Horse captured the critical Beersheba wells. Allenby then rolled up the enemy line. When the attack slowed down there he smashed through the Turkish positions at Gaza. Again cavalry proved its worth. Lightly equipped Turkish soldiers might be able to outmarch their more heavily equipped British counterparts but they could not outmarch horse cavalry, which constituted a quarter of Allenby's force of seven infantry and three cavalry divisions. In 17 days Allenby had reduced his enemy by a third and gained 50 miles.[20]

Falkenhayn, meanwhile, was forced to split his resources between Jaffa and Jerusalem. Fortunately for Allenby, Yilderim arrived piecemeal. After limited fighting in the Jordan foothills, on 9 December Allenby took Jerusalem. Since 28 October the EEF had lost 21,000 men, the Turks 28,000.[21] After the capture of Jerusalem Allenby consolidated his gains.

On 5 July 1917, meanwhile, Arab forces took Akaba on the gulf leading to the Red Sea. This provided a secure base from which they could receive supplies and assist Allied operations in Palestine and Syria. The British also assisted in the creation of an Arab Northern Army (ANA) commanded by Sharif Faisal, third son of the King of Hejaz, with Lawrence as his advisor.[22]

The Allied Supreme War Council, meanwhile, decided that while victory was not likely on the Western Front until 1919, victory over the Ottoman Empire was possible in 1918. Lloyd George therefore ordered Allenby to continue to Damascus and to Aleppo to trap Turkish forces in Mesopotamia.

Events delayed the new offensive. Heavy rains made resupply difficult and Russia's defeat and the consequent shift of German troops west allowed Ludendorff to launch his Western Front offensive in March. Desperate for manpower, London ordered Allenby to transfer to France two complete divisions to France plus separate battalions sufficient to constitute three more: some 60,000 men in all. Two Indian divisions from Mesopotamia and fresh troops from India, all of which had to be trained, replaced them.[23]

While training his men Allenby planned a new offensive. This time he would feint an attack inland and deliver the main blow along the left or Mediterranean Sea flank. In the meantime he used cavalry to patrol aggressively in the Jordan Valley and even staged two large cavalry raids toward the city of Amman, which was supporting Turkish forces at Medina. This new threat forced Liman von Sanders, who succeeded Falkenhayn on 1 March 1918, to deploy a third of his troops east of the Jordan River.

Allenby then transferred substantial resources northward until he had three-quarters of his resources along only one quarter of the front. His deception measures for the Jordan Valley, made possible by British air supremacy, included 15,000 canvas stuffed horses, a dummy headquarters, false radio traffic, sledges to kick up large clouds of dust, and even men marching about to give the false impression of large numbers.

Allenby brilliantly combined the principles of mass and surprise. Forward observers adjusted artillery fire and armoured cars operated with horse cavalry. All arms – infantry, cavalry, artillery, engineers, and the Royal Flying Corps – worked smoothly together and irregular Arab forces, advised by Lawrence, provided useful support. Allenby used fire and manœuvre to secure key mountain passes and envelop the principal Turkish units.

The ensuing battle began early on the morning of 19 September with an intense 15-minute artillery barrage. The infantry then attacked and created a lane for the cavalry, which drove north. By day's end one division controlled the pass near the small village of Megiddo, which gave its name to the campaign. The next morning another division hit Turkish headquarters at Nazareth, forcing Liman von Sanders to flee. By 21 September the British had 25,000 prisoners; for all intents and purposes the Turkish Seventh and Eighth Armies ceased to exist. Only a part of Fourth Army managed to escape through Dera.[24]

Consolidating their gains, Allenby's troops resumed the offensive. They took Damascus 1–2 October and throughout that month a mobile column of cavalry and a few armoured cars pursued shattered Turkish remnants through Syria and Lebanon to beyond Aleppo. There they received their only check, at the hands of Turkish troops under Mustapha Kemal. On 30 October 1918, at Mudros Turkey signed an armistice ending the fighting. In five weeks Allenby's men had taken 360 enemy guns and either killed or taken prisoner three-quarters of the 104,000-man enemy force in Palestine.[25]

Mesopotamia

Mesopotamia was another important theatre of the war. The area of present-day Iraq, this great plain is drained by the Tigris and Euphrates Rivers, which also provide its chief avenues of communication. Campaigning in Mesopotamia was difficult, especially in summer when water had to be transported for men and horses and temperatures could reach 120°F for as much as ten hours a day. Sunstroke, heatstroke, diarrhoea, malaria, typhoid, yellow fever, and cholera all took a heavy toll.[26] The Mesopotamian theatre was originally a backwater under the Indian Army's direction. Many of the officers were incompetent, the men were not well-trained, its artillery was obsolescent, and logistical support was inadequate.

The area, however, was important to Britain, especially after conversion of her capital ships from coal to oil. The fleet depended on oil from the refinery at Abadan Island at the head of the Persian Gulf. The largest city of the region, Baghdad, lay 415 miles upriver.

Prior to Turkey's entry into the war the British sent a reinforced brigade to the mouth of the Shatt-al-Arab to protect Abadan. After Britain declared war on Turkey and increased its strength to a division, an Indian Expeditionary Force commanded by General Sir Arthur A. Barrett moved upriver to Basra. The Turks were slow to react and Basra fell on 22 November. Several weeks later Barrett's troops occupied Qurna, above Basra at the confluence of the Tigris and Euphrates. This meant that the Abadan refinery, 50 miles to the rear, was secure and the British controlled the only access.[27]

During the first half of 1915 British forces were reinforced to two infantry divisions, a cavalry brigade, and artillery detachments, all commanded from Basra by General Sir John E. Nixon. His arrival in April marked a turning point. London favoured a defensive strategy to protect the oil fields, but before Nixon left India, Sir Beauchamp-Duff, commander-in-chief of the Indian Army, counselled an advance on Baghdad up the Tigris. This was not known to London until later. In April the British repulsed Turkish attacks on Ahwaz and Qurna, north and west of Basra respectively, trying to cut the oil pipeline.

When Barrett became ill General Charles V. F. Townshend replaced him. On 11 May Nixon ordered Townshend to carry out a reconnaissance in force up the Tigris. On the 31st Townshend, commanding an Indian division and a cavalry brigade assisted by a small naval flotilla, routed the Turks in an amphibious operation at Qurna. The easy victory gave the British a false impression of Turkish military ability. Townshend's amphibious force continued its advance and on 3 June took Amara (El-Amarah).

Nixon now secured grudging approval from London to continue the advance to Kut el Amara, more than 100 miles farther upriver. It fell to the British on 26–28 September, but the long march, weather, and low water in the Tigris prevented Townshend from pursuing the Turks, the bulk of whom escaped northward.[28]

Despite the fact that the British river supply line was now twice as long as that of the Turks (200 miles to Basra versus 100 to Baghdad), London authorized Nixon to move against Baghdad if he was satisfied that the forces available were sufficient. London promised to send out two divisions from France as soon as possible, but these were only to help with occupation duties.[29] Nixon, who was prepared to gamble, depreciated Turkish ability and overestimated that of his own forces.

Townshend opposed an advance on Baghdad without reinforcements, and so informed Nixon. He explained the weather, lack of water, and supply shortage. Indeed, Townshend's force required more than 200 tons of supplies a day but, partly as a result of pillage, was receiving only 150. Nonetheless Nixon ordered the offensive to proceed. In late November Townshend dutifully began a march on Baghdad, supplied by river boats and improvised camel and donkey transport.[30]

The Turks received reinforcements and in the Battle of Ctesiphon (22–26 November 1915), on the outskirts of Baghdad, they halted his advance. Townshend lost 4,600 men and Turkish commander Nur-al-Din 9,500 but, unlike Townshend, Nur-al-Din continued to receive reinforcements.[31]

The Turks then forced the British to fall back. On 3 December, after an epic retreat, Townshend's troops arrived exhausted back at Kut-el-Amara. Townshend wired Nixon that he had one month's full rations for British troops and two months' worth for the Indians, as well as plenty of ammunition. Nixon replied that every effort would be made to relieve him and that he hoped this could be done within two months; meanwhile, Townshend was to send ahead his cavalry and as many ships as possible. Nixon's telegram gave Townshend pause; he informed Nixon that within two months he would be surrounded by six enemy divisions and he suggested it would be best if he retreat to Ali Gharbi. Nixon ordered Townshend to stay put; at Kut he would be tying down superior numbers of enemy troops. By 7 December the Turks had closed the ring around Kut and begun a siege.

In January 1916 Nixon gave up his command, ostensibly for health reasons. That same month the two Indian divisions arrived from France. Commanded by General Fenton J. Aylmer they tried to reach Kut-el-Amara but the Turks halted them. In March General George F. Gorringe, who succeeded Aylmer, attempted a surprise attack on the south bank of the Tigris. It was repulsed by the Turkish Sixth Army, now led by German Field Marshal Colmar von der Goltz. The relieving forces suffered some 23,000 casualties while trying to rescue the 13,000 trapped men. The Russians also mounted a half-hearted operation of their own from northwestern Persia, but it soon bogged down.

At Kut-el-Amara, meanwhile, food finally gave out. On 29 April 1916, after an unsuccessful effort to ransom the garrison, Townshend surrendered, ten days after von der Goltz died from spotted fever. The Turks took 2,700 British and 6,500 Indian troops prisoner. Townshend was treated well but most of his men suffered horribly in captivity and many died.[32]

A shocked London now took over direction of the Mesopotamian Front, including reorganizing and greatly increasing the forces there. Nixon's successor, General Sir Percy Lake, had already begun developing the communications and transport that made possible sustained operations in the interior. Throughout the summer and autumn supplies of all kinds and troop reinforcements poured into Basra. The British built a rail line north that reached Amara in November and increased their river fleet. Additional aircraft brought air superiority.[33]

In August General Sir Stanley Maude assumed command from Lake of all British forces in the area. He now had available two corps of two divisions each: I Corps commanded by General A. S. Cobbe and III Corps under General Sir William R. Marshall. Maude also had a division in reserve along with two cavalry brigades. Of roughly 350,000 Empire troops in Iraq, 150,000 were fighting men and two-thirds of these were Indian. Khalil Pasha's Sixth Turkish Army of 48,000 men opposed them.

Having received permission to resume offensive operations, on 13 December Maude began a slow, methodical advance toward Baghdad, making maximum use of artillery support. While this approach was unlikely to trap large numbers of Turkish troops, it insured success with minimal British casualties. Maude retook Kut during 22–23 February 1917. After feinting an attack on the Turkish left that forced the enemy to spread his defences, his men crossed the Tigris on the enemy's right flank and then pressed forward on both flanks. Baghdad fell on 11 March. A Turkish effort to retake the city collapsed when the troops destined for it were diverted to the Palestine front. Maude then took Samarrah, a railhead 90 miles north of Baghdad. There was little fighting in the summer because of the extreme heat. In all, Maude's force of 45,000 men had suffered 18,000 casualties.[34]

A new campaigning season opened in September with the British continuing their wide advance. On 19 November Maude died of cholera and corps commander General Marshall replaced him. In summer 1918 London siphoned away troops from his Mesopotamian Expeditionary Force to Palestine, the Balkans, and India.

Combat in Mesopotamia had not ended, however. In mid–October 1918, with the Turks seeking an armistice, London directed Marshall to take as much of northern Iraq as possible. In a drive beginning on 23 October he employed frontal assaults in combination with flanking attacks and also made good use of aircraft and armoured car companies known as Lewis-gun detachments after the light machine gun they carried.

On 29 October Turkish forces surrendered. The armistice declared the next day ended the fighting, although it was not until 14 November that the British occupied Mosul, Iraq's major northern city. The Mesopotamian campaign was finally at an end. It had cost the British some 93,000 casualties, nearly a third of them dead. The advance on Baghdad was mounted purely for political reasons and the Mesopotamian Front tied down 350,000 Empire troops. It did, however, achieve its political goals; Britain maintained control of the area for decades to come.[35]

Africa

Capturing German colonies in Africa was a major Allied war aim. Britain's control of the seas not only made it possible for her to tap the resources of her far-flung empire and the neutral states but also made it virtually impossible for Germany to resupply her colonies. The Allies, principally the British, claimed they were waging the war overseas in order to deny the Germans trading access and to protect neighbouring Allied colonies, but these statements masked a simple desire for territorial acquisition.[36]

There were diplomatic efforts to preserve neutrality in Africa, especially in the Congo basin as provided by the 1885 Berlin Conference. The Germans had the chief interest in this as they had the most to lose.[37] But the Germans weakened their cause by sinking Belgian vessels on Lake Tanganyika. In any case the British were determined to conquer German Africa.

Fighting in Africa occurred on both land and sea; it also revealed great distrust between the British and French. Neither the Allies nor Germany were prepared for African fighting; German colonial officials, financially strapped even in the best of times, were especially hard pressed.

In 1914 Africa contained the bulk of Germany's overseas possessions: Togoland, the Cameroons, German Southwest Africa, and German East Africa. Despite assistance from Belgian and French forces the British conquered German Africa only with difficulty. Togoland was the exception. The most difficult campaign was for German East Africa, which did not capitulate until after the armistice in Europe.

African campaigning differed greatly from that in Europe. Roads were few but there was great mobility in the campaigns. Extremes of weather and terrain took their toll as did the omnipresent tsetse fly and other disease-bearing insects. Troops were also routed on occasion by angry bees, elephants, and rhinoceroses.

This was a White Man's war with Blacks often treated harshly. For the Allied prisoners held by the Germans in Southwest Africa the greatest indignity they suffered was being guarded by Black troops. As one prisoner put it, "We felt very depressed . . . We had never expected the Germans would descend so low as to guard white men with Hottentots."[38] Most Europeans in Africa thought it was unseemly for Africans to see Europeans fighting one another.

Many outstanding war leaders emerged from the fighting in Africa. These included South African Jan Smuts, who led the conquest of German Southwest Africa, but the pre-eminent figure was undoubtedly Lieutenant Colonel Paul von Lettow-Vorbeck in East Africa, the only German commander to occupy British territory in any theatre.

The war in Africa had its notable moments. Among these was the epic November 1917 long-distance flight by Zeppelin *L59* (*Afrikaschiff*) from Bulgaria in an attempt to reach German East Africa with a cargo of provisions for the garrison. It got as far as Khartoum, only to be recalled by a still-disputed radio message.[39] Also, one of the most prolonged naval engagements in history occurred on the Rufiji River between a German cruiser and two British monitors.

Togoland

Fighting in Africa began easily enough for the Allies. A radio station in German Togoland coordinated German warships in African waters, and taking it was important to the Allied cause at sea. On 7 August 1914, without waiting for instructions from London, four companies of British-led native troops and a detachment of French-led Senegalese troops invaded the colony. Togoland fell on 26 August and the British and French promptly divided it.[40]

Cameroons

Securing the Cameroons was much more difficult. It was sparsely populated – only about half a million people, of whom 2,000 were Europeans. Most of

191

the fighting was conducted in a steaming climate, with temperatures in excess of 100°F, heavy rains, swamps, and the ever-present tsetse fly. Aside from naval forces, about 7,000 British and 11,000 French and Belgian troops took part. Virtually all the troops on the Allied side were black Africans, apart from the Indian 5th Light Infantry and a West Indies regiment.

On 7 September the British invaded the Cameroons from Nigeria; the French then invaded from the south and east. The Cameroons finally fell in February 1916 when the last German troops crossed into Spanish territory. The cost to the Allies was 4,000 British casualties (1,668 dead, mostly of diseases) and 2,567 French. This did not include a large number of bearers, whom the Europeans did not bother to count. As with Togoland, France and Britain then divided the colony.[41]

Southwest Africa

The British had good reason to be thankful that they had treated their enemy generously following the Boer War. The 1910 creation of the Union of South Africa handed over effective political power to the Boers. Many of Britain's former enemies, including Jan Smuts and Louis Botha, became staunch allies. On the outbreak of war in Europe, Botha cabled London that the British government could remove all its imperial troops since a newly formed South African Defence Force would protect the Union. On 10 August London did just that but asked Botha to conduct a campaign against the Germans in Southwest Africa. Botha agreed although he was aware of strong anti-British sentiment among many of his people.

On 19 September a British force landed at Lüderitz Bay, but South African participation was delayed by a revolt at home. Although most Boers remained loyal to Britain, about 12,000 in the Orange River Colony and Transvaal took advantage of the withdrawal of British troops to raise the standard of revolt. Some 30,000 Loyalists opposed them. In the ensuing fighting the rebels lost 540 killed and wounded and the government side 347.[42]

After crushing the Boer revolt, Union of South Africa troops proceeded with their campaign to take Southwest Africa. The Union of South Africa's army that invaded the German colony on 14 January 1915, was 50,000 strong, but it was an assortment of regulars, volunteers, a Rhodesian regiment, and some imperial troops. The force included a squadron of armoured cars that had been supplied by the Royal Navy. There were clashes between Afrikaaners and English-speaking troops. Botha, the first prime minister of any

British colony personally to lead his troops into battle, held them together for the common goal.

Botha skilfully blended his fighting forces and employed Zulu-style double envelopments. On 9 July 1915, German resistance ceased. The conquest of Southwest Africa was the only land campaign of the war carried out by a British dominion on its own. South African and Rhodesian casualties were remarkably light: only 266 dead of all causes and 263 wounded. The Germans lost 1,331 killed. South African troops then transferred to German East Africa or to Europe.[43]

German East Africa

The campaign for German East Africa was much more difficult, the longest anywhere in the entire war. The colony itself was vast: with 384,180 square miles of territory it was larger than France and Germany combined. Lieutenant-Colonel Paul von Lettow-Vorbeck, commander in German East Africa, was a thoroughgoing professional. Foreseeing the inevitability of war with the other colonial powers, especially Britain, he worked hard to prepare his German troops and 12 companies of native Askaris. A proponent of the offensive, Lettow-Vorbeck in August 1914 launched raids against the British in Kenya with the goal of tying down as many British and Allied troops as possible and preventing them from joining the fighting in Europe. He never had more than 3,000 Europeans and 11,000 Askaris plus uncounted thousands of carriers.

Roads were few and bearers were absolutely essential. Cut off from his homeland, Lettow-Vorbeck improvised weapons, fuel, medicine, and clothing. Realizing the value of a friendly native population he made certain the Africans were treated with justice, which inspired exceptional loyalty in his African troops. Despite their lack of supplies they fought bravely against British Empire troops who discounted the fighting abilities of native soldiers. Indifferent and overly confident Allied commanders ignored reports that the German Askaris were well-trained. Actually the two Indian brigades sent out to fight the Germans in East Africa were poorly trained. British stupidity, racial arrogance, and mistakes gave Lettow-Vorbeck vital time.[44]

Lettow-Vorbeck secured much needed supplies from the German light cruiser *Königsberg*. This station ship at Dar-es-Salaam in German East Africa enjoyed some initial success as a commerce raider in the Indian Ocean. On 6 August 1914, she took *The City of Winchester*, the first British merchant ship captured in the war, and in September she sank a small British cruiser. The *Königsberg* developed engine problems, however, and larger British warships blockaded her in the remote Rufiji River delta. Their deeper drafts prevented the British warships from moving upriver against her, until the Admiralty sent out from Gallipoli two 6.5-foot draft monitors, the *Mersey* and *Severn*. Originally ordered by the government of Brazil for river work, London sequestered them at the outbreak of the war and they were towed 5,000 miles to the battle area. In early July 1915 the monitors, assisted by spotter aircraft, engaged the *Königsberg* and forced her scuttling. Commander Max Loof and his crew salvaged the cruiser's ten 4.1-inch (105 mm) guns, which proved of great value to the German land forces. Her crew also removed 1,000 105 mm shells; thousands of rounds of 47 mm ammunition for small field guns; 1,800 rifles with 3 million rounds of ammunition; two new 60 mm guns; six machine guns; and tons of dynamite, medicine, food, clothing, tools and other valuable supplies, along with coal and lumber. The *Königsberg* had tied down 27 British warships.[45]

The British opened the fighting in German East Africa on 8 August 1914, by bombarding the coast towns of Bagamoyo and Dar-es-Salaam. They then sent in Indian forces, but the numerically inferior Germans repulsed that landing force in the Battle of Tanga (2–5 November 1914). Fighting remained desultory until November 1915 when the British gained naval control of Lake Tanganyika and took Tanga (7 July 1916) and Bagamoyo (15 August 1916). General Jan Smuts, commanding a force of South Africans and Portuguese, pushed operations. Dar-es-Salaam fell on 4 September and Tabora on 19 September 1916. Lettow-Vorbeck and his forces were driven back into the southeastern corner of the colony.

In October 1917 Lettow-Vorbeck invaded Portuguese Mozambique, where he carried out an aggressive and successful guerrilla campaign, taking Portuguese outposts and maintaining himself on captured supplies. He then re-entered German East Africa and captured several small posts before, on 2 November 1918, invading British Northern Rhodesia. Upon learning of the armistice in Europe, he negotiated the surrender of his undefeated army. Lettow-Vorbeck had tied down over 130,000 Allied troops and prevented their use on the Western Front, except for one South African brigade.[46]

Pacific islands

Fighting also occurred in Asia where Germany had Qingdao in China, German New Guinea, and a number of smaller islands: the Bismarcks, the Solomons, Samoa, the Carolines, the Marshalls, the Marianas, and Palau.

British forces, mostly from Australia and New Zealand, aided by the Japanese, soon took the German Pacific islands. At the end of August 1914 New Zealand troops transported by Australian and French cruisers captured German Samoa. An Australian invasion force then sailed to New Guinea to take the powerful radio station at Rabaul. Landing there on 11 September, Australian troops secured the island in a week. It was the only fighting of the war in the South Pacific and cost about 40 casualities in all. In 1916 Britain annexed the Gilbert and Ellice Islands.

For Japan the conflict in Europe was a heaven-sent opportunity to eliminate Germany as a major power in Asia as she had earlier eliminated Russia. In the fall of 1914 Japanese naval units took the northern Marianas, the Carolines, and Marshall Islands. A 1917 secret treaty between Britain and Japan, to which Australia later objected, defined permanent claims to Germany's South Pacific possessions, assigning those north of the Equator to Japan and those south of it to Australia. The Paris Peace Conference, however, accorded the islands mandate status, emphasizing national self-determination. Australia received a mandate over German New Guinea. New Zealand was awarded trust of German Samoa, and Japan was entrusted with German Micronesia.[47]

Qingdao

A key goal of Japanese policy was to gain the German cession in China. This brought the only major land battle of the First World War in east Asia, the 23 August–7 November 1914, siege of the German fortress city of Qingdao (Tsingtao). Located halfway between Tianjin (Tientsin) and Shanghai at the tip of the Shandong (Shantung) Peninsula, Qingdao commanded the entrance to Jaiozhou (Kiaochow) Bay, home base for Germany's East Asia Squadron. Berlin had used the 1897 murder of two German missionaries to pressure China into a 99-year lease on 214 square miles of territory surrounding the bay. By 1913 it was a European-style city with extensive port facilities and one of the world's largest dry docks.

Qingdao's harbour defences consisted of a series of small forts with heavy guns in revolving turrets. Powerful Fort Bismarck with heavy howitzers and guns in reinforced concrete casemates anchored the centre of the German defensive line. Flanking forts contained smaller guns and many small guns were positioned between them. The German defences appeared impressive, but most of the artillery was obsolete, there was little ammunition, and German Governor Captain Alfred Meyer-Waldeck had only 4,600 troops.

On 15 August 1914, Japan issued an ultimatum giving the Germans one week to surrender and evacuate Qingdao. Meyer-Waldeck refused. Not wishing to fall victim to a reprise of the Japanese 1904 attack on Port Arthur, Admiral Spee promptly took his squadron to sea, leaving at Qingdao only the obsolete Austrian cruiser *Kaiserin Elizabeth*, a torpedo boat, and five small gunboats. The Germans also had an observation balloon and one Rumpler Taube monoplane.

Japanese Admiral Sadakichi Kato commanded a powerful assault fleet of four battleships, two cruisers, and 15 destroyers along with torpedo boats, minesweepers, and submarines. On 27 August Kato's ships arrived off Qingdao and established a blockade. The British contributed the *Triumph*, a pre-Dreadnought battleship, and a token land force of a battalion from Tianjin and later half a battalion of Sikhs.

On 2 September the first Japanese troops disembarked at Longkou (Lungkow) Bay, 100 miles north of Qingdao. On the 18th Japanese land commander General Mitsuomi Kamio landed additional forces at Laoshan Bay, only 30 miles from his objective. Kamio's plan centred on the use of heavy artillery and General Kishino Watanabe's 24th Brigade had more than 100 large guns and howitzers. In their first two landings the Japanese put 23,000 troops ashore but by the end of the siege had committed over 50,000 men, while another 10,000 served in the fleet. The Germans were outnumbered more than 13 to one.

Although not successful, an attack by three Japanese army aircraft against German gunboats harassing the shore advance was one of the first encounters between aircraft and ships. The Germans used their one plane to good effect for observation and intelligence gathering and their balloon to direct long-range artillery fire. In one of the earliest air-to-air combats, Lieutenant Günther Plüschow and Japanese pilots shot at one another with pistols.

The Japanese took the thinly held outer German defences on 28 September, whereupon the Germans retreated to their middle defensive line in the Hai Po valley. It took the Japanese most of October to get their heavy guns and ammunition into position, and most fighting that month was between ships and the shore.

The first major Allied naval bombardment occurred on 6 October but achieved little because the range was too long. In a closer attempt on 14 October the *Triumph* was hit by a German shore battery. On the 17th the German sub *S90* carried out a night attack on the *Takashio*, a cruiser working as a minelayer; three torpedoes set off her mines and the resulting explosion sank her and killed all but three of her 253-man crew; however, the concussion from the blast split the *S90*'s seams, forcing her to scuttle.

On 31 October, after positioning their heavy guns, the Japanese began a bombardment that continued until Qingdao surrendered. On 1 November the *Kaiserin Elizabeth* fired her remaining shells at the Japanese, after which her crew scuttled her in the harbour.

On 1 November Japanese troops began an advance by the eighteenth-century method of digging parallels. The next night they dug a second parallel, reducing No-Man's Land to only 300 yards. With the German artillery largely neutralized by artillery fire and, in any case, nearly out of ammunition, shortly after midnight on 7 November the Japanese attacked the centre of the middle defensive zone. That morning after fierce hand-to-hand fighting, and out of ammunition, Meyer-Waldeck surrendered.

The siege of Qingdao cost the Japanese 1,445 killed and 4,200 wounded. British losses were 14 killed and 61 wounded. Despite the artillery bombardment the defenders suffered only 200 killed and 500 wounded. From a tactical standpoint the siege was one of history's last large-scale actions involving coastal artillery. It was also one of the first major battles in which air, land, and sea power all played significant roles. Despite their relatively high casualty rate the Japanese military demonstrated mastery of combined operations far beyond the capability of most 1914 armies. The battle also had long-term geopolitical consequences. With Germany no longer a Pacific power and the British Empire severely weakened after the war around the globe, the two principal Pacific rivals left were the United States and Japan.[48]

China

During the war the Japanese also made a blatant effort to secure control of the rest of China. In January 1915 Tokyo secretly presented the Yuan Shikai regime in Beijing its so-called "Twenty-One Demands". The first four groups of demands would cede Shandong to Japan and increase the Japanese presence and control in Manchuria. The fifth set would give Japan virtual control of the Chinese government. In May 1915, after failing to receive help from abroad and faced with the threat of a major Japanese military presence, China accepted most of the Twenty-One Demands except the fifth group. In June 1916 Yuan Shikai died and the government passed to one unscrupulous general after another. Again Japan sought to take advantage. In return for large loans (actually bribes) to Beijing, in January 1917 Japan received secret Chinese guarantees of Japanese hegemony in Shandong, Manchuria, and Inner Mongolia.

After the United States' April 1917 entry into the war President Wilson hinted that the principle of self-determination would also apply to China. Many Chinese leaders assumed that the United States would press for the removal of the Japanese military presence in China once the war ended. On 14 August 1917, China declared war on Germany and Austria-Hungary, persuaded by President Wilson that this would allow China to secure a seat at the peace conference and present her case. Although no combat units were available, China did send labour battalions to France, Mesopotamia, and Africa. By so doing China secured an end to German and Austrian extra-territoriality and Boxer Rebellion indemnity payments and the return of their cessions at Tianjin and Hankow. China was to be disappointed, however, by decisions at the post-war peace conference.[49]

The war overseas ended, as was inevitable, in defeat for the Central Powers. It did, however, tie down substantial Allied resources. Although attracting much attention and evoking admiration for the courage and tenacity of the defeated, it was not decisive in determining the conflict's outcome. Fighting in Europe alone decided the war.

Chapter Eight

The home fronts

While soldiers were struggling and dying at the front the conflict also profoundly affected those at home. It would not be too extreme to say that the
war touched either directly or indirectly every country of the world. It
especially affected people living in the warring states and those on the war's
periphery, such as Scandinavia and Switzerland; but all were affected, even
those geographically far removed from the fighting such as Latin America.
Many nations, cut off from their colonial masters or trading partners, out of
necessity developed their own industries and forged new market relationships.
Japan and the United States especially benefited.

Initial solidarity

Initially the First World War brought national solidarity for the states involved. Many national leaders had welcomed the war as a means to end social
and economic conflict within their states. Even in multinational Austria-
Hungary there was near unanimous support for the government; vocal Czech
and Croat dissidents agreed to cease political agitation for the duration and all
but the Empire's ethnic Serbs supported war against Serbia.

Those who had challenged class and political differences vied with one
another to demonstrate their patriotism. Socialists and trade union leaders,
who before the war had advocated international class solidarity, demonstrated
that they were Germans or Frenchmen before they were socialists. Such unity,
however, did not last.

France was typical. In August 1914 Premier René Viviani established a
national government that included Jules Guesde, the first Socialist in a Third

Republic cabinet. The government also shelved its plan to arrest dissidents and suspended laws banning religious orders. But the *union sacrée*, the ideological union of all French people on the basis of patriotism, was more apparent than real; it foundered in the bloodletting of the war. By 1917 the French government had to contend with army mutinies, anti-war agitation, work stoppages, even domestic sabotage in munitions factories and power plants. France survived because most Frenchmen and Frenchwomen accepted the direction of their intellectual, spiritual, and political leaders, because national living standards were not seriously diminished by the war, and because they had an energetic and capable leader.[1]

Although there was no formal abdication of power the Chamber of Deputies initially yielded to the generals. Military reverses brought the reassertion of parliamentary leadership and the removal of General Joffre as French Army commander. In November 1917 following the disastrous spring Nivelle Offensive Georges Clemenceau, a veritable one man committee of public safety, became premier. "War is too important a business to be left to generals", he said.[2] Determined to have the last word, even in military policy, Clemenceau was also bent on fighting on until final victory. When deputies in the Chamber of Deputies asked what his government's policy would be, he replied "Je fais la guerre!" (I make war!)[3]

In Britain politics were "adjourned" for the duration of the war. Nonetheless the war had a profound political impact. It led to the demise of the Liberal Party, the rehabilitation of the Conservatives, and the rise of Labour.

As in France the politicians in Britain at first yielded to the generals and Secretary of State for War Lord Kitchener was soon running things. Even politicians deferred to him.[4] In the course of the war civilian leadership reasserted itself. Prime Minister Asquith, under severe criticism for increased shipping losses from U-boats and heavy casualties in the Battle of the Somme, resigned in December 1916.[5] His successor, Lloyd George, constantly sparred with BEF commander Field Marshal Haig over military matters. Although he shrank from challenging Haig directly, Lloyd George was appalled by the bloodletting on the Western Front and did all he could to sabotage Haig's strategy in favour of peripheral operations.[6]

The United States

In the United States President Wilson dominated foreign policy. He favoured a strictly neutral stance but when this proved impossible and the United States entered the conflict, Wilson, who knew nothing of military matters, largely deferred to his commander in the field, General Pershing, although he did assert himself in 1919 in the shaping of the peace.[7]

Italy's situation was different from that of her allies. She entered the war not by popular demand but in a cynical manœuvre by her leaders to secure territory. The two largest mass organizations in Italy, the Socialist Party and the Catholic Church, opposed the war as did some prominent political leaders. In Italy there was no *union sacrée.*[8]

In Germany the old power structure consisting of the army and Prussian aristocracy continued little changed throughout the conflict except that dictatorship by the Kaiser gave way to dictatorship by the High Command.[9] Army authority was confirmed on 31 July 1914, in the declaration of a state of siege for all Germany except Bavaria. It gave local army commanders precedence over civilian authorities and provided for the suspension of civil liberties. Moltke, a commander of limited abilities, had been quite close to the Kaiser; Falkenhayn, his competent replacement, took care to keep the Kaiser at arm's length and avoided sharing decisions with him and civilians in general. When Falkenhayn stumbled, a coalition of civilians, including Chancellor Bethmann-Hollweg, clamoured for his removal in the expectation that this would end military interference in the civilian government. They failed to realize the dangers inherent in Generals Hindenburg and Ludendorff.[10]

In any case imperial Germany's constitutional framework denied the political parties meaningful control over policy; the Reichstag remained, as Bismarck intended, largely a debating club. Its positions were often ignored, as the July 1917 Peace Resolution demonstrated. Contrary to myth it was not the Reichstag but Ludendorff who instituted the so-called German Revolution of 1918, including the responsibility of the chancellor to the Reichstag. But this was done in order that Germany might secure better peace terms. The final irony is that the army leadership escaped responsibility for its role in Germany's defeat. By sacrificing the Kaiser, the army leadership helped preserve discipline and unity. As Martin Kitchen has observed,

> Even in the moment of defeat, threatened revolution and radical democratization, the officer corps was able to preserve its traditions and its unique position in German society. It did not go the way of the monarchy but remained a powerful, independent and harmful force in the new republic.[11]

The war had profound effects on Russia. While modern in many ways, in others Russia remained virtually medieval. In August 1914 the monarchy benefited from a wave of patriotic support both in the Duma and throughout all Russia. This soon ended. As the war continued and defeats and economic dislocation multiplied discontent increased.

In Russia war profiteering and corruption were widespread. Political ineptitude, economic dysfunction, and war-weariness toppled the tsarist regime. But what happened in Russia probably sprang, more than anything else, from a failure of leadership. The monarchy had steadfastly resisted all attempts to modernize the government, regarding these as threats to its authority. Tsar Nicholas II sincerely believed he had inherited his authority from God and did not have the right to dilute or delegate it in any way. His wife, the inflexible, conservative, German-born Empress Alexandra, was ill-at-ease in court society and withdrew into her family. Increasingly the royal family was isolated from the people over whom they ruled.

Between 1914 and 1917 Russia mobilized 12 million men for the army. The inclusion of skilled industrial workers and agricultural labourers in this cost some productivity, but the call-up was from a population of 167 million, whereas France called up almost as many men from a population of 40 million and Germany more than that number from 65 million. Indeed, in 1902 Russia's surplus rural population had been estimated at 22 million people.[12] More troublesome were the serious shortage of trained bureaucrats capable of running a modern industrial war and the government's utter inability to deal with wartime economic problems. Indeed, many economic shortages had been solved by late 1915, and the March 1917 Revolution actually resulted not from industrial backwardness but from the social consequences of overly rapid industrialization.

By 1917, largely cut off from the outside world and forced to make do on its own, Russia had made great economic strides, especially in production of war matériel. The problem was that uneven growth and bottlenecks, especially in transportation, brought severe economic dislocation. At the heart of industrial snarls and shortages of food and other goods was the collapse of the railway system. Barely adequate in peacetime, rail transportation could not supply the demands both of the cities and the army. Overly rapid industrialization also brought rampant inflation, but it was the inability to deliver grain for the cities, in part the result of hoarding, and the lack of consumer goods that produced revolution. Throughout, the tsarist regime was barely aware of what was transpiring and clearly incapable of dealing with it.[13]

Russia's fate rested with the central government. Throughout the war Russian politics were a contest between the tsar and his entourage who wanted to maintain the medieval prerogatives of the monarchy, and leaders in the State Duma who wanted to introduce genuine reform. By mid-1915 the crown and the Duma were on a collision course.

In September 1915 with the military situation desperate, the tsar left for the front, believing that his presence at military headquarters would inspire the army. His departure worsened an already bad situation. He was merely in the way at military headquarters, but his presence there led to his being held responsible for Russian military reversals. This also left the tsarina in charge of the government. She was far more reactionary and vindictive than he, and the result was confusion and rampant disaffection within the Duma. Increasingly the peasant Grigorii Rasputin, who claimed to be a holy man, influenced government policy and the selection of officials at the highest levels of government. His strong sway over the royal family stemmed from his perceived ability to preserve the life of the young Tsarevich Alexis, who suffered from hemophilia. By the end of 1916 the national government was in chaos.

By November 1916 members of the Duma began openly to attack Rasputin and liberals also assailed the Empress. On 30 December Rasputin was murdered by three noblemen, two of them close kinsmen of the tsar. Hailed at the time, this violent act came too late to heal the rift between the crown and the Russian people.

On 8 March strikes and riots broke out in the working-class section of Petrograd. Two days later security forces called out to put down the disturbances refused to fire on their own people. Duma President Mikhail Rodzianko wired the tsar, still at the front, urging the "immediate appointment of people in whom the nation has trust and who will be empowered to form a government that commands the confidence of the people". Certain that delay would be fatal, he also informed the Russian Army front commanders and Nicholas' Chief of Staff Alekseev. Nicholas, however, referred to the telegram as "nonsense" and spent the next few hours playing dominoes.[14]

Riotous troops then seized the Liteinyi Arsenal and secured 40,000 rifles, 30,000 revolvers, and 400 machine guns. More than 66,000 soldiers joined the demonstrators. Rodzianko again telegraphed the tsar and urged immediate action, but it was already too late. Nicholas at last acted, not to establish genuine responsible government but to order dissolution of the Duma and to crush the revolution by force. Firm resolution earlier might have saved the regime but by then it was too late. More than 100,000 troops had gone over to the rioters. Nicholas set out by train for Petrograd but revolutionary workers stopped him at Pskov.

There were now two sources of political power in Petrograd. The Duma refused to obey an imperial decree ordering its dissolution and instead established a provisional government. A small group of socialist deputies simultaneously announced the creation of the Executive Committee of the Petrograd Soviet [council] of Workers' and Soldiers' Deputies.

On 14 March the Soviet issued its "Order Number One" to all military units, inviting them to arrest their officers, elect revolutionary committees, and await instructions. This was virtually the end of the Russian Army as a fighting force. Hundreds of thousands of Russian soldiers left for home.

On 15 March the Duma's Provisional Committee sent two of its members to receive the tsar's abdication. Utterly alone, he abdicated the same day. If Russia had not gone to war in 1914 the tsarist regime might have stumbled on for some time. The new regime was itself toppled by revolution before the year was out, victim of its decision to continue Russia's involvement in the war.[15]

Austria-Hungary had her own serious problems. One of the great surprises of the war was how well the Dual Monarchy held together until near the end. There were problems with desertion in the army, led by Czechs who no doubt resented the fact that two-thirds of the officers were Germans and most of the rest were Hungarians. In this the Dual Monarchy's military merely reflected its political problems.[16] Most soldiers did their duty regardless of their nationality, however.

The war did hit hard economically. No provisions were made for a war lasting more than a few weeks and Vienna merely relied on Berlin supplying what it needed. Austrian shell output never reached more than a million rounds per month, even in 1916 when the Germans produced seven million and the Russians more than four million. One of the chief problems was the lack of centralization, with both Vienna and Budapest going their separate ways, and as the war wore on the ties binding Hungary to Austria grew more tenuous.

Shortages and rationing were soon a way of life. Fuel was short and in Hungary even baths became a major event. On one occasion Budapest had no fuel for an entire week. Count Széchenyi lamented: "All my male servants are mobilized; all my female servants are in munitions factories. There is not a scrap of coal in my house. I have no gas, electric lights or lamps, and very little food; the condition of things compels me to spend all my time in bed."[17]

Vienna's mid-January 1918 announcement of a reduction in the daily flour ration brought demonstrations and strikes. A greater threat was the Bolshevik Revolution in Russia and propaganda calling for peace without victory, which had a considerable impact throughout Central Europe. Efforts to "re-educate" returning prisoners of the Russians after the Treaty of Brest-Litovsk were only partially successful.[18]

National minority leaders of the Dual Monarchy were soon active abroad. Czechs Tamás Masaryk and Eduard Beneš and Slovak Milan Stefánik carried out propaganda efforts arguing for dissolution of the Habsburg empire. In April 1915 refugee Serb, Croat, and Slovene leaders formed a Yugoslav

Committee.[19] Still there was no serious internal threat to the Dual Monarchy's survival until the military collapse of the Central Powers.

In January 1918 Czech, Pole, and Yugoslav representatives to the Austria Reichsrat called for sovereign constituent assemblies in the empire's different linguistic divisions. Three months later Czechs and Yugoslavs demonstrated in Prague and took an oath to continue the struggle for independence. In June the French government recognized the Czechoslovaks' "right to independence".[20] And in a particularly ominous development, in September Bulgaria, guarding the southern approaches to the empire, collapsed.

Too late, on 16 October 1918, Emperor Karl issued a manifesto proclaiming federalization. In Budapest this was taken as repudiation of the *Ausgleich* and the Hungarian government immediately proclaimed an end to the Dual Monarchy. Romanians and Slovaks then announced their intention to secede from Hungary. Within the next two weeks the old empire completely collapsed as the subject peoples set up their own national congresses.

Total war

The First World War, unlike Europe's last major conflict (the Franco-German War of 1870–71), involved entire societies. The American Civil War of 1861–5, probably the first Machine Age war, demonstrated industrial war's insatiable appetite for munitions and other war supplies. That national leaders had to mobilize the entire nation if their country were to survive was little understood. The British Army had expected to mobilize 100,000 men in event of a European war, but 5.7 million men served out of a population of 46.4 million. France mobilized eight million men, more than 67 per cent of the entire adult male population between the ages of 18 and 40 (20 per cent of the entire population of 40 million). Government spending underwent the same quantum leap. Immediate prewar French government expenditures ran at five billion francs a year; the 1918 budget was 190 billion francs.[21]

All warring governments greatly increased control over their citizens during the war. Each imposed some degree of censorship, attempting to control the flow of news to their citizens both for reasons of morale and for military security. Correspondents were kept from the front and the candour with which events were reported varied from country to country. Censorship proved most severe in Russia, which had no tradition of a free press. In Germany the military controlled newspapers, which could print only those stories cleared by a central press office. This led to little real war news. German officials also banned dancing, theatrical comedy, and ragtime music, and required that public performances present patriotic and serious themes.[22] In Britain editors were liable to prosecution for publishing anything that might be deemed a military or naval secret. "It is not always easy to decide what information may or may not be dangerous", said Lord Kitchener, "and whenever there is any doubt, we do not hesitate to prevent publication." The government also authorized the reading of private mail.[23]

Governments extended power over their national economies. In this the Entente benefited from its substantially greater economic base, probably the key factor in its victory. The British and French were able to utilize their merchant fleets to tap the resources of their far-flung empires as well as those of the world's neutral states.

In August 1914 no country was prepared for a long war, and few in Europe envisioned its vast wastages and costs. This lack of foresight created serious difficulties for all the powers early on, but it is clear that the Western Allies were much more successful than the Central Powers in mobilizing their societies for war and coordinating their economic policies; they consequently suffered less.

As the war continued without abatement, increasing economic difficulties had a severe impact on political stability. Because their collective resources were much greater and they had access to the world's trade, the Western democracies were able to feed their populations. The Central Powers and Russia were unable to do this adequately. Germany spent 83 per cent of its budget on the military, and only two per cent on the civilian sector. Comparable figures for Britain were 62 per cent and 16 per cent.[24]

Each power responded differently to the crisis. Britain allowed the government to increase output of war goods without taking over the economy or applying undue regulation. In August 1914 Parliament's Defence of the Realm Act (DORA) gave the government extraordinary power in a number of areas including the economy. DORA's provisions were periodically amended and expanded as the need to manage the economy grew. With time came price controls; import/export regulation; subsidies for agriculture; manipulation of labour to specific wartime industries; and in 1918 food rationing.

Liberal leader Lloyd George loudly criticized Lord Kitchener and the War Office over the early British shortage of shells. In May 1915 Prime Minister Asquith appointed him to the new cabinet post of minister of munitions; the position itself symbolized the new age of machines in war. Lloyd George's energy and determination to eliminate red tape and increase shell production became legendary. Lloyd George was instrumental in putting Britain on a war footing and greatly increasing shell production. As an indication of the claims of the war his office grew from what had been the War Contracts Office with

20 clerks in 1914 to a bureaucracy of 65,000 clerks in 1918, overseeing the work of three million men and women in munitions plants.[25] All this paid the expected dividends. Britain entered the war with only 1,330 machine guns. In four years of war she produced 5,090,442 rifles, 239,840 machine guns, 25,031 artillery pieces, 2,818 tanks, and 54,798 aircraft.[26] But, as with all the warring nations, mobilization of the national resources meant Britain would not emerge from the conflict unimpaired.[27]

For the most part a cooperative spirit prevailed in Britain, as Unions voluntarily collaborated with the government. Britain never resorted to wholesale drafts of civilian labourers or to the construction of government-owned plants for munitions production. Wartime production was achieved with existing privately held facilities.

To increase industrial production in France the government had to demobilize from the army half a million skilled workers; it also temporarily assigned other soldiers to war work. Loss of industrial capacity in territory captured by the German Army in 1914 forced the French into growing economic dependence on Britain. These lands had produced three-quarters of the nation's coal and four-fifths of her iron and steel.[28] As late as 1916 the French and British were competing in shipping and commodities, and in the process driving up prices, a fact that appalled Jean Monnet, a member of the French purchasing commission in London. His ideas led to the creation of the powerful Allied Maritime Transport Committee, the first institutionalized example of a supranational pooling of resources. Ultimately French reliance on Britain for essential imports gave Britain control over much of the French economy. Within France itself Minister of Commerce Etienne Clémentel used this to justify his own control over supplies to individual firms. His consortium system helped hold down prices, thereby putting less pressure on wages and living standards.[29]

Despite the crippling presence of German soldiers occupying productive areas of the nation, French industry achieved a great deal. French daily shell output rose from 9,000 in September 1914 to 300,000 in 1915. In 1914, France was producing five artillery pieces per day; by 1918 that had risen to 60. During the war she produced more than 50,000 aircraft and some 4,800 tanks.[30]

The French National Assembly introduced an income tax in 1916 but the rates were so low that they generated little revenue. Only about one-fifth of the French war costs were paid by taxation. To raise the money required to fight the war, the French resorted to borrowing and printing paper money. The result was a dramatic rise in inflation and a large post-war debt.[31] By 1916 the cost of living had risen by 40 per cent over its pre-war level and by August 1917 by 80 per cent. There were also price controls, at first only on bread.

The government introduced piecemeal rationing in 1917, and in 1918 maximum prices were established.[32] During the war there were no serious supply shortages in France and peasants, farmers, and workers all did reasonably well financially. In a material sense the lower middle class was perhaps the hardest hit.[33]

The economic burdens fell unevenly within the warring states. Generally speaking most people were worse off financially although some, such as war contractors and munitions workers, did well. Economic disparity heightened the sense of class conflict, which in the case of Russia manifested itself sooner and in the case of Italy later.

Inflation, driven by military expenditures, gripped all the warring states. In order to pay the great costs of the war all governments resorted to borrowing and printing money, which produced inflation. Prices rose less in France and Britain, and Britain paid for more of her war effort by taxation (income taxes went up to 30 per cent of income) than any other belligerent.[34] In Italy the cost of living doubled from 1914 to 1916 and then doubled again by 1919.[35] Inflation was highest among the Central Powers, largely because they were less able to wage a protracted war.

Germany was hard hit by the British blockade, certainly one of the most important factors in her defeat. The naval blockades of Germany and Austria-Hungary probably resulted in the death of more than a million people and may have been the single most important factor in the Allied victory.[36] Even in peacetime Germany imported 20 per cent of her food and much of her raw materials. Her military planners knew that after 18 months of a blockade the food situation would become critical, but they expected to win the war before that happened.

Under Hindenburg and Ludendorff the High Command took full control of the economy, demanding greater production of war goods. In 1916 German General Wilhelm Groener, a highly capable administrator who in 1914 had headed the German Army railroad section, became head of a new war office to supervise the economy. War socialism (*Kriegssozialismus*) was already well underway in Germany. Groener worked out what became known as the Hindenburg Programme, forwarded by OHL to the government in the summer of 1916. It called for a reorganization of German industry so that every individual who did not possess essential skills could be released for service at the front. Industries not deemed essential to the war effort would take second place and might be shut down. The plan also provided for substantial increases in the output of weapons: by the spring a threefold increase in artillery and machine guns and a 100 per cent increase in artillery.

In effect German industrialists assumed command of what came to be known as the "corporatist" solution to Germany's wartime production problems. A labour office ensured that "he who does not work, does not eat". The Auxiliary Labour Bill of December 1916 subjected all German males between the ages of 17 and 60 to war service for the fatherland and to military discipline. The bill was worded so that it applied exclusively to the working class; for all practical purposes, workers could not leave their jobs without the permission of their employers. All this was to give OHL full control over the war economy. In Martin Kitchen's words it "marked a radical break with earlier attempts to achieve a modicum of cooperation between capital and labor. It was designed to destroy the labor movement and was a death sentence to those companies deemed non-essential to the war effort."[37]

The blockade denied Germany strategic raw materials from overseas, especially nitrates for explosives and fertilizer, foodstuffs, cotton, and copper. It was raw materials rather than factories that Germany lacked to sustain her war production. Stripping the occupied Belgian, French, and Russian lands brought only temporary relief. More important was the work of Walther Rathenau in securing raw materials to boost Germany's production. On his initiative a Raw Materials Board (*Kriegsrohstoffabteilung*) was established in Berlin. Rathenau also organized a crash programme to develop *ersatz*, or substitute, materials. The firms of Haber-Bosch and Franck-Caro developed a process that helped provide nitrogen for the explosives industry and rayon became a substitute for cotton. The Germans had less success in developing substitutes for oil and rubber.

Nonetheless German war matériel production soared. By 1918 she was producing more ammunition than at any time in the Second World War. But the corporate managers took what they could with little regard for the interests of the nation as a whole. Profits soared as business merely passed on the costs to the army and to the German people. This fuelled inflation, which in the last year of the war was running four times that of 1914.[38]

A combination of manpower shortages, lack of fertilizers, and poor weather led to a sharp decline in German agricultural output. Daily civilian rations went from 1,350 calories in 1916 to a starvation diet of only 1,000 calories in 1917. When the potato crop failed in 1916 many Germans were hard hit. The winter of 1916/1917 was known appropriately as the "Turnip Winter" (*Rübenwinter*).[39]

The war deprived the German people of basic necessities. The food problem had arisen early. In the winter of 1916/1917 it was coal. Then came serious shortages of such essentials as clothing (especially shoes) and housing. Even soap was in short supply.[40]

Food prices in Germany increased 65 per cent in the first year of the war alone. A government cut in the bread ration in April 1917 sparked massive workers' strikes in Berlin and Leipzig, followed by other demonstrations that summer and a January 1918 strike by munitions workers. Such unrest helped prompt the Reichstag's July 1917 Peace Resolution, which called for peace on the basis of no annexations. But after the defeat of Russia and the signing of the Treaty of Brest-Litovsk it was ignored.[41] As at the end of the Second World War, as her population starved Germany was producing more armaments than she had trained men to use them.

In Austria-Hungary the near-solidarity of 1914 was more apparent than real. The prolonged war and government's failure to address economic problems awakened the nationality issue just beneath the surface. Although the Dual Monarchy did have problems with Slavic soldiers being reluctant to fight Russians, one of the great surprises of the war was how well the monarchy held together during most of the conflict. Part of the reason was that the Austrian government simply suspended the Reichstag. When it was reconvened in May 1917, however, separatism had grown past the point at which the empire might be held together. A factor in this was the death of Franz Josef at the end of 1916. Emperor since 1848, he had long since ceased to control events but he had provided a symbolic continuity and legitimacy to the empire. His great nephew and successor Karl immediately tried to negotiate a way out of the war.

Austria-Hungary mobilized eight million men out of a 1914 population of 50 million people. The Dual Monarchy was hard hit economically. As with Germany, the British naval blockade exacted a toll. Austria-Hungary also suffered from low industrial productivity and corruption in war supply. As historian Robert Paxton summed up, "The Habsburg case shows how ineffective political autocracy was in waging total war."[42]

Societal effects

Not only did the war affect national economies, it profoundly altered social structures as well. In 1914 political power in European states was still exercised by small groups of men drawn from the upper classes. Seemingly secure, by 1918 these elites had either disappeared or were badly weakened. Although on a positive note the war appeared to have strengthened republicanism, including giving the beleaguered Third French Republic a new lease on life, a profound distrust of governing classes everywhere accompanied a more general disillusionment with government itself. Alienation fostered the rise of communism and fascism after the war.

The war also exacerbated the desire for national homelands. Many in Europe felt that their only security lay in a state that was inclusive of their nationality. In 1914 all European powers had restive minorities within their borders; even Britain had the Irish and a rebellion in Dublin in 1916. The war, in large part caused by nationalism, only partially resolved this problem; but in 1919 Europe was more aligned along lines of nationality than ever before.

In 1914 class conflict, specifically the growing strength of socialism, had threatened the stability of European governments. But pre–war socialists generally followed the thinking of Eduard Bernstein, considering themselves "evolutionary" rather than "revolutionary". When war broke out a rush to the colours in all countries obscured this class conflict but war-weariness brought it to the fore again and made socialism more radical. The most obvious example of this was Russia, but there was serious unrest in other countries, particularly Germany and Italy.

After the war, heightened by cruel economic times, class conflict intensified and became a serious problem in most European states. Even in the Western democracies the working classes became more radical and unionized. The war brought French trade unions a million new members.[43] In 1920 the Socialist Party split, most of its members joining the new, more radical French Communist Party.

Italy was hard hit by the war. Less well off economically than her Western allies, she was not well suited to the demands of industrial war. During the conflict about half the males in rural areas were taken into the military. This depleted the countryside of labourers, especially in the rural south where 75 per cent of the rural work-force was male. Women and children did some of the work, but the rural standard of living declined because the government took not only men, but livestock and goods and paid less than fair value for them. The number of Italians in unions increased five-fold between 1914 and 1919. Labourers were radicalized by the war, which seemed to benefit chiefly industrialists and some factory workers.[44]

Political changes

The war also brought profound political changes, although some of what seemed significant at the time was actually slight. In Germany the so-called "revolution" of November 1918 consisted mainly of a change at the top: the replacement of the Kaiser with a republic; the actual social and political framework was little changed. In January 1919 a small number of radical

Spartacists did attempt to seize power and effect a genuine revolution but were crushed by the military and government. Real economic and social change in Germany came later, the result of chronic inflation that was fuelled by the war but was in fact more the product of deliberate government policy to break the shackles of the peace treaty.

Europe's middle classes were hard hit by the war, for inflation robbed them of their savings. Their economic losses, coupled with social changes, produced disillusionment. Since the middle classes were the backbone of Europe's democracies, their disenchantment gave a tremendous boost to fascism, especially in Italy and Germany.

Advancement of women

The war dramatically affected the status of women, many of whom served the war effort directly. In Britain 23,000 women nurses and 15,000 orderlies worked in military hospitals, some overseas. Women also volunteered as ambulance drivers and in 1914 the Women's Hospital Corps staffed a surgical unit in Paris. Englishwomen also joined a number of organizations to support the war effort. The Women's Emergency League trained army cadets in signalling; the Women's Auxiliary Force, formed in 1915, trained part-time workers in first-aid, cooking and sewing and provided canteens and entertainment, air-raid shelter stewards, and hospital visitations. Englishwomen also joined the First Aid Nursing Yeomanry (FANY), which trained nurses to render battlefield aid.

As manpower needs grew, women donned uniforms. In 1917 the British government created the Women's Army Auxiliary Corps (WAAC) to perform such jobs as cooks, drivers and typists; and the WRNS (Women's Royal Naval Service) to serve as signallers, make mine nets, and work on torpedoes. In 1918 came the WRAFs (Women's Royal Air Force), with women as drivers and fitters.

But many more British women went to work in non-traditional trades. In Britain in 1911 one-third of women worked, primarily as domestics or in the textile industry. Just in industry the number of women and girls over the age of ten went from 2,179,000 in 1914 to 2,971,000 in 1918. The war presented new opportunities in high-paying, skilled manufacturing jobs, government service, and education, especially after the introduction of compulsory military service for men beginning in January 1916. Increases were greatest in transport. Between 1914 and 1918 the number of women in public transport rose 14-fold; it doubled in commerce and increased by a third in industry. Women came to hold many positions in the munitions industries. For example, in 1914 Woolwich Arsenal employed only men but two years later half of its 100,000 workers were women. In July 1917, 819,000 women worked in the munitions industry; a year later that figure was up by more than 100,000.

In contrast to France, however, few women in Britain moved into jobs that could have translated into postwar industries. In France the largest increase in female employment occurred in chemical, wood, and transport manufacturing industries directly tied to the war. In 1914 women made up only one-twentieth of this work-force; by 1918 they were one-quarter.[45]

In Germany only a relatively small number of women entered the labour force for the first time during the war. This was in part because of the increasing difficulty that the war imposed on families in Germany and the traditional custom of doing piecework at home. But many women worked at home producing goods for the German military. Other women did move into war-related industries. For example, a 1916 trade union survey revealed an increase from 63,000 to 266,000 women in metalworking.[46] In Italy during the war there was a dramatic shift in the employment of women; by 1918 about 196,000 members of the industrial work-force (22 per cent) were women.[47]

For women workers the war was a mixed experience. Labouring conditions were hard and many women lived in barracks and worked 12-hour shifts for wages far less than those paid men. Women were also the first to be laid off at the end of the war, and many simply returned to their prewar status. Although some progress was temporary in that it was for the war only, the First World War accelerated trends in the professions and politics then already underway. Women's rights achieved greater gains in the four years of the war than during the preceding generation of female activism. In at least one area most European women gained lasting progress; virtually all governments granted them the right to vote after the war.[48] In 1919 Lady Astor was elected to the House of Commons, the first woman to serve in a European parliament.[49]

Securing workers was a major problem for all the warring powers. Britain utilized her vast empire and France brought many workers from North Africa and Asia to repair roads, unload ships, and till fields. By mid-1917 roughly 50,000 Chinese coolies were digging trenches in France and substantial numbers of labourers came from Indo-China as well. What these non-Europeans saw and learned in Europe had an impact on their own societies later. Vietnamese nationalist Ho Chi Minh spoke for thousands of his countrymen in France when, after the war, he pressed Allied leaders to grant Vietnam autonomy.[50] Developing nations welcomed the general weakening of colonial ties during the war and President Wilson's talk of "self determination of peoples". How these matters would be worked out in the post-war period remained to be seen.

Chapter Nine

The peace lost

Paris Peace Conference

At the beginning of 1919 representatives of the victorious powers assembled at Paris to hammer out peace treaties with the Central Powers.[1] Eventually there were five of these, all named after locations in greater Paris: the Treaty of Versailles (28 June 1919) with Germany; St. Germain-en-Laye (10 September 1919) with Austria; Trianon (4 June 1919) with Hungary; Neuilly (27 November 1919) with Bulgaria; Sèvres (10 August 1920) with Turkey. The overall peace agreement is usually erroneously referred to as the "Versailles settlement".

Paris was an unfortunate if inevitable site for the conference. Having come under enemy fire during the war the French capital hardly offered a neutral setting. Many Germans believe that having Paris as a setting portended a dictated peace. They claimed that an armistice implied a negotiated settlement between equals; but the Allies did not intend to have a negotiated peace any more than the Germans intended one in the case of Russia in 1918.

Twenty-seven countries sent delegations to Paris. The smaller states and President Woodrow Wilson favoured open negotiations, but such an approach proved unworkable as even Wilson soon acknowledged. Locked in civil war, Russia was a notable absence.

Two representatives each from Britain, France, the United States, Italy, and Japan met as the Council of Ten, the main deliberative body of the conference. It was an outgrowth of the Supreme Inter-Allied War Council that had decided policy issues in the last year of the war. The Japanese were little interested in European matters. They sought aggrandizement in Asia, notably the German cession in China and the German North Pacific islands, along with a statement of racial equality. They only got the former. Once these issues were settled the Japanese took little interest in the other negotiations.[2] This meant that most decisions of the peace conference were settled by Woodrow Wilson of the United States, David Lloyd George of Britain, Georges Clemenceau of France, and Vittorio Orlando of Italy.

Many Americans believed then and since that the peace settlement was driven by French greed. But Wilson, not Clemenceau, was its key figure and it was the Americans who dictated its final shape. French and British leaders knew that they could not have won the war without the United States and that her support would be critical in maintaining any peace settlement.

The idealistic Wilson arrived in Europe aboard the liner *George Washington* on Friday, 13 December – a poor omen for the superstitious. He then spent a month travelling in Britain, France, and Italy, explaining his principles to the people of Europe and visiting with Europe's statesmen. Wilson suffered from a Messiah complex, believing that he had a mandate from the world's peoples to be the arbiter of peace, but he had scant knowledge of Europe. In Rome he told journalists: "the soul of one people is crying out to the soul of another, and no people in the world with whose sentiments I am acquainted want a bargaining peace. They all want settlements based upon right."[3] There was one key pre-conference trip that Wilson neglected: a visit to the Western Front battlefields. It might have adjusted his perspective.

Wilson was not interested in honouring the wartime partition treaties; he wanted to recast Europe's boundaries along "clearly recognizable lines of nationality". His chief interest at Paris, however, was in establishing an international organization to promote peaceful settlement of future disputes. On most key issues Wilson stood with the British against the French.

Prime Minister David Lloyd George headed the British delegation. The fiery Welshman and canny politician wanted chiefly to end the German threat to Britain's naval superiority and to reassert Britain's traditional leadership in manufacturing and trade. He also sought colonial gains in Africa and the Middle East. Once the naval issue was disposed of to British satisfaction Lloyd George favoured normalizing relations with Germany as quickly as possible to restore a key trading partner.[4]

Premier Georges Clemenceau was 78 years old, a French patriot, and a realist who had twice seen the Germans invade his country. His primary goal was French security. As historian Charles Mee notes, "after all, unlike the English and the Americans, whose armies clamoured to go back home, Clemenceau lived there".[5] To Clemenceau's way of thinking, security meant reducing and controlling Germany's capacity to wage war; it also required active post-war collaboration between France, Britain, and the United States. He also sought war damages from the Germans and a share of the German and Ottoman colonies.[6]

Premier Vittorio Orlando and the Italian delegation mainly desired territory at the expense of Austria and the new state of Yugoslavia. This meant conflict between the provisions of the 1915 secret Treaty of London that promised Italy territory along the Adriatic coast and Wilson's ideal of self-determination. Orlando proved inflexible when it came to the largely Italian-speaking port of Fiume (Rijeka to the Yugoslavs), which was not included in territory earlier promised to Italy. Accordingly he left the conference for a time, and because Italy was only marginally a great power Orlando was not one of the principal players at Paris.[7]

The chief issues to be resolved at Paris were the creation of a league of nations, French and Belgian security and the future of the Rhineland, the creation of a Polish state and Eastern European frontiers, the disposition of German and Ottoman colonies, and disarmament.

League of Nations

On Wilson's insistence, discussion of the league was made the priority, in part because Wilson assumed such an organization would take care of any loose ends from the settlement. Clemenceau was more concerned with concrete guarantees, but the French delegation believed that the right kind of league could be useful in maintaining the peace.

French constitutional lawyer Léon Bourgeois had spent years working on a draft for just such an organization. The league he and the French delegation envisioned would have mandatory membership and its own independent military force to keep the peace. Wilson wanted a voluntary organization and overran objections by stating that any state refusing membership would be branded an "outlaw". Wilson and Lloyd George also wanted the emphasis on the rule of law and peaceful settlement of disputes. At US insistence the committee on the league rejected the Bourgeois draft and adopted the Miller–Hurst draft of American David Hunter Miller and Briton C. J. Hurst as its basic document.

The covenant of the League, remarkably produced in less than two weeks, closely reflected Wilson's position. As it finally emerged the League of Nations included a Secretariat (the executive), a Council (France, Britain, Italy, Japan, and the United States as permanent members, and four non-permanent members selected by the Assembly); and an Assembly of all powers. The covenant also provided a Mandates Commission to supervise treatment of natives in the former German and Turkish colonies.

Emphasizing the peaceful settlement of disputes, the League's strongest enforcement weapon was sanctions. Although the League had serious short-comings, most of which would still be evident in its near-duplicate successor, the United Nations, it was nonetheless a novel creation and it sparked great interest and enthusiasm. One problem with this, as Clemenceau was quick to point out, was that many people assumed the League was a panacea, a cure for the world's security problems when other guarantees were what really mattered.

Rhineland

Clemenceau took little interest in negotiations over the League; his chief interest remained French security. Clemenceau and his aides wanted all German territory west of the Rhine River (the Rhineland) taken from Germany and made into one or more independent states. They also wanted these states to maintain forever a joint Allied military occupation force to guarantee the settlement. Lloyd George and Wilson were not thinking in terms of taking German territory and wanted an immediate withdrawal of military forces once a peace treaty had been signed. Here was a vast chasm to be bridged.

Certain aspects of the Rhineland settlement were easily resolved. Alsace and Lorraine went back to France. This was a foregone conclusion and there was little protest in Germany. France was also awarded the coal production of the Saar basin for a 15-year period because the Germans had destroyed or damaged many of the French mines. The Saar itself would be under League of Nations' administration. In 1935 its inhabitants would vote to determine their future: continuation under League administration or union with France or Germany. If, as expected, the German population there voted to rejoin their fatherland, Germany would have to repurchase the mines at a price to be determined by outside experts.

In order to improve its defensive position vis-à-vis Germany, Belgium received the two small border enclaves of Eupen and Malmédy. Luxembourg was placed outside the German customs union and secured control of her railroads.[8]

But there was sharp confrontation over the Rhineland itself. Wilson and Lloyd George opposed taking it from Germany. Warning of a potential "Alsace-Lorraine in reverse" they said the Germans would not be able to accept the loss of the Rhineland and would soon resort to war to take it back. Clemenceau found it difficult to accept the fact that the Americans and British would deny France the security it had fought for for so long and at such a cost.

He brushed away charges that France wanted to annex the Rhineland, saying that the territory could be one or more states and could adopt whatever form of government it wished.

The impasse was finally broken in March 1919 when Lloyd George and Wilson agreed to secure France's eastern border with a treaty of guarantee if France would drop its demand for an independent Rhineland. Britain and the United States would come to the assistance of France if Germany ever invaded. French leaders such as Poincaré and Foch argued that this was inadequate and accused Clemenceau of selling out French security, but Clemenceau hoped that by compromising he would at least achieve his goal of maintaining Anglo–American–French cooperation in the peace settlement.[9] The Rhineland would remain German, but it was to be permanently demilitarized. In addition the right (east) bank of the Rhine would be demilitarized to a depth of 50 kilometres (about 30 miles).

The length of the military occupation of the Rhineland also had to be worked out. Agreement was reached on a staggered withdrawal. The British would occupy for five years a northern zone around the Rhine bridgehead at Köln (Cologne), the Americans a centre zone at Koblenz (Coblenz) for ten years, and the French a southern zone with its Rhine crossing at Mainz for 15 years. Foch charged that the peace had been lost and predicted that Germany would invade France again within a generation.[10]

Italy's frontiers

Italy's northern frontier was another difficult problem. Here Orlando and the Italian delegation encountered Wilson's opposition to the secret wartime Treaty of London. Italy's case for territory, originally based on the threat from Austria-Hungary, had been weakened since the 1918 collapse of the Dual Monarchy. In 1919 Italy was the dominant Central European power.

Italy did receive the Austrian Tyrol (the so-called Trentino, today the Alto Adige) to the Brenner Pass and Austria's former coastal provinces of Gorizia-Gradisca, the port of Trieste, and Istria. Wilson refused, however, to yield on the matter of the coastal city of Fiume in Dalmatia. Orlando at first tried to barter Italian support for the League of Nations. Fiume was largely Italian but its surrounding areas were heavily Slavic, and the Yugoslavs wanted the port as much as did the Italians. Lloyd George and Clemenceau favoured giving it to Italy in return for other territorial considerations, but Wilson remained adamant. Remembering the warm welcome he had received in Italy before the conference and incorrectly assuming that it meant support for his pro-gramme, Wilson appealed directly to the Italian people, urging them to reject exaggerated and unjust demands.

Orlando was so shaken by this that he left the conference, remarking that he would let the Italian people choose between him and Wilson. Orlando remained in Italy from late April to early May waiting for an apology from Wilson that never came. The Italian delegation returned to Paris "fuming", it was said, just in time to sign the final treaty.[11]

In September 1919 Italian volunteers under Gabriele d'Annunzio marched into Fiume and seized it, much to the delight of the Italian people. In the November 1920 Treaty of Rapallo Yugoslavia and Italy agreed that Fiume would be Italian. In general, however, most Italians were upset at what they regarded as their minimal gains from the war. More than 600,000 dead and severe economic dislocation fuelled popular resentment that helped bring Benito Mussolini and his Fascists to power in 1922.

Eastern Europe

In 1919 the situation in Eastern Europe was quite fluid. Attempting to maintain its military presence in the Baltic states Germany stressed unsuccess-fully the Bolshevik threat. Estonia, Latvia, and Lithuania owed their in-dependence to fear in Western capitals over the spread of Communism. In 1919 Western leaders sought to erect in Eastern Europe a *cordon sanitaire* to contain Communism.[12]

Poland

Poland was the most difficult Central European problem to resolve. A free and independent Poland with access to the sea was one of Wilson's Fourteen Points.[13] France in particular sought a strong Poland to take the place of Russia in containing Germany. Poland had disappeared from the map at the end of the eighteenth century, gobbled up by Prussia, Russia, and Austria. It was a foregone conclusion that some sort of Polish state would re-emerge. The problems were in what form and exactly where.

A Commission on Polish Affairs recommended that there be a corridor across Posen and West Prussia to give Poland access to the Baltic through the port of Danzig at the mouth of the Vistula River. Heavily German Danzig was placed under League of Nations administration. This arrangement regarding Poland's western frontier was in line with the Fourteen Points but it cut off 1.5 million Germans in East Prussia from the rest of Germany. Although the Germans were given free transit across the corridor, in 1939 Hitler used the corridor as a pretext for war. With the benefit of hindsight, the best thing might have been simply to move Poland and eliminate the corridor but Wilson rejected this as "major surgery". Poland also received Upper Silesia. A plebiscite was held in March 1920, after which the districts of Marienwerder and Allenstein were awarded to Germany.

Also vexing was a solution to Poland's Eastern border. The situation there was so confused that it was not until December 1919 that a commission headed by Englishman Lord Curzon set the border. Neither the Russians nor the Poles recognized the line, and the two then went to war. After Poland was victorious on the battlefield, in the March 1921 Treaty of Riga the Soviet Union recognized a border that ran east of the so-called "Curzon Line" close to the Russo-Polish border of 1772.

Many Poles were unhappy with their borders and wanted to push them farther. Their subsequent expansionism, while successful, alienated their neighbours and isolated Poland in her fatal confrontation with Germany. The Curzon Line reappeared during the Second World War when Stalin insisted that it be the western boundary of the Soviet Union and obtained Allied agreement to this. Both the Soviet Union and Germany regarded Poland as a temporary entity (*Saisonstaat*) and sought its destruction at the earliest possible opportunity. The August 1939 Nazi–Soviet Non-Aggression Pact guaranteed fulfilment of their desire.

Czechoslovakia

Two other new states appeared. Czechoslovakia consisted of the Czech provinces of Bohemia and Moravia (which had been under Austrian administration), Slovakia (formerly part of Hungary), and Ruthenia. The Allies added the latter, with its largely Ukrainian population, to provide a land bridge to Romania. Although there were many differences between them, Czechs and Slovaks united in the belief that they would fare better together than separately. The state did suffer the serious handicap of being multinational in population. Even the more numerous Czechs were a minority in their own country and there were a large number of Germans in the western fringes of the country. Still Czechoslovakia provided one of the few success stories in Eastern Europe between the wars until the West abandoned her to

Hitler in 1938. In the late 1930s Czechoslovakia had the highest standard of living in the region and was its only democracy.[14]

Yugoslavia

To the south of Czechoslovakia was another new state. It began as the Kingdom of Serbs, Croats, and Slovenes under the Serbian Karadjordjević dynasty. In 1929 it changed its name to Yugoslavia. The state drew its inspiration from the 1917 Corfu Manifesto whereby the national groupings had declared their intention to merge into one large entity. Serbia was its most populous component and nucleus. In 1914 Yugoslavian territory was divided among the Kingdoms of Serbia and Montenegro and the Dual Monarchy. Austria controlled Carniola, Styria, and Dalmatia; Hungary administered Slavonia, Bačka, and the Banat of Temesvár. Austria and Hungary jointly administered Bosnia-Herzegovina.

Yugoslavia secured all these territories (save the eastern Banat) at Paris. But welding the disparate elements together in one state would prove difficult since Yugoslavia suffered from serious internal problems. There were subtle and not so subtle national, linguistic, economic, and religious divisions.

Romania

Romania, unlucky at war, was fortunate at peace. She was greatly enlarged as a result of arrangements at Paris. Romania kept the Dobrudja, won from Bulgaria in the 1913 Balkan War, the eastern Banat, and Transylvania – with its large Magyar population. To her surprise Romania also gained Bessarabia, a consequence of Allied efforts to contain Communist Russia.

After the war, Romania, Czechoslovakia, and Yugoslavia formed the Little Entente to work together in foreign policy matters and prevent a Habsburg restoration. Since the three states of this bloc had profited at the expense of the former Central Powers, they maintained a strong Western orientation.

Austria

Shrinking to a small homogeneous state of only 6.5 million people, Austria was hard hit economically. A third of the population lived in Vienna, the nerve centre of the former empire. Because the surrounding successor states feared a return of Austro-Hungarian domination and wanted to establish their own industrial bases, they now raised trade barriers against her. Over-industrialized Austria and its factories were cut off from their traditional sources of raw materials and markets. Economic dislocation was severe and there was considerable Austrian sentiment at the time for *Anschluss* (union) with Germany, a step blocked by France and the Little Entente.

Hungary

Hungary lost 65 per cent of its prewar territory including Slovakia, Croatia, Slavonia, Syrmia, the Banat, and Transylvania. The loss of Transylvania with its large Magyar population was especially grievous. Bitterness in Hungary over this helps to explain why Hungarian leaders were open to revisionist opportunities offered by Hitler in the late 1930s. Hungary was, however, much better balanced economically than Austria.

Bulgaria, Greece, and Turkey

In the Treaty of Neuilly Bulgaria gave up western Thrace to Greece and western Macedonia to Yugoslavia. Cut off from direct access to the Mediter-ranean and comparatively poor, she was now one of the weakest of Balkan states. In the Treaty of Sèvres Turkey gave up her non-Turkish populations. France received a mandate over Syria (and Lebanon), while Britain obtained Iraq and Palestine. Greece secured a mandate over Smyrna in western Anatolia pending a plebiscite. The Straits were to be internationalized. The Treaty of Sèvres did not last, however. Turkish nationalists, headed by war hero Mustapha Kemal, seized control of the government and went to war against Greece, defeating her. Turkey demanded and received a new treaty. The Treaty of Lausanne of 24 July 1923, restored to Turkey the land she had lost in Europe and Asia Minor.[15]

Reparations and "war guilt"

One of the bitterest controversies of the peace settlement concerned repara-tions. The Allies had told the Germans that they would be liable for war damages, and the precedent for assessing reparations in the war had been set by the Germans themselves in the Treaty of Brest-Litovsk. At Paris reparations were "justified" by Article 231 of the Treaty of Versailles, which placed the blame for the war on Germany and her allies. British election politics, meanwhile, drove up the amount of reparations by adding pensions and widow's benefits to the total. Following a series of conferences in 1920 reparations were finally set at $33 billion.[16]

John Maynard Keynes, a member of the British delegation, resigned in protest. In 1920 he published *The Economic Consequences of the Peace* in which he claimed that the settlement was a piece of French villainy to keep Germany down. He further charged that reparations hampered the recovery of world economies and that there was no way that Germany could pay the sums demanded of her. Immensely influential, his book helped spread dissatisfaction with the treaty in Britain and the United States. In 1946 Frenchman Etienne Mantoux published *The Carthaginian Peace or the Economic Consequences of Mr. Keynes*. Mantoux held that Germany had adequate resources to pay the sums demanded of her if she had really desired peace, and he maintained that Hitler spent more money rearming than the Allies had demanded in reparations.

In fact Germany made money from the bizarre financial triangle that developed. In the 1920s US bankers loaned money to Germany in order to help her rebuild her economy. These loans enabled Germany to make reparations payments of some $9 billion between 1918 and 1932; this was not even the interest owing on the principal.[17] The countries that received the payments used the money to make payments on war debts owed the United States. Probably it would have been best to have cancelled reparations altogether, but the United States refused to cancel the war debts it was owed. "They hired the money didn't they?" President Calvin Coolidge asked.[18]

German disarmament

Another controversy pertained to the size and nature of the German military. The British and Americans wanted Germany to have a small professional army modelled after their own military establishments. The French disagreed, fearing that this would simply be a cadre army, rapidly expandable later. But the new German Army, or Reichswehr, following Anglo-Saxon suggestions, was restricted to a 100,000 all-volunteer force with its men serving 12-year enlistments. Germany would have no air force, no tanks, no heavy artillery, and the German Navy was limited to 6 pre-dreadnought battleships, 6 light cruisers, 12 destroyers, and no submarines. There was talk of a general reduction in world armaments, but only Wilson genuinely sought it. Later this provided German nationalists a powerful argument in that only the vanquished disarmed.[19]

Shandong

Another controversy at Paris centred on the matter of the Chinese province of Shandong (Shantung). China sent a delegation to Paris headed by Foreign Minister Lou Cheng-hsiang. The Japanese delegation expected big-power acceptance of Japan's control of the former German cession on the Shandong peninsula, while China counted on President Wilson's support for her own cause. The dispute nearly wrecked the conference.[20]

Wilson had already endured an Italian walkout and the Japanese now threatened the same. After tortured deliberation Wilson, who feared a breakup of the conference, supported the Japanese, although he did secure concessions on the timing of the return of the province to China and the setting aside of Japanese political rights there.[21]

News of this American "betrayal" had immediate repercussions in China. The Chinese government refused to sign the peace treaty and student demonstrations and general riots broke out in nearly every major Chinese city. This became known as the May 4th Movement after the date when the news from Paris reached China. It was a major event in the modern Chinese revolutionary movement. Communism in China certainly benefited from it.[22]

Collapse of the Versailles settlement

No other twentieth-century treaty involved as much controversy as the Treaty of Versailles. For the next quarter of a century it entered into virtually any discussion of European affairs. All knew the peace settlement was flawed, but was it necessarily doomed to failure? Contrary to what many believed it neither dismembered Germany nor substantially affected her power. Germany certainly suffered from the war and afterwards, but the Treaty of Versailles left the German nation and its infrastructure essentially intact.

The ink was barely dry on the signatures to the treaties when the wartime alliance of France, Britain, and the United States collapsed. The United States Senate rejected the Paris settlement and retreated into isolation. When the Anglo-American Treaty of Guarantee evaporated Britain declared itself no longer bound by its provisions and returned to a policy of non-interference in Continental matters. With Russia already lost and Britain unwilling to keep up her military strength, only France was left to enforce the settlement. There were those in France who urged their leaders to act alone and seize the Rhineland, but even staunch patriots such as Raymond Poincaré rejected such an extreme course.

Two great questions remained after 1919: how would the Germans adjust to their new internal regime of democracy, and would they accept their new borders? Unfortunately the two were intertwined as many Germans believed the Weimar Republic had been delivered in the baggage trains of the Allies. Given time and favourable conditions many might have adjusted to democracy, but no patriotic German accepted the new frontiers as final. And it was the leaders of the new Weimar Republic, not the Kaiser or the army, who had to bear the onus of defeat and the lies about a "stab in the back". They bore the consequences of the catastrophic self-inflicted inflation of 1923 and the onslaught of the Great Depression. In retrospect it is amazing that the new German republic lasted as long as it did.

Although few realized it at the time, in the final analysis enforcement of the Versailles Treaty was left to the Germans themselves. Half again as populous and more powerful economically than France, Germany would decide whether the settlement lasted.

Germany's new leaders soon set out to break the settlement. When Germany refused to pay reparations, in 1923 French Premier Raymond Poincaré acted. A stickler for the law who believed that if Germany could break any part of the settlement she could nullify all of it, Poincaré, in concert with Belgian and Italian leaders, sent French troops into the Ruhr.

Britain and the United States protested and Germany tried to buy time to bring about a French withdrawal by following a programme of "passive resistance" and printing paper money to pay the salaries of idled workers. Poincaré refused to budge. France had fulfilled the terms of the 1871 Treaty of Frankfurt and now it was Germany's turn. France would stay in the Ruhr until Germany agreed to live up to the terms of the Treaty of Versailles. Catastrophic inflation, ultimately leading to an exchange rate of 4.2 trillion marks to the dollar, now wrecked the German economy and her leaders agreed to resume reparations payments. The pauperization of the German middle class was perhaps the most important factor in the rise of Adolf Hitler. Frenchmen at first applauded Poincaré for his tough stand but later looked at the cost of the Ruhr occupation and turned him out of office in 1924. Never again in the inter-war years would France attempt an independent policy vis-à-vis Germany.[23]

Still the next decade saw relative harmony on the international scene. France maintained Europe's largest standing army but this dominance was more apparent than real: the peace rested not so much on French strength as on German weakness. The Great Depression further destabilized the world. Its effects, together with the United States' refusal to join the League, made international police actions, already unlikely, a virtual impossibility.

In January 1933 Adolf Hitler became German chancellor. With the Western democracies unwilling to enforce the settlement they had made two decades earlier Hitler easily broke the shackles of Versailles. He rearmed Germany, in April 1935 securing British approval for this step in the naval sphere. In March 1936, in his most significant breach of the First World War settlement, Hitler sent troops to remilitarize the Rhineland. The Frence and British did nothing. Not content with this or the *Anschluss* of Austria with Germany, Hitler planned war to secure the territorial prizes of military victory denied Germany in 1914–18. Italy, another power not content with the 1919 peace arrangements, joined Germany to form the Rome–Berlin Axis. Japan again sought to take advantage of European circumstances to acquire Manchuria and perhaps all China. The Second World War, which officially began in September 1939, may actually have begun in Manchuria in 1931.

The war had its seeds in the Paris settlement, not for its flaws – and there were many – but because it was not enforced. Treaties are less important for their terms than whether they are enforced. Especially because it was a compromise arrangement the Paris peace settlement required vigilance. During debate in the French Chamber of Deputies over ratification of the Treaty of Versailles Clemenceau rose to defend it. The treaty was, he agreed, full of imperfections but his critics had missed the point: "M. Louis Marin [a right-wing deputy] went to the heart of the matter when . . . he said with a touch of despair: 'Your treaty condemns France to eternal vigilance.'" That was indeed the case: "Peace is only war pursued by other means . . . I see life as a perpetual conflict in war and peace . . . ; that conflict you cannot suppress."[24]

The failure to follow Clemenceau's lead insured that the 1920s and 1930s were only a period of truce before the struggle was renewed.

Notes

Chapter One

1. Recent studies address the nature of these tensions whether – governing elites' negative reactions to working-class unrest or aggressive Social Darwinism for which lower classes shared enthusiasm. See Robert J. W. Evans and Hartmut Pogge von Strandmann, *The coming of the First World War* (Oxford, 1988); also Geoff Eley, *Reshaping the German right: radical nationalism and political change after Bismarck* (Ann Arbor, MI, 1980); and David Blackbourn, *Class, religion, and local politics in Wilhelmine Germany: The Centre Party in Württemberg before 1914* (Weisbaden, 1980).
2. For a summary of the war guilt debate see John W. Langdon, *July 1914. The long debate, 1918–1990* (New York, 1991).
3. For a brief introduction see Arthur J. May, *The Hapsburg Monarchy, 1867–1914* (New York, 1951).
4. *Ibid.*, p. 158; Imanuel Geiss (ed.), *July 1914. The outbreak of the First World War: selected documents* (London, 1967), p. 51. Gary W. Shanafelt, "Franz Ferdinand", in Spencer C. Tucker (ed.), *The European powers in the First World War* (New York, 1996), pp. 268–9. Hereinafter cited as *European powers*. See also Gordon Brook-Shepherd, *Archduke of Sarajevo. The romance and tragedy of Franz Ferdinand of Austria* (Boston, 1984), pp. 149–51.
5. Ottokar Czernin, *In the World War* (London, 1919), p. 38. For an excellent short account of the Dual Monarchy and the coming of the war see Samuel R. Williamson, *Austria-Hungary and the origins of the First World War* (New York, 1991).
6. British doctors had misdiagnosed his cancer of the throat. See Lamar Cecil, *Wilhelm II. Prince and emperor, 1859–1900* (Chapel Hill, NC, 1989), pp. 88–95.
7. Alan Palmer, *Bismarck* (New York, 1976), p. 242.
8. See George F. Kennan, *The fateful alliance. France, Russia, and the coming of the First World War* (New York, 1984).
9. See Peter Padfield, *The great naval race. Anglo-German naval rivalry, 1900–1914* (New York, 1974); also Arthur J. Marder, *From dreadnought to Scapa Flow* (5 vols; London, 1961), I.
10. Holger Herwig, *"Luxury" fleet. The Imperial German Navy, 1888–1918* (London, 1980), pp. 3 ff.

11. Schlieffen's article, "Der Krieg in der Gegenwart", appeared in January 1909. See Geiss, *July 1914*, pp. 36 ff.

12. General Friedrich von Bernhardi, *Germany and the next war*, trans. Allen H. Powles (New York, 1914), p. 152.

13. Fritz Fischer, *World power or decline. The controversy over Germany's aims in the First World War* (New York, 1974), p. 4.

14. Martin Kitchen, "Civil-military relations in Germany during the First World War", in R. J. Q. Adams (ed.), *The Great War, 1914–18. Essays on the military political and social history of the First World War* (College Station, TX, 1990), p. 62.

15. Otto Friedrich, *Blood and iron. From Bismarck to Hitler the von Moltke family's impact on German history* (New York, 1995), p. 236.

16. Herwig, *"Luxury" fleet*, p. 2.

17. Keith Eubank, *Paul Cambon. Master diplomatist* (Norman, OK, 1960), pp. 145–55.

18. Douglas Porch, *The conquest of Morocco* (New York, 1983), pp. 144–7.

19. Geiss, *July 1914*, pp. 51–2.

20. *Ibid., July 1914*, pp. 57–8; Williamson, *Austria-Hungary and the origins of the First World War*, pp. 190–92.

21. Volker R. Berghahn, *Germany and the approach of war in 1914* (New York, 1973), pp. 188–95.

22. Geiss, *July 1914*, p. 81, 136, 160; Williamson, *Austria-Hungary and the origins of the First World War*, pp. 192–203.

23. Berghahn, *Germany and the approach of war in 1914*, p. 202.

24. Sidney B. Fay, *The origins of the World War* (2nd ed., rev. NY, 1966), II: 291–321; Berghahn, *Germany and the approach of war in 1914*, p. 202.

25. Fay, *The origins of the World War*. II: p. 266; Williamson, *Austria-Hungary and the origins of the First World War*, p. 190.

26. John F. V. Keiger, *France and the origins of the First World War* (New York, 1983), p. 160.

27. Fritz Fischer, *War of illusions, German policies from 1911 to 1914*, tr. Marion Jackson (New York, 1975), p. 704 ff.

28. Geiss, *July 1914*, p. 336.

29. Keiger, *France and the origins of the First World War*, pp. 161–2.

30. *Ibid.*, pp. 231–2, 275, 337.

31. *Ibid.*, pp. 339–40.

32. Barbara W. Tuchman, *The guns of August* (New York, 1962), p. 122.

33. See David G. Herrmann, *The arming of Europe and the making of the First World War* (Princeton, NJ, 1996).

34. *Ibid.*, pp. 195–6.

35. Hubert C. Johnson, *Breakthrough! Tactics, technology, and the search for victory on the Western Front in World War I* (Novato, CA, 1994), p. 5.

36. Anthony Livesey, *Great battles of World War I* (New York, 1989), p. 47.

37. See John Ellis, *The social history of the machine gun* (New York, 1975).

38. *Ibid.*, pp. 62, 113; Johnson, *Breakthrough!*, p. 17; Peter Simkins, *World War I. The Western Front* (New York, 1991), pp. 87–8.

39. Boyd Dastrup, *King of battle: A branch history of the U.S. Army's field artillery* (Fort Monroe, VA, 1992), pp. 126–9.

40. Johnson, *Breakthrough!*, p. 4; Boyd Dastrup, *The field artillery: History and sourcebook* (Westport, CT, 1994), pp. 44–5. See also Bruce I. Gudmundsson, *On artillery* (Westport, CT, 1993).

41. Philip J. Haythornthwaite, *World War One source book* (London, 1992), p. 181; David T. Zabecki, *Steel wind. Colonel Georg Bruchmüller and the birth of modern artillery* (Westport, CT, 1995), pp. 7 and 10; Randal Gray, *Chronicle of the First World War* (New York, 1991), II: 284.
42. In the British Army the total was 58 per cent from artillery and mortar shells, and slightly less than 39 per cent from machine gun and rifle bullets. Simkins, *World War I*, p. 124.
43. Robert Gardiner (ed.), *Steam, steel & shellfire. The steam warship 1815–1905* (Annapolis, MD, 1992), pp. 158–61.
44. Robert Gardiner (ed.), *The eclipse of the big gun. The warship 1906–45* (Annapolis, MD, 1992), p. 15.
45. Jon Sumida, "Fisher's naval revolution", *Naval history* (August 1996), p. 21.
46. Gardiner, *The eclipse of the big gun*, pp. 15–17.
47. *Ibid.*, p. 8.
48. Gardiner, *Steam, steel and shellfire*, pp. 134–45.
49. For discussion of early submarines see *ibid.*, pp. 147–57.
50. Theodore Roscoe, *On the seas and in the skies. A history of the U.S. Navy's air power* (New York, 1970), pp. 27–31.
51. Anthony Livesey, *The historical atlas of World War I* (New York, 1994), p. 15.
52. Gray, *Chronicle of the First World War*, I: 284; II: 290.
53. Livesey, *The historical atlas of World War I*, p. 156.
54. Herrmann, *The arming of Europe and the making of the First World War*, pp. 70–74; Correlli Barnett, *The Great War* (New York, 1980), p. 133.
55. Martin Van Creveld, *Supplying war: Logistics from Wallenstein to Patton* (London, 1977), p. 110.
56. For a discussion of tactics and technology in the war see Johnson, *Breakthrough!*.

Chapter Two

1. All national population figures are from William R. Griffiths, *The Great War* (Wayne, NJ, 1986), p. 7.
2. Figures vary. The usual for the German Army is over 1,000,000 men, but for the sake of continuity I have used those for armies and navies in Randal Gray, ed., *Chronicle of the First World War* (2 vols; Oxford, 1991).
3. Herrmann, *The arming of Europe*, p. 221.
4. These and other naval strength figures are from Paul G. Halpern, *A naval history of World War I* (Annapolis, MD, 1994).
5. Philip J. Green, "Austria-Hungary, Army 1914–18", in *European powers*, pp. 85–8; Stone, *Eastern Front*, p. 125. See also Gunter E. Rothenberg, *The army of Francis Joseph* (West Lafayette, IN, 1976) and István Deak, *Beyond nationalism: A social & political history of the Habsburg Officer Corps, 1848–1918* (Oxford, 1990).
6. Williamson, *Austria-Hungary and the origins of the First World War*, p. 51.
7. John W. Bohon, "Russia, army", *European Powers*, pp. 610–12.
8. Norman Stone, *The Eastern Front, 1914–1917* (New York, 1975), pp. 29–30 and 41.

9. Paddy Griffith, *Battle tactics of the Western Front. The British Army's art of attack, 1916–18* (New Haven, CT, 1994), pp. 9–10. Basil H. Liddell Hart, *The real war, 1914–1918* (Boston, 1930), p. 42.

10. Richard Hough, *The Great War at sea* (New York, 1983), p. 55.

11. Eugene L. Rasor, "Blockade, naval of Germany", *European Powers*, pp. 134–5.

12. Bernadotte E. Schmitt and Harold C. Vedeler, *The world in the crucible, 1914–1919* (New York, 1984), p. 28.

13. Gary P. Cox, "Schlieffen Plan", *European Powers*, pp. 633–5.

14. Anthony Livesey, *Great battles of World War I* (New York, 1989), p. 12.

15. Cox, "Schlieffen Plan", *European Powers*, p. 635.

16. Otto Friedrich, *Blood and iron*, pp. 227–31.

17. Gerhard Ritter, *The Schlieffen Plan: critique of a myth* (New York, 1958).

18. Jan Karl Tanenbaum, "Michel, Victor", *European Powers*, pp. 482–3.

19. Colonel Grandmaison was head of the Operations Branch at the War Ministry (1908–1911) and Brigadier General Foch was commandant of the Ecole Supérieure de Guerre (1908–11). Foch's book, *The principles of a war* (1903) stressed the importance of the commander's will and necessity of offensive operations.

20. Gary P. Cox, "French War Plan XVII", *European Powers*, p. 275.

21. For an excellent analysis of Plan XVII see S. R. Williamson, "Joffre reshapes French strategy, 1911–1913", in Paul M. Kennedy (ed.), *The war plans of the Great Powers* (London, 1979).

22. The seventeenth since the 1870–71 Franco-German War.

23. Johnson, *Breakthrought!*, pp. 35–6.

24. Jan Karl Tanenbaum, "Joffre, Joseph Jacques Césaire", in *European Powers*, p. 388.

25. Samuel Williamson, *Austria-Hungary and the origins of the First World War*, p. 50; Alan Clark, *Suicide of the empires: the battle on the Eastern Front, 1914–1918* (New York, 1971), pp. 50–53. See also Graydon A. Tunstall, *Planning for war against Russia and Serbia: Austro-Hungarian and German Military Strategies, 1871–1914* (Boulder, CO, 1993).

26. Sir Alfred Knox, *With the Russian Army, 1914–1917* (New York, 1921), p. 47; Sir Edmund Ironside, *Tannenberg: the first thirty days in East Prussia* (London, 1925), pp. 2–9 and 22–3.

27. Gray, *Chronicle of the First World War*, I: 261.

28. G. H. Perris, *The Campaign of 1914 in France and Belgium* (London, 1915), pp. 7–12.

29. At Dinant on 23 August von Hausen's Saxon troops shot over 600 men, women, and children in the main square. Barnett, *The Great War*, p. 26.

30. Simkins, *World War I*, p. 21.

31. John Keegan, *Opening moves: August 1914* (New York, 1971), pp. 92–8.

32. Griffiths, *The Great War*, pp. 29–30.

33. Green, "Great Britain, Army", *European Powers*, pp. 312–13.

34. Field Marshal Sir John French, *1914* (London, 1919), pp. 5–7; Livesey, *Great battles of World War I*, p. 16; Simkins, *World War I*, pp. 22–3.

35. Simkins, *World War I*, p. 24.

36. Tuchman, *The guns of August*, pp. 381, 417.

37. *Ibid.*, pp. 34–5 and 412–13.

38. Livesey, *Great battles of World War I*, pp. 21–2.

39. Tuchman, *The guns of August*, p. 434.

40. Griffiths, *The Great War*, p. 36.

41. Tuchman, *The guns of August*, p. 438.
42. One of the Renault taxis is today displayed at the French military museum at Les Invalides in Paris.
43. Griffiths, *The Great War*, pp. 36–7.
44. Erich von Falkenhayn, *The German General Staff and its decisions, 1914–1916* (New York, 1920), pp. 10–19.
45. B. J. Liddell Hart, *Foch. The man of Orleans* (Boston, 1932), p. 108. See also Field Marshal French's praise of Foch in French, *1914*, pp. 197–8.
46. Ferdinand Foch, *The memoirs of Marshal Foch* (New York, 1931), pp. 117–39.
47. French, *1914*, pp. 163–74.
48. Winston Churchill, *The world crisis* (New York, 1955), I: 365–90.
49. Different dates are given for this action. I have used Gray, *Chronicle of the First World War*, I: 52, 54.
50. Simkins, *World War I*, p. 38.
51. For an excellent study of trench warfare and everyday life (and death) in the trenches, see John Ellis, *Eye-deep in hell. Trench warfare in World War I* (New York, 1977).
52. Simkins, *World War I*, p. 53.
53. Griffiths, *The Great War*, p. 53.
54. Robert Asprey, *The German high command at war. Hindenburg and Ludendorff conduct World War I* (New York, 1992), pp. 154–5 and 162; Liddell Hart, *The "Real" War*, p. 116.
55. Simkins, *World War I*, pp. 57–8 and 60.
56. David K. Yelton, "Champagne, First Battle of", *European Powers*, pp. 180–81.
57. Green, "Great Britain, army", *European Powers*, pp. 312–15.
58. Stone, *The Eastern Front*, p. 45.
59. John F. V. Keiger, *France and the origins of the First World War* (New York, 1983), p. 96.
60. Griffiths, *The Great War*, p. 43.
61. Stone, *The Eastern Front*, pp. 47–8.
62. *Ibid.*, 48–59; N. N. Golovin, *The Russian Army in the World War* (New Haven, 1931), p. 23.
63. Asprey, *The German high command at war*, pp. 57–8.
64. Griffiths, *The Great War*, p. 44; John W. Bohon, "East Prussia campaign (August–September 1914)", *European Powers*, p. 231. See also David Kahn, *The codebreakers: The story of secret writing* (New York, 1973).
65. Max Hoffmann, *The War of Lost Opportunities* (New York, 1925), pp. 20–23.
66. Griffiths, *The Great War*, p. 45.
67. Asprey, *The German high command at war*, p. 70. On Hindenburg, see J. W. Wheeler-Bennett, *Hindenburg, the wooden titan* (New York, 1967). On Ludendorff: D. J. Goodspeed, *Ludendorff, genius of World War I* (Boston, 1966) and Roger Parkinson, *Tormented warrior. Ludendorff and the supreme command* (New York, 1979). See also Max Hoffmann, *War diaries and other papers* (London, 1929).
68. Liddell Hart, *The real war*, pp. 110–11.
69. Griffiths, *The Great War*, p. 47.
70. Livesey, *Great battles of World War I*, pp. 34–7.
71. Asprey, *The German high command at war*, pp. 88–91; Griffiths, *The Great War*, pp. 48–9.
72. Griffiths, *The Great War*, pp. 49–52; Livesey, *The historical atlas of World War I*, p. 36; John W. Bohon, "East Galicia, 1914 Campaign", *European Powers*, pp. 227–8.

73. Stone, *The Eastern Front*, p. 96.
74. See James J. Bloom, "Poland: German offensive of September–November 1914", *European Powers*, pp. 564–7; also Stone, *The Eastern Front*, pp. 92–107.
75. See Cyril Falls, *Military Operations: Macedonia* (2 vols.: London, 1933 and 1935); also Philip C. Green, "Balkan Front, 1914", *European Powers*, pp. 100–1.
76. See Gary W. Shanafelt, "Potiorek, Oskar", *European Powers*, p. 569.
77. These and the following naval strength figures are from Halpern, *A Naval History of World War I*, pp. 7–9.
78. See *Ibid.*, pp. 30–32; Herwig, *"Luxury" fleet*, p. 149; also David Woodward, "Heligoland, The First Sea Battle", *Warships and sea battles of World War I*, Bernard Fitzsimons (ed.) (London, 1973), pp. 18–25.
79. Samuel Eliot Morison, *The Oxford history of the American people* (New York, 1965), p. 864.
80. Barrie Pitt, "Revenge at Sea", *Warships and sea battles of World War I*, pp. 26–32. See also Geoffrey Bennett, *Coronel and the Falklands* (London, 1962).
81. Quoted in Halpern, *A Naval history of World War I*, p. 39.
82. Patrick Beesly, *Room 40. British naval intelligence 1914–18* (New York, 1982), pp. 4–20.
83. *Ibid.*, pp. 36–7 and 39–42; Martin Gilbert, *The First World War. A Complete History* (New York, 1994), p. 110; and Jürgen Rohwer, "German cruiser raids, 1914", *European Powers*, pp. 291–3.
84. Herwig, *"Luxury" fleet*, p. 218.
85. Simkins, *World War I*, p. 56.

Chapter Three

1. Simkins, *World War I*, p. 57.
2. Gray, *Chronicle of the First World War*, I: 82.
3. David K. Yelton, "Champagne, first battle of", *European Powers*, pp. 180–81.
4. Simkins, *World War I*, p. 63.
5. James J. Bloom, "Neuve Chapelle, battle of", *European Powers*, pp. 505–6. On Neuve Chapelle see Robin Prior and Trevor Wilson, *Command on the Western Front. The military career of Sir Henry Rawlinson, 1914–18* (Oxford, 1992), pp. 19–73.
6. Zabecki, *Steel Wind*, p. 11.
7. David K. Yelton, "Woëvre battle", *European Powers*, p. 751.
8. David K. Yelton, "Artois, second battle of", *European Powers*, p. 76.
9. On its use in the war see L. F. Haber, *The poisonous cloud: chemical warfare in the First World War* (Oxford, 1986); and William Moore, *Gas attack: chemical warfare, 1915 to the present day* (London, 1987).
10. For an excellent oral history of the gas attack and Second Ypres, see Lyn Macdonald, *1915: The death of innocence* (New York, 1995).
11. Moore, *Gas attack*, p. 11.
12. Griffiths, *The Great War*, p. 67.
13. Moore, *Gas attack*, pp. 1–2; 23–5; Griffiths, *The Great War*, p. 67.
14. Simkins, *World War I*, pp. 61–2.
15. Moore, *Gas attack*, pp. 72–85.
16. Simkins, *World War I*, p. 68.

17. *Ibid.*, p. 71; Prior and Wilson, *Command on the Western Front*, pp. 77–93.
18. David K. Yelton, "Artois, second battle of," *European Powers*, pp. 76–7.
19. Livesey, *The Historical atlas of World War I*, p. 76.
20. Bernadotte E. Schmitt & Harold C. Vedeler, *The World in the crucible, 1914–1919* (New York, 1984), p. 80.
21. David K. Yelton, "Champagne, second battle of", *European Powers*, pp. 181–2.
22. Liddell Hart, *The real war 1914–1918*, p. 189.
23. Simkins, *World War I*, p. 73.
24. Yelton, "Champagne, second battle of", *European Powers*, pp. 182–3.
25. Prior and Wilson, *Command on the Western Front*, pp. 100–34.
26. *Ibid.*, pp. 133–4; David K. Yelton, "Artois, third battle of", *European Powers*, p. 78; Liddell Hart, *The real war 1914–1918*, pp. 186–8.
27. Philip J. Haythornthwaite, *World War One source book* (London, 1992), pp. 72 and 93.
28. Simkins, *World War I*, p. 80.
29. Antonio Salandra, *Italy and the Great War. From neutrality to intervention*, tr. Zoe K. Pyne (London, 1932), pp. 268–70. Also Denis Mack Smith, *Italy* (Ann Arbor, MI, 1969), pp. 292–305.
30. James J. Sadkovich, "Isonzo, battles of, nos. 1–4", *European Powers*, pp. 365–7.
31. Griffiths, *The Great War*, p. 68.
32. General A. A. Brusilov, *A soldier's note-book* (London, 1930), pp. 170–1.
33. Asprey, *The German high command at war*, pp. 154–5 and 161–5; Griffiths, *The Great War*, pp. 53–4.
34. Livesey, *The Historical atlas of World War I*, p. 70.
35. Griffiths, *The Great War*, p. 55.
36. *Ibid.*, pp. 55–6; Asprey, *The German high command at war*, pp. 186–91.
37. Dan Van Der Vat, *The ship that changed the world. The escape of the Goeben to the Dardanelles in 1914* (Bethesda, MD, 1986), pp. 22–30 and 183–9; and Alan Moorehead, *Gallipoli* (New York, 1956), pp. 11–31.
38. Moorehead, *Gallipoli*, p. 38.
39. On the Dardanelles and Gallipoli see Moorehead, *Gallipoli*, Robert Rhodes James, *Gallipoli. The history of a noble blunder* (New York, 1965); and Michael Hickey, *Gallipoli* (London, 1995). See also Winston S. Churchill, *The world crisis. Volume II* (New York, 1923). For a useful memoir see Major John Gillam, *Gallipoli diary* (Stevenage, Herts, UK, 1989).
40. Moorehead, *Gallipoli*, p. 34.
41. John Charmley, *Churchill, the end of glory* (New York, 1993), p. 110.
42. *Ibid.*, pp. 35–8; Winston Churchill, *The world crisis*, II: 85–90.
43. Moorehead, *Gallipoli*, pp. 36–40; Rhodes James, *Gallipoli*, pp. 31–3.
44. Churchill, *The world crisis*, II, 90–91.
45. *Ibid.*, pp. 94 and 103–4.
46. Moorehead, *Gallipoli*, pp. 53–4 and 74.
47. *Ibid.*, pp. 55–6. On Churchill's role see Trumbull Higgins, *Winston Churchill and the Dardanelles* (London, 1963).
48. Moorehead, *Gallipoli*, pp. 58–9.
49. *Ibid.*, pp. 60–69 and 76–7.
50. Churchill, *World crisis*, II: 234–7; George H. Cassar, *The French and the Dardanelles* (London, 1971); pp. 104–5.
51. Moorehead, *Gallipoli*, pp. 78–9.

NOTES

52. *Ibid.*, pp. 80–84, 104–6, 120–21, and 133–6.
53. *Ibid.*, pp. 157–218.
54. *Ibid.*, pp. 219–313.
55. *Ibid.*, pp. 314–55 and 360–61.
56. Philip J. Green, "Balkan front, 1915", *European Powers*, pp. 101–2.
57. For this part of the war see Cyril Falls, *History of the Great War: Military operations, Macedonia* (2 vols., London, 1933–5) and Alan Palmer, *The gardeners of Salonika: The Macedonian campaign, 1915–1918* (New York, 1965).
58. Alan Palmer, *The Gardeners of Salonika* (New York, 1965), pp. 18–19.
59. Green, "Balkan front, 1915", *European Powers*, pp. 102–3.
60. Jan Karl Tanenbaum, "Salonika campaign, 1915", *European Powers*, pp. 622–3.
61. Malcolm Muir, Jr., "Dogger Bank, naval battle of", *European Powers*, pp. 220–21; Paul Kennedy, "Dogger Bank, clash of the battle cruisers", *Warships and sea battles of World War I*, pp. 44–51. See also, Churchill, *The world crisis*, II: 118–44.
62. Herwig, *"Luxury" fleet*, p. 163.
63. The sinking remains controversial; some documents related to it are classified and the British government refuses to allow salvage operations. See Thomas A. Bailey and Paul B. Ryan, *The Lusitania disaster* (New York, 1975) and Colin Simpson, *The Lusitania* (Boston, 1972).
64. Herwig. *"Luxury" fleet*, pp. 164–5.
65. Richard P. Hallion, *Rise of fighter aircraft 1914–1918* (Annapolis, MD, 1984), pp. 8–13.
66. Lee Kennett, *The first air war, 1914–1918* (New York, 1991), pp. 94 and 170.
67. *Ibid.*, pp. 50 and 219.
68. A sortie is defined as one flight by one aircraft.
69. Richard R. Muller, "Zeppelins", *European Powers*, pp. 766–7.
70. Kennett, *The first air war*, p. 49.
71. *Ibid.*, pp. 48–53.
72. Earl H. Tilford, Jr., "Air warfare, strategic bombing", *European Powers*, p. 14.
73. Raymond H. Fredette, *The sky on fire. The first Battle of Britain 1917–1918 and the birth of the Royal Air Force* (New York, 1976), pp. 157, 221–6.
74. R. D. Layman, *Naval aviation in the First World War. Its impact and influence* (Annapolis, MD, 1996).
75. Stanley Sandler, "Warships, aircraft carriers", *European Powers*, pp. 731–2.

Chapter Four

1. Griffiths, *The Great War*, p. 69.
2. Memorandum from Falkenhayn to Kaiser Wilhelm II, 25 December 1915, Falkenhayn, *German General Staff*, pp. 239–50.
3. The standard work on the battle is Alistair Horne, *The price of glory. Verdun, 1916* (New York, 1962). For an excellent memoir by a German participant see William Hermanns, *The holocaust. From a survivor of Verdun* (New York, 1972).
4. *Verdun. Vision and comprehension. The battlefield and its surroundings* (Drancy, France, 1990), pp. 2 and 32.
5. Barnett, *The Great War*, p. 68. Driant had written several books, including one entitled *La guerre de forteresse*. Horne believes that his circumvention of the military chain of command

236

would have led to his court-martial (Joffre was livid), had he not been killed. Horne, *The price of glory*, pp. 51–3.

6. *Ibid.*, pp. 36, 39–40, and 55–7.
7. *Verdun, vision and comprehension*, p. 50; Griffiths, *The Great War*, p. 70.
8. Griffiths, *The Great War*, p. 70.
9. Horne, *The price of glory*, p. 81.
10. *Verdun, vision and comprehension*, pp. 50 and 60.
11. Horne, *The price of glory*, pp. 125 and 149.
12. Stephen Ryan, *Pétain the soldier* (New York, 1969), pp. 86–7.
13. Simkins, *World War I*, p. 103.
14. Spencer C. Tucker, "Verdun, battle of", *European Powers*, pp. 714–18.
15. Horne, *The price of glory*, pp. 327–8.
16. Display in the military museum at Verdun.
17. Simkins, *World War*, p. 102.
18. Norman Stone concluded that Falkenhayn's strategy of attrition warfare offered Germany a better chance of victory. Stone, *The Eastern Front, 1914–1917*, pp. 11–12.
19. On the Somme see Lyn Macdonald, *Somme* (London, 1983) and Martin Middlebrook, *First day on the Somme* (New York, 1972).
20. Simkins, *World War I*, p. 108.
21. Tim Travers, "The Somme: the reason why", *MHQ: The Quarterly Journal of Military History* (vol. VII, no. 4; Summer 1995): 66–7. On planning for the attack see Prior and Wilson, *Command on the Western Front*, pp. 137–70.
22. Denis Winter, *Haig's command. A reassessment* (New York, 1991), pp. 55–6; Barnett, *The Great War*, pp. 73 and 75.
23. David T. Zabecki, "Somme, Battle of", *European Powers*, p. 649.
24. Simkins, *World War I*, p. 105; Prior and Wilson, *Command on the Western Front*, pp. 137–8.
25. Peter Simkins, *Kitchener's army. The raising of the new armies, 1914–16* (Manchester, 1988), pp. 79–100.
26. Simkins, *World War I*, p. 105; Prior and Wilson, *Command on the Western Front*, pp. 137–8.
27. Middlebrook, *First day on the Somme*, pp. 100–2.
28. *Ibid.*, pp. 103–5.
29. *Ibid.*, pp. 244–6.
30. Winter, *Haig's command*, pp. 62–3.
31. Zabecki, "Somme, battle of", *European Powers*, pp. 649–50; Middlebrook, *First day on the Somme*, dust jacket and pp. 103 and 244–5.
32. Prior and Wilson, *Command on the Western Front*, pp. 196–226.
33. *Ibid.*
34. For a short introduction to the subject see Kenneth Macksey, *The tank pioneers* (New York, 1981).
35. Robert Cowley, "The Somme: the last 140 Days", *MHQ: The Quarterly Journal of Military History* (vol. VII: no. 4, Summer 1995): 81; Churchill, *The world crisis*, III: 185–7; A. J. Smithers, *Cambrai. The first great tank battle 1917* (London, 1992), pp. 37–53.
36. Quoted in Griffiths, *The Great War*, p. 115.
37. John F. Votaw, "Tanks", *European Powers*, pp. 684–5; Smithers, *Cambrai*, pp. 49–50; Prior and Wilson, *Command on the Western Front*, pp. 228–9.
38. Churchill, *The world crisis*, III: 186.

39. Barnett, *The Great War*, p. 84.
40. Johnson, *Breakthrough!*, pp. 170–73.
41. Gray, *Chronicle of the First World War*, II, 297.
42. Zabecki, "Somme, battle of", *European Powers*, pp. 650–51.
43. Eugene L. Rasor, "Jutland, battle of", *European Powers*, p. 390.
44. Peter Kemp, "Prelude to Jutland", *Warships & sea battles of World War I*, pp. 73–4.
45. Churchill, *The world crisis*, II: 124.
46. Commander John Irving, *The smoke screen of Jutland* (New York, 1967), p. 143.
47. Churchill, *The world crisis*, II: 106.
48. Rasor, "Jutland, battle of", *European Powers*, pp. 390–93.
49. James J. Sadkovich, "Isonzo, battles of, nos. 5–9", *European Powers*, p. 368.
50. Griffiths, *The Great War*, p. 73.
51. James J. Sadkovich, "Trentino offensive", *European Powers*, pp. 695–6.
52. Sadkovich, "Isonzo, battles of, nos. 5–9", *European Powers*, pp. 368–70.
53. Winston Churchill, *The unknown war* (New York, 1931), p. 360.
54. Ulrich Trumpener, "Naroch, Lake, battle of", *European Powers*, p. 501.
55. Brusilov, *A soldier's note-book*, pp. 213–18.
56. Gray, *Chronicle of the First World War I*, I: 287.
57. Bohon, "Brusilov Offensive", *European Powers*, pp. 145–7; Brusilov, *A soldier's note-book*, pp. 218–43.
58. Brusilov, *A Soldier's Note-Book*, pp. 243–9.
59. Bohon, "Brusilov offensive", *European Powers*, pp. 145–7; Brusilov, *A soldier's note-book*, pp. 218–43; 254–75.
60. Walther Hubatsch, *Germany and the Central Powers in the World War, 1914–1918* (Lawrence, KS, 1963), p. 74; Carl O. Schuster, "Romania", *European Powers*, p. 600.
61. *Ibid.*, pp. 600–2; Ulrich Trumpener, "Romanian campaign, 1916", *European Powers*, pp. 602–3; Justin D. Murphy, "Bucharest, treaty of", *Ibid.*, pp. 147–9.
62. Charles H. Bogart, "Greece", *European Powers*, pp. 320–21; Haythornthwaite, *The World War One source book*, pp. 237–41.

Chapter Five

1. For a reappraisal of Asquith see George H. Cassar, *Asquith as war leader* (London, 1994).
2. Barnett, *The Great War*, p. 101; Simkins, *World War I*, p. 135. See also David French, *The strategy of the Lloyd Gerorge coalition, 1916–1918* (London, 1995).
3. David L. Longfellow, "Nivelle, Robert", *European Powers*, pp. 514–15.
4. B. H. Liddell Hart, *Foch. The man of Orleans* (Boston, 1932), p. 237.
5. Griffiths, *The Great War*, pp. 116–19; Simkins, *World War I*, pp. 135–7. Haig's diary suggests he was not displeased with the outcome of the conference. Winter, *Haig's command*, p. 83.
6. David L. Longfellow, "Nivelle (Chemin des dames) offensive", *European Powers*, p. 512.
7. Ludendorff, *My war memories, 1914–1918* (2 vols.; London, 1919), II, 3–11; Steven D. Fisher, "ALBERICH, Operation of Siegfried Line", *European Powers*, pp. 32–3; Simkins, *World War I*, pp. 147–8.
8. Longfellow, "Nivelle offensive", *European Powers*, pp. 512–13.

9. Simkins, *World War I*, pp. 144–6.
10. Gray, *Chronicle of the First World War*, II, 36; Spencer C. Tucker, "Vimy Ridge, battle of", *European Powers*, pp. 725–6.
11. Asprey, *The German high command at war*, p. 309.
12. Tucker, "Vimy Ridge", *European Powers*, pp. 725–6.
13. John F. Votaw, "Tanks", *European Powers*, p. 685.
14. Longfellow, "Nivelle offensive", *European Powers*, pp. 513–14; Simkins, *World War I*, pp. 149–52.
15. Gray, *Chronicle of the First World War*, II: 40. For the mutinies see Richard Watt, *Dare call it treason* (New York, 1963).
16. Simkins, *World War I*, p. 161. This has also been described as "Squat, do little, and keep the losses small." Gordon Wright, *France in modern times. 1760 to the present* (Chicago: Rand McNally, 1960), p. 398.
17. Watt, *Dare call it treason*, pp. 241–5; Ryan, *Pétain the soldier*, p. 140.
18. Wright, *France in modern times*, p. 399.
19. See Arthur S. Link, *Woodrow Wilson and the progressive era, 1910–1917* (New York, 1954).
20. Herwig, *"Luxury" fleet*, p. 197.
21. So called because many of them sailed from Queenstown, Ireland. During the war Great Britain employed 221 Q-ships, and from November 1914 through September 1917 they fought 70 U-boat engagements and sank 13, or nine per cent of the total of 145 U-boats sunk during the war. See Randall Metscher, "Q-Ships", *European Powers*. The best recent full-length study is Carson I. A. Ritchie, *Q-ships* (Lavenham, 1985).
22. See Barbara W. Tuchman, *The Zimmermann telegram* (New York, 1958).
23. For the expedition see Frank E. Vandiver, *Black Jack. The life and times of John J. Pershing* (College Station, TX, 1977), II: 595–668.
24. Thomas A. Bailey, *A diplomatic history of the American people* (New York, 1958), p. 583.
25. Barnett, *The Great War*, p. 112.
26. The best short account of the United States in the war is Robert H. Ferrell, *Woodrow Wilson & World War I, 1917–1921* (New York, 1985).
27. Samuel Eliot Morison, *The Oxford history of the American people* (New York, 1965), pp. 862–4.
28. See John J. Pershing, *My experiences in the World War* (2 vols.; New York, 1931) and Vandiver, *Black Jack*.
29. Simkins, *World War I*, p. 171.
30. Morison, *Oxford history of the American people*, p. 866; Alexander Rudhart, *Twentieth century Europe* (Philadelphia, 1975), p. 31.
31. Samuel Flagg Bemis, *A diplomatic history of the United States* (New York, 1965), p. 614.
32. Herwig, *"Luxury" fleet*, p. 220.
33. Churchill, *The world crisis*. IV: p. 78.
34. Elizabeth D. Schafer, "Asdic", *European Powers*, p. 81.
35. Morison, *Oxford history of the American people*, p. 862; Paul G. Halpern, "Convoy system, naval", *European Powers*, pp. 197–9.
36. Halpern, *A naval history of World War I*, pp. 348–50.
37. *Ibid.*, pp. 162–5. The definitive account of naval warfare in the Mediterranean is Paul G. Halpern, *The naval war in the Mediterranean, 1914–1918* (Annapolis, MD, 1987).
38. Halpern, *A naval history of World War I*, pp. 376–9.
39. Konrad H. Jarausch, *The enigmatic chancellor. Bethmann Hollweg and the hubris of Imperial*

Germany (New Haven, CT, 1973), pp. 348–78.

40. Andrew A. Wiest, *Passchendaele and the Royal Navy* (Westport, CT, 1995), pp. 75–9; Wiest argues that the Royal Navy must share blame with Haig for the Passchendaele campaign because it had a prominent role in the planning and prosecutiön. *Ibid.*, p. xxiii.

41. Barnett, *The Great War*, p. 118.

42. Philip Warner, *Passchendaele. The tragic victory of 1917* (London, 1987), pp. 33–4.

43. Van Micahel Leslie, "Messines, battle of", *European Powers*, pp. 478–9. See also Alexander Barrie, *War underground. The tunnellers of the Great War* (London, 1988).

44. Simkins, *World War I*, pp. 163–5; James J. Bloom, "Passchendaele", *European Powers*, p. 546.

45. Bloom, "Passchendaele", *European Powers*, pp. 546–7.

46. Simkins, *World War I*, p. 166.

47. A useful and poignant memoir is Edwin Campion Vaughan, *Some desperate glory. The World War I diary of a British officer, 1917* (New York, 1988).

48. Gray, *Chronicle of the First World War*, II: 68.

49. Bloom, "Passchendaele", *European Powers*, p. 548; Simkins, *World War I*, pp. 166–8.

50. Lyn Macdonald, *They called it Passchendaele* (New York, 1989), p. 233.

51. Bloom, "Passchendaele", *European Powers*, p. 548.

52. Barnett, *The Great War*, pp. 132–4.

53. On the battle see Smithers, *Cambrai*.

54. *Ibid.*, p. 71.

55. Philip J. Green, "Cambrai, battle of", *European Powers*, p. 158.

56. Anthony John Trythall, *"Boney" Fuller: Soldier, strategist, and writer, 1878–1966* (Rutgers, NJ, 1977), p. 56.

57. Green, "Cambrai, battle of", *European Powers*, pp. 158–9.

58. It is untrue that at Flesquières one German defender knocked out up to 16 tanks with a single field gun. Smithers, *Cambrai*, pp. 119–21 and 124.

59. Barnett, *The Great War*, p. 135.

60. Griffiths, *The Great War*, p. 125.

61. See James J. Sadkovich, "Isonzo, battles of, nos. 10 and 11", *European Powers*, pp. 370–2.

62. The standard works are: Cyril Falls, *The battle of Caporetto* (Philadelphia, 1966); and Ronald Seth, *Caporetto: The scapegoat battle* (New York, 1965).

63. A misnomer. Actually one of the first to propose abandoning linear tactics was French Captain André Laffaraque who wrote a pamphlet on the subject in 1915. They should more properly be called "infiltration tactics" or "storm troop tactics". See Zabecki, *Steel wind*, p. 23 and Bruce I. Gudmundsson, *Stormtroop tactics. Innovation in the German Army, 1914–1918* (Westport, CT, 1995).

64. See Erwin Rommel, *Infantry attacks*. Trans. G. E. Kidde (Washington, 1944), pp. 168–207. Also Gudmundsson, *Stormtroop tactics*.

65. James J. Sadkovich, "Caporetto", *European Powers*, pp. 166–8.

66. Mario Caracciolo, *L'Italia nella guerra mondiale* (Roma, 1935).

67. Sadkovich, "Caporetto", *European Powers*, pp. 166 and 169.

68. John W. Bohon, "Kerensky, Aleksandr", *European Powers*, p. 357; and Tom Cagley, "Kerensky Offensive", *Ibid.*, p. 401.

69. John W. Bohon, "Russia, home front and revolutions of 1917", *European Powers*, p. 617.

70. Bohon, "Kerensky, Aleksandr", *European Powers*, p. 399.

71. Michael Pearson, *The sealed train. Lenin's eight-month journey from exile to power* (New York, 1975), pp. 286–7. See also Edmund Wilson, *To the Finland Station* (New York, 1960).

72. Cagley, "Kerensky offensive", *European Powers*, p. 400.

73. Cagley, "Kerensky offensive", *European Powers*, p. 401; Brusilov, *A soldier's note-book*, p. 310.

74. Cagley, "Kerensky offensive", *European Powers*, p. 401.

75. For more on this innovative artillerist see David Zabecki, *Steel wind*.

76. Spencer C. Tucker, "East Galicia, German counteroffensive", *European Powers*, p. 228.

77. Bohon, "Kerensky, Aleksandr", *European Powers*, pp. 399–400.

78. Hoffmann, *The War of lost opportunities*, pp. 188–91.

79. See David T. Zabecki, "Riga, battle of", *European Powers*, pp. 597–9.

80. Griffiths, *The Great War*, pp. 108–9.

81. Bohon, "Kerensky, Aleksandr", *European Powers*, p. 400. On Kornilov see same author, "Kornilov, Lavr", *Ibid.*, pp. 408–9.

82. Bohon, "Russia, home front and revolutions of 1917", *European Powers*, pp. 617–8.

83. Barnett, *The Great War*, p. 164.

84. George B. Leontaritis, *Greece and the First World War: From neutrality to intervention, 1917–1918* (New York, 1990), pp. 5–79.

Chapter Six

1. George F. Kennan, *Russia leaves the war* (New York, 1967), p. 322.

2. See John W. Wheeler-Bennett, *Brest-Litovsk: the forgotten peace, March 1918* (London, 1938).

3. The vote was 7 to 6.

4. Wheeler-Bennett, *Brest-Litovski*, p. xii.

5. John W. Bohon, "Brest-Litovsk, treaty of", *European Powers*, pp. 140–2.

6. J. W. Wheeler-Bennett, *Hindenburg, the wooden titan* (London, 1967), p. 132. Figures on population loss vary. John W. Bohon cites 63 million. See Bohon, "Brest-Litovsk, Treaty of", *European Powers*, pp. 140–42. On the treaty see also J. W. Wheeler-Bennett, *Brest-Litovsk*, pp. 270–71, 273, 392–408.

7. This view is held by most German historians. See Fischer, *World power or decline*, p. 91; Hajo Holborn, *A history of modern Germany, 1840–1945* (New York, 1969), pp. 490–4.

8. Alexander Rudhart, *Twentieth century Europe* (Philadelphia, 1975), p. 107.

9. Fischer, *Germany's aims in the First World War*, p. 506.

10. Wheeler-Bennett, *Brest-Litovsk*, p. 363.

11. Justin Murphy, "Bucharest, treaty of", *European Powers*, pp. 147–9.

12. Bemis, *A diplomatic history of the United States*, pp. 625–7.

13. Fischer, *Germany's aims in the First World War*, p. 608. For OHL's spring 1918 war aims see pp. 586–608.

14. Hermann von Kuhl, *Genesis. Execution and collapse of the German offensive in 1918*, trans. Army War College (2 vols, Washington, DC, 1933), II, 1; Erich Ludendorff, *Ludendorff's own story* (2 vols; New York, 1919), II: 158–63. David T. Zabecki, "Ludendorff offensives", *European Powers*, pp. 442–3.

15. Wheeler-Bennett, *Hindenburg*, p. 135.

16. Asprey, *The German high command at war*, p. 349; Barnett, *Great War*, p. 147.

17. Griffiths, *The Great War*, p. 132.
18. Simkins, *World War I*, p. 183.
19. Griffiths, *The Great War*, pp. 132–7.
20. *Ibid.*, p. 137.
21. Hubert Gough, *The Fifth Army* (London, 1931), pp. 222–3; Ryan, *Pétain the soldier*, p. 158; Simkins, *World War I*, pp. 184–5.
22. Zabecki, "Ludendorff offensive", *European Powers*, p. 443.
23. Barnett, *The Great War*, p. 151. Simkins, *World War I*, pp. 188–9.
24. See E. Ray Lewis, "Paris gun", *European Powers*, pp. 539–40.
25. Robert Blake (ed.), *The private papers of Douglas Haig, 1914–1919* (London, 1952), pp. 296–7; Warner, *Haig's command*, pp. 183–4; Griffiths, *The Great War*, p. 140.
26. Georges Clemenceau, *Grandeur and misery of victory* (London, 1930), p. 32.
27. Wright, *France in modern times*, p. 400.
28. Griffiths, *The Great War*, p. 140.
29. Simkins, *World War I*, p. 190.
30. Morison, *Oxford history of the American people*, p. 866.
31. Zabecki, "Ludendorff offensive", *European Powers*, p. 455; Rod Paschall, *The defeat of Imperial Germany, 1917–1918* (Chapel Hill, NC, 1989), p. 147.
32. Simkins, *World War I*, p. 190; Griffiths, *The Great War*, p. 141.
33. Paschall, *The defeat of Imperial Germany*, pp. 147–8.
34. Gilbert, *The First World War*, p. 414.
35. Macksey, *The tank pioneers*, p. 34; Simkins, *World War I*, p. 193.
36. Simkins, *World War I*, p. 194.
37. See Paul G. Halpern, *A naval history of World War I*, pp. 411–16. See also Barrie Pitt, *Zeebrugge: St. George's Day, 1918* (London, 1958).
38. Morison, *The Oxford history of the American people*, p. 871.
39. Barnett, *The Great War*, p. 153.
40. Zabecki, "Ludendorff offensive", *European Powers*, p. 445.
41. Jere Clemens King, *Generals and politicians: conflict between France's high command, parliament and government, 1914–1918* (Berkeley CA, 1951), p. 225; Liddell Hart, *The real war*, pp. 412–14.
42. Simkins, *World War I*, p. 197; Zabecki, "Ludendorff Offensive", *European Powers*, pp. 445–6; Zabecki, *Steel wind*, p. 68.
43. Griffiths, *The Great War*, pp. 142–3; Simkins, *World War I*, p. 198; Edward M. Coffman, *The War to end all wars: the American military experience in World War I* (New York, 1968), pp. 156–7.
44. Simkins, *World War I*, p. 197.
45. Griffiths, *The Great War*, pp. 150–2.
46. Asprey, *The German high command at war*, pp. 439–40.
47. Barnett, *The Great War*, p. 158.
48. Gray, *Chronicle of the First World War*, II: 284.
49. On planning for this see Prior and Wilson, *Command on the Western Front*, pp. 301–15.
50. Quoted in D. J. Goodspeed, *Ludendorff. Genius of World War I* (Boston, 1966), p. 259.
51. Gordon Brook-Shepherd, *November 1918* (Boston, 1918), p. 66.
52. Vandiver, *Black Jack*, II: 936–40.
53. James H. Hallas, *Squandered victory. The American First Army at St. Mihiel* (Westport, CT, 1995), pp. 261–4.

NOTES

54. Ulrich Trumpener, "Vittorio Veneto campaign", *European Powers*, pp. 726–7.
55. Richard C. Hall, "Bulgaria", *European Powers*, pp. 150–1; R. Ernest Dupuy and Trevor N. Dupuy, *The Harper encyclopedia of military history* (New York, 1993), p. 1079.
56. Kitchen, "Civil–military relations in Germany during the First World War", R. J. Q. Adams (ed.), *The Great War, 1914–18. Essays on the military, political and social history of the First World War* (College Station, TX, 1990), p. 59.
57. Goodspeed, *Ludendorff*, pp. 271–2.
58. Vandiver, *Black Jack*, II: 985; Ferrell, *Woodrow Wilson and World War I*, pp. 132–3.
59. Stanley Weintraub, *A stillness heard round the world. The end of the Great War: November 1918* (New York, 1985), p. 47.
60. *Ibid.*, pp. 152–7.
61. Charles Bracelen Flood, *Hitler, the path to power* (Boston, 1989), p. 35.
62. On the latter see Arthur Mendel, "On interpreting the fate of Imperial Russia", in Theofanis George Stavrou (ed.), *Russia under the last tsar* (Minneapolis, 1969).
63. William L. Langer, *The encyclopedia of world history* (New York, 1974), p. 976.

Chapter Seven

1. Alan F. Wilt, "Persian front", *European Powers*, p. 551.
2. Ekkehart B. Guth & Thomas G. Oakes, "Ottoman Empire, army", *European Powers*, pp. 526–7.
3. Griffiths, *The Great War*, p. 80.
4. Montecue J. Lowry, "Caucasian front", *European Powers*, p. 174.
5. *Ibid*; Griffiths, *Great War*, p. 81; *The Harper encyclopedia of military history*, p. 1047.
6. Gilbert, *Atlas of World War I*, p. 41.
7. Lowry, "Caucasian front", *European Powers*, pp. 174–5; Wilt, Persian front", *Ibid.*, p. 552; Langer, *Encyclopedia of world history*, p. 966.
8. Lowry, "Caucasus front', *European Powers*, p. 175.
9. Wilt, "Persian front", *European Powers*, p. 552; A. J. Barker, *The bastard war. The Mesopotamian campaign of 1914–1918* (New York, 1967), pp. 134–45; Langer, *An encyclopedia of world history*, p. 966.
10. Lowry, "Caucasus front", *European Powers*, p. 175.
11. Wilt, "Persian front", *European Powers*, pp. 552–3.
12. Jack McCallum, "Sinai Campaign", *European Powers*, pp. 643–4; also Archibald P. Wavell, *The Palestine campaigns* (London, 1931), pp. 12–31.
13. Jan Karl Tannenbaum, "Sykes–Picot agreement", *European Powers*, pp. 677–8.
14. David L. Bullock, "Senussi and Sultan of Darfur rebellions", *European Powers*, pp. 636–7; Jack McCallum, "Sinai Campaign", *Ibid.*, p. 643.
15. Wavell, *The Palestine campaigns*, pp. 61–2.
16. *Ibid.*, pp. 53–6. For Lawrence see B. H. Liddell Hart, *Lawrence in Arabia and after* (London, 1934).
17. Moberly, *Mesopotamia*, III, pp. 259–61.
18. David L. Bullock, "Palestine and Syria", *European Powers*, pp. 536–7. See same author, *Allenby's War: The Palestine–Arabian campaign, 1916–1918* (London, 1988). Also Wavell, *The Palestine campaigns*, pp. 59–90.

19. Bullock, "Palestine and Syria", *European Powers*, p. 537.
20. Wavell, *The Palestine campaigns*, pp. 98–141.
21. *Ibid.*, pp. 108–10; Bullock, "Palestine and Syria", *European Powers*, p. 537.
22. Wavell, *The Palestinian campaigns*, pp. 141–72; Bullock, "Palestine and Syria", *European Powers*, p. 537.
23. Wavell, *The Palestine campaigns*, pp. 173–89.
24. Bullock, "Palestine and Syria", p. 538; Wavell, *The Palestine campaigns*, pp. 192–213.
25. Bullock, "Palestine and Syria", p. 538; Wavell, *The Palestine campaigns*, pp. 192–213.
26. Barker, *The bastard war*, pp. 76 and 81.
27. Alan F. Wilt, "Mesopotamia", *European Powers*, p. 476.
28. Barker, *The bastard war*, pp. 51–6, 59, 65–9, 77–90.
29. F. J. Moberly, *The campaign in Mesopotamia, 1914–1917* (4 vols., London, 1923–1927), II: 28.
30. Barker, *The bastard war*, pp. 77, 93–9, and 119.
31. *Ibid.*, pp. 101–11; and Wilt, "Mesopotamia", *European Powers*, p. 478.
32. Barker, *The bastard war*, pp. 112–260; Wilt, "Mesopotamia", *European Powers*, p. 477.
33. Barker, *The bastard war*, pp. 262–75.
34. Wilt, "Mesopotamia", p. 477; Barker, *The bastard war*, pp. 276 332.
35. Wilt, "Mesopotamia", *European Powers*, pp. 477–8; Barker, *The bastard war*, pp. 358–98.
36. The standard work on the subject is Byron Farwell, *The Great War in Africa, 1914–1918* (New York, 1986). See also Karl P. Magyar, "Africa", *European Powers*, pp. 5–9.
37. Farwell, *The Great War in Africa*, pp. 23–5 and 34–5.
38. Quoted in *Ibid.*, p. 101.
39. *Ibid.*, pp. 338–41.
40. *Ibid.*, pp. 21–30.
41. *Ibid.*, pp. 31–71.
42. *Ibid.*, pp. 72–84.
43. *Ibid.*, pp. 97–103.
44. *Ibid.*, pp. 105–26.
45. *Ibid.*, pp. 127–60.
46. *Ibid.*, pp. 161–357.
47. Elizabeth D. Schafer, "South Pacific", *European Powers*, pp. 655–6. See also Edmund Dane, *British campaigns in Africa and the Pacific, 1914–1918* (London, 1919).
48. See David Zabecki, "Qingdao, siege of", *European Powers*, pp. 579–82.
49. See Thomas E. La Fargue, *China and the World War* (Stanford, CA, 1937).

Chapter Eight

1. For an excellent short synthesis see Jean-Jacques Becker, *The Great War and the French people* (Oxford, 1985). It provides a wealth of information on popular attitudes in France during the war. For a general work see John Williams, *The other battleground. The home fronts: Britain, France and Germany, 1914–1918* (Chicago, 1972).
2. Robert O. Paxton, *Europe in the 20th century* (2nd edn; Fort Worth, TX, 1991), p. 103.
3. *Ibid.*

4. J. M. Winter, *The experience of World War I* (New York, 1989), p. 47.
5. George Cassar concludes that Asquith faced more difficult problems than his successor, that he had resolved the big problems of munitions supply and manpower, and that "all the strategic elements that would produce victory, save for the convoy system, were in place when he passed the mantle of leadership to Lloyd George". George Cassar, *Asquith as war leader*, p. 236.
6. Griffiths, *The Great War*, pp. 116–18.
7. Morison, *The Oxford history of the American people*, p. 868. See also, Ferrell, *Woodrow Wilson & World War I*.
8. James J. Sadkovich, "Italy, home front", *European Powers*, pp. 374–5; H. James Burgwyn, *The legend of the mutilated victory. Italy, the Great War, and the Paris Peace Conference, 1915–1919* (Westport, CT, 1993), p. 29.
9. For an excellent short discussion of this see Kitchen, "Civil–military relations in Germany during the First World War", *The Great War, 1914–18*, pp. 39–64.
10. *Ibid.*, pp. 39–40, 44. See also Karl-Heinz Janssen, *Der Kanzler und der General. Die Führungskrise um Bethmann-Hollweg und Falkenhayn, 1914–1916* (Göttingen, 1967).
11. *Ibid.*, p. 61.
12. Gray, *Chronicle of the First World War*, II, 288. Norman Stone puts the Russian mobilization at 14 million. Stone, *Eastern Front*, pp. 213–14.
13. Stone, *Eastern Front*, pp. 295–7.
14. W. Bruce Lincoln, *The Romanovs* (New York, 1981), p. 722.
15. *Ibid.*, pp. 695–725; John W. Bohon, "Russia, home front and revolutions of 1917", *European Powers*, pp. 616–17. Also Nicholas V. Riasanovsky, *A History of Russia* (New York, 1977), pp. 505–7.
16. Stone, *Eastern Front*, pp. 125–7.
17. Arthur J. May, *The passing of the Hapsburg Monarchy, 1914–1918* (2 vols; Philadelphia, 1966), II: 701.
18. Stone, *Eastern Front*, pp. 123–4; Gordon Brook-Shepherd, *The last Habsburg* (New York, 1968), p. 161.
19. Z. A. B. Zeman, *The break-up of the Habsburg Empire 1914–1918* (London, 1961), p. 66.
20. Brook-Shepherd, *The last Habsburg*, pp. 161–2.
21. Paxton, *Europe in the 20th century*, p. 98; Gray, *Chronicle of the First World War*, II, 288.
22. Suzanne Hayes Fisher, "Germany, home front", *European Powers*, p. 298.
23. Glenn R. Sharfman, "Censorship", *European Powers*, pp. 178–80.
24. Winter, *The experience of World War I*, p. 40.
25. Paxton, *20th century Europe*, p. 101.
26. Gray, *Chronicle of the First World War*, II, 290, 296–7.
27. See David French, *The strategy of the Lloyd George coalition, 1916–1918* (Oxford, 1995).
28. Paxton, *Europe in the 20th century*, p. 102.
29. Winter, *The experience of World War I*, p. 54.
30. Gray, *Chronicle of the First World War*, II, 290, 296–7.
31. Paxton, *Europe in the 20th century*, p. 102.
32. Bernard A. Cook, "France, home front", *European Powers*, pp. 263–5.
33. Becker, *The Great War and the French people*, p. 325.
34. Paxton, *Europe in the 20th century*, p. 101.
35. James J. Sadkovich, "Italy, home front", *European Powers*, p. 376.
36. See Richard Bessel, *Germany after the First World War* (Oxford, 1993), pp. 78, 144–5, and

179; also Leo Grebler and Wilhelm Winkler, *The cost of the World War to Germany and to Austria-Hungary* (New Haven, CT, 1940), pp. 38–42. Grebler and Winkler estimate loss of potential life through the declining birth rate in Germany at about 3,000,000 people and in Austria-Hungary at more than 1,600,000. *Ibid.*, pp. 78 and 179.

37. Kitchen, "Civil-military relations in Germany during the First World War", *The Great War, 1914–18*, pp. 46–8.
38. Winter, *The Experience of World War I*, pp. 52–5.
39. Alexander Rudhart, *Twentieth century Europe* (Philadelphia, 1975), p. 30.
40. Gerald D. Feldman, *Army, industry, and labor in Germany, 1914–1918* (Princeton, NJ, 1966), p. 459.
41. Suzanne Hayes Fisher, "Germany, home front", *European Powers*, p. 299. The Social Democrats did split on the issue, however.
42. Gray, *Chronicle of the First World War*, II, 288; Paxton, *Europe in the 20th century*, pp. 108–9.
43. Cook, "France, home front", *European Powers*, p. 264.
44. Sadkovich, "Italy, home front", *European Powers*, p. 376.
45. Brenda Taylor, "Women in the war", *European Powers*, p. 752; Arthur Marwick, *The deluge. British society and the First World War* (Boston, 1966), pp. 88–94; Also Barnett, *The Great War*, pp. 141–2.
46. Taylor, "Women in the war", *European Powers*, p. 752.
47. Sadkovich, "Italy, home front", *European Powers*, p. 375.
48. Taylor, "Women in the war", *European Powers*, p. 754.
49. Paxton, *Europe in the 20th century*, p. 111.
50. William J. Duiker, *The rise of nationalism in Vietnam, 1900–1941* (Ithaca, NY, 1976), p. 196.

Chapter Nine

1. A good balanced history of the conference is Ferdinand Czernin, *Versailles 1919. The forces, events and personalities that shaped the treaty* (New York, 1964). For vignettes of the process see Harold Nicolson, *Peacemaking 1919* (New York, 1939) and Charles L. Mee, Jr., *The end of order, Versailles 1919* (New York, 1980). For the French point of view, see M. Tardieu, *The truth about the treaty*. See also Churchill, *The world crisis*, vol. 5 and Arno J. Mayer, *Politics and diplomacy of peacemaking: containment and counterrevolution at Versailles, 1918–1919* (New York, 1967).
2. Blaine T. Browne, "Japan", *European Powers*, p. 385.
3. Carl H. Pegg, *Contemporary Europe in world focus* (New York, 1956), p. 6.
4. *Ibid.*, pp. 7–8.
5. Mee, *The end of order*, p. 66.
6. Pegg, *Contemporary Europe*, p. 8.
7. Glenn R. Sharfman, "Orlando, Vittorio E.", *European Powers*, pp. 522–3.
8. Pegg, *Contemporary Europe*, pp. 10–13 and 15.
9. Clemenceau, *Grandeur and misery of victory*, p. 192.
10. Pegg, *Contemporary Europe*, pp. 14–15.
11. Sharfman, "Orlando", *European Powers*, pp. 522–3. On Italy at the conference see

Burgwyn, *The legend of the mutilated victory*, pp. 245–309.

12. Pegg, *Contemporary Europe*, pp. 17–18.
13. See Louis L. Gerson, *Woodrow Wilson and the rebirth of Poland, 1914–1920* (New Haven, CT, 1953).
14. *Ibid.*, pp. 18–21.
15. *Ibid.*, pp. 20–24.
16. See Bernard Baruch, *The making of the reparation and economic sections of the treaty* (New York, 1920).
17. Ferrell, *Woodrow Wilson & World War I*, p. 143.
18. John David Hicks, *Republican ascendancy, 1921–1933* (New York, 1960), p. 136.
19. Pegg, *Contemporary Europe*, pp. 25–6.
20. See G. Zay Wood, *The Shantung question. A study in diplomacy and world politics* (New York, 1922).
21. For a reappraisal see Bruce A. Elleman, "Did Woodrow Wilson really betray China at Versailles?" *The American Asian Review*, vol. XIII, no. 1 (Spring 1995): 101–28.
22. La Fargue, *China and the World War*, pp. 173–237.
23. Arnold Wolfers, *Britain and France between two wars. Conflicting strategies of peace since Versailles* (Hamden, CT, 1963), pp. 57–60.
24. Wright, *Modern France*, p. 407.

Select bibliography

(All titles listed once only, in most appropriate area)

Causes of the War and its Outbreak

Albertini, Luigi. *The origins of the war of 1914* [3 vols] (Oxford, 1952).

Berghahn, Volker R. *Germany and the approach of war in 1914* (New York, 1973).

Bestuzhev, I. V. Russian foreign policy, February–June 1914. *Journal of Contemporary History* 1 (1966).

Bosworth, R. J. B. *Italy and the approach of the First World War* (New York, 1983).

Brook-Shepherd, Gordon. *Archduke of Sarajevo. The romance and tragedy of Franz Ferdinand of Austria* (Boston, 1984).

Cassels, Lavender. *The Archduke and the assassin: Sarajevo, June 28th 1914* (London, 1984).

Contamine, Henri. *La revanche, 1871–1914* (Paris, 1957).

Dedijer, Vladimir. *The road to Sarajevo* (New York, 1966).

Eubank, Keith. *Paul Cambon, master diplomatist* (Norman, OK, 1960).

Fay, Sidney B. *The origins of the World War after Sarajevo* [2 vols], 2nd edn rev. (New York, 1930).

Fischer, Fritz. *War of illusions, German policies from 1911 to 1914*. Translated by Marion Jackson (New York, 1975).

Geiss, Imanuel (ed.). *July 1914. The outbreak of the First World War: selected documents* (London, 1965).

Grey, Sir Edward. *Twenty-five years, 1892–1916* [2 vols] (New York, 1925).

Hayne, M. B. *The French Foreign Office and the origins of the First World War, 1898–1914* (Oxford, 1993).

Helmreich, Jonathan E. *Belgium and Europe: a study in small power diplomacy* (The Hague and Paris, 1976).

Herrmann, David G. *The arming of Europe and the making of the First World War* (Princeton, NJ, 1996).

Joll, James. *The origins of the First World War*, 2nd edn (London, 1992).

Keiger, John V. *France and the origins of the First World War* (New York: St. Martin's Press, 1983).

Kennan, George F. *The fateful alliance: France, Russia, and the coming of the First World War* (New York, 1984).

Kennedy, Paul M., ed. *The war plans of the Great Powers, 1880–1914* (London, 1979).

Lafore, Laurence. *The long fuse. An interpretation of the origins of World War I*, 2nd edn (Philadelphia, 1971).

Langdon, John W. *July 1914. The long debate, 1918–1990* (New York, 1991).

Lee, Dwight E. *Europe's crucial years: the diplomatic background of World War I, 1902–1914* (Hanover, NH, 1974).

Lieven, D. C. B. *Russia and the origins of the First World War* (New York, 1983).

Massie, Robert K. *Dreadnought. Britain, Germany, and the coming of the Great War* (New York, 1991).

Miller, Steven E., Sean M. Lynn-Jones, & Stephen Van Evera (eds). *Military strategy and the origins of the First World War* (Princeton, 1991).

Padfield, Peter. *The great naval race. Anglo-German naval rivalry, 1900–1914* (New York, 1974).

Porter, Charles W. *The career of Théophile Delcassé* (Philadelphia, PA, 1936).

Remak, Joachim. *Sarajevo: the story of a political murder* (New York, 1959).

Renouvin, Pierre. *La crise européenne et la Première Guerre Mondiale* (Paris, 1962).

Ritter, Gerhard. *The Schlieffen Plan: critique of a myth* (New York, 1958).

Steinberg, Jonathan. *Yesterday's deterrent: Tirpitz and the birth of the German battle fleet* (New York, 1966).

Steiner, Zara. *Britain and the origins of the First World War* (New York, 1977).

Stokes, Gale. The Serbian documents from 1914: a preview. *Journal of Modern History* 48 (1976).

Taylor, A. J. P. *War by time-table. How the First World War began* (New York, 1969).

Tuchman, Barbara W. *The Guns of August* (New York, 1962).

Tuchman, Barbara W. *The proud tower. A portrait of Europe before the War, 1890–1914* (New York, 1966).

Wilfong, W. Thomas: Rebuilding the Russian Army, 1905–1914: the question of a comprehensive plan for national defense (Ph.D. diss., Indiana University, 1977).

Williamson, Samuel R., Jr. *Austria-Hungary and the origins of the First World War* (New York, 1991).

Williamson, Samuel R., Jr. *The politics of grand strategy: Britain and France prepare for war, 1904–1914* (Cambridge, MA, 1969).

Wilson, Keith, ed. *Decisions for war, 1914* (New York, 1995).

Wilson, Keith. *The policy of the Entente* (Cambridge, 1985).

General Histories of the War

Baldwin, Hanson W. *World War I* (New York: Grove Press, 1962).

Barnett, Correlli. *The swordbearers: supreme command in the First World War* (New York, 1964).

Barnett, Correlli. *The Great War* (New York, 1980).

Churchill, Winston S. *The World Crisis*, [6 vols] (New York, 1923–1931).

Cruttwell, C. R. M. F. *A history of the Great War 1914–1918* (London, 1934).

Falls, Cyril. *The Great War* (New York, 1959).

Ferro, Marc. *The Great War, 1914–1918* (New York, 1973).

Gilbert, Martin. *The First World War. A complete history* (New York, 1994).

Liddell Hart, Basil H. *The real war, 1914–1918* (Boston, 1930).
Livesay, Anthony. *Great battles of World War I* (New York, 1989).
Marshall, S. L. A. *World War I* (New York, 1964).
Schmitt, Berdnadotte E. and Harold C. Vedeler. *The world in the crucible, 1914–1919* (New York, 1984).
Stokesbury, James L. *A short history of World War I* (New York, 1981).
Taylor, A. J. P. *A history of the First World War* (New York, 1966).
Winter, J. M. *The experience of World War I* (New York, 1989).

Austria-Hungary

Bardolff, C. von. *Soldat im alten Österreich* (Jena, 1938).
——. *Der Militär-Maria Theresien-Orden. Die Auszeichnungen im Weltkrieg. 1914–1918* (Vienna, 1944).
Bridge, F. R. *From Sadowa to Sarajevo: the foreign policy of Austria-Hungary, 1866–1918* (London, 1972).
Brook-Shepherd, Gordon. *The last Habsburg* (New York, 1968).
Conrad von Hötzendorf, Franz. *Aus meiner Dienstzeit* [5 vols] (Vienna, 1921–5).
Cornwall, Mark. *The last years of Austria-Hungary: essays in political and military history, 1908–1918* (Exter, UK, 1990).
Czernin, Ottokar. *In the World War* (London, 1919).
Deak, István. *Beyond nationalism: a social & political history of the Habsburg officer corps, 1848–1918* (Oxford, 1990).
Galántai, József. *Hungary in the First World War.* Translated by Éva Grusz and Judit Pokoly (Budapest, 1989).
Glaise-Horstenau, Edmund von. *The collapse of the Austro-Hungarian Empire* (London and Toronto, 1930).
Horthy, N. *Memoirs* (New York, 1957).
Károlyi, M. *Fighting the world* (London, 1925).
Kiszling, Rudolf. *Österreich-ungarns Anteil am ersten Weltkrieg* (Graz, 1958).
May, Arthur J. *The passing of the Hapsburg Monarchy, 1914–1918* [2 vols] (Philadephia, PA, 1966).
Michel, Bernard. *La chute de L'Empire Austro-Hongrois 1916–1918* (Paris, 1991).
Rauchensteiner, Manfried. *Der Tod des Doppeladlers: Österreich-Ungarn und der erste Weltkrieg* (Vienna, 1993).
Regele, O. *Feldmarschall Conrad* (Vienna, 1955).
Rothenberg, Gunther. *The army of Francis Joseph* (West Lafayette, IN, 1976).
Shanafelt, Gary. *The secret enemy: Austria-Hungary and the German Alliance, 1914–1918* (Boulder, CO, 1985).
Silberstein, Gerard E. *The troubled alliance: German-Austrian relations, 1914–1917* (Lexington, KY, 1970).
Sondhaus, Lawrence. *The naval policy of Austria-Hungary, 1867–1918. Navalism, industrial development, and the politics of dualism* (West Lafayette, IN, 1994).
Tunstall, Graydon A. *Planning for war against Russia and Serbia: Austro-Hungarian and German military strategies, 1871–1914* (Boulder, CO, 1993).
Valiani, Leo. *The end of Austria-Hungary* (London, 1973).

Vermes, Gabor. *István Tisza: The liberal vision and conservative statecraft of a Magyar nationalist* (Boulder, CO, 1985).
Zeman, Z. A. B. *The break-up of the Habsburg Empire 1914–1918* (London, 1961).

Belgium

Aaronson, Theo. *Defiant dynasty: the Coburgs of Belgium* (Indianapolis and New York, 1968).
Albert I. *Les Carnets de guerre* (Brussels, 1953).
Bronne, Carlo. *Albert Ier: Le Roi sans terre* (Paris, 1965).
Davignon, Henry. *Belgium and Germany: texts and documents* (Edinburgh and New York, 1915).
Fuehr, Alexander. *The neutrality of Belgium: a study of the Belgian case under its aspects in political history and international law* (New York and London, 1915).
Galet, Émile Joseph. *Albert, King of the Belgians, in the Great War* (Boston, 1931).
Pierenne, Henri. *La Belgique et la guerre mondiale* (New Haven, CT, 1928).
Thomas, Daniel H. *The guarantee of Belgian independence and neutrality in European diplomacy, 1830's–1930's* (Kingston, 1983).

Bulgaria

Bell, John D. *Peasants in power: Alexander Stamboliski and the Bulgarian National Union, 1899–1923* (Princeton, 1977).
Crampton, Richard J. *Bulgaria, 1878–1918: a history* (Boulder, CO, 1983).
Stoichev, Iran K. *Builders and military leaders of the Bulgarian army, 1879–1942* (Sofia, 1941).

France

Azan, Paul. *Franchet D'Espèrey* (Paris, 1949).
Bankwitz, Philip & Charles Farwell. *Maxime Weygand and civil–military relations in modern France* (Cambridge, MA, 1967).
Beaufre, General André. *La France de la Grande Guerre, 1914/1919* (Paris, 1971).
Becker, Jean-Jacques. *The Great War and the French People.* Translated by Arnold Pomerans (Oxford, 1985).
Brunn, Geoffrey. *Clemenceau* (Cambridge, MS, 1943).
Clemenceau, Georges. *Grandeur and misery of victory* (New York, 1930).
Fayolle, Marie-Émile. *Cahiers secrets de la Grande Guerre* (Paris, 1964).
Foch, Ferdinand. *The Memoirs of Marshal Foch* (London, 1931).
Franzius, Enno. *Caillaux: statesman of peace* (Stanford, CA, 1976).
Fridenson, Patrick (ed.). *The French home front, 1914–1918.* Translated by Bruce Little (Oxford, 1977).
Galliéni, Joseph. *Les Carnets de Galliéni* (Paris, 1932).
Galliéni, Joseph. *Mémoires: Defense de Paris* (Paris, 1920).
Griffiths, Richard, *Marshal Pétain* (London, 1970).
Hunter, T. M. *Marshal Foch: A study in leadership* (Ottawa, 1961).
Jackson, John Hampden. *Clemenceau and the Third Republic* (New York, 1948).

Joffre, Marshall Joseph. *The personal memoirs of Joffre* [2 vols] (New York, 1932).

King, Jere Clemens. *Foch versus Clemenceau: France and German dismemberment, 1918–1919* (Cambridge, MA, 1960).

King, Jere Clemens. *Generals and politicians: conflict between France's high command, parliament, and government, 1914–1918* (Berkeley, CA, 1951).

Lanrezac, Charles Louis Marie. *Le Plan de campagne français et le premier mois de la querre (2 août– 3 septembre, 1914)* (Paris, 1921).

Liddell Hart, Captain Basil. *Foch: man of Orleans* (London, 1931).

Lottman, Herbert R. *Pétain, hero or traitor* (New York, 1985).

Mangin, Charles. *Lettres de guerre, 1914–1918* (Paris, 1950).

Marshall-Cornwall, Sir James. *Foch as military commander* (London, 1972).

Pedroncini, Guy. *Les Mutineries de 1917* (Paris, 1967).

Pedroncini, Guy. *Pétain: général en chef, 1917–1918* (Paris, 1974).

Poincaré, Raymond. *Au service de la France – neuf années de souvenirs* [10 vols] (Paris, 1926–1933).

Ryan, Stephen. *Pétain the soldier* (New York, 1969).

Thomazi, A. *La Marine française dans la Grande Guerre (1914–1918)* [4 vols] (Paris, 1925–1929).

Varillon, Pierre. *Joffre* (Paris, 1956).

Watson, David R. *Georges Clemenceau: a political biography* (New York, 1974).

Watt, Richard. *Dare call it treason* (New York, 1963).

Weygand, Maxime. *Foch* (Paris, 1947).

Weygand, Maxime. *Mémoires* [3 vols] (Paris, 1950–1957).

Wright, Gordon. *Raymond Poincaré and the French Presidency* (New York, 1967).

Germany

Asprey, Robert B. *The German high command at war. Hindenburg and Ludendorff conduct World War I* (New York, 1991).

Baden, Prince Max von. *Erinnerungen und Dokumente* (Stuttgart, 1968).

Balfour, Michael. *The Kaiser and his times* (London, 1964).

Berglar, Peter. *Walther Rathenau: seine Zeit, sein Werk, seine Persönlichkeit* (Bremen, 1970).

Berlau, A. Joseph. *The German Social Democratic Party, 1914–1921* (New York, 1949).

Bernstorff, Johann Heinrich von. *Deutschland und Amerika: Erinnerungen aus dem fünfjährigen Kriege* (Berlin, 1920).

Bernstorff, Johann Heinrich von. *Erinnerungen und Briefe* (Zurich, 1936).

Bethmann Hollweg, Theobald von. *Betrachtungen zum Weltkrieg* [2 vols] (Berlin, 1921).

Cowles, Virginia. *The Kaiser* (London, 1963).

Craig, Gordon A. *Germany, 1866–1945* (New York, 1978).

Craig, Gordon A. *The politics of the Prussian army, 1640–1945* (London, 1964).

Falkenhayn, Erich von. *The German general staff and its decisions, 1914–1916* (New York, 1920).

Feldman, Gerald D. *Army, industry, and labor in Germany 1914–1918* (Princeton, 1966).

Fischer, Fritz. *Germany's aims in the First World War* (New York, 1967).

Fischer, Fritz. *World power or decline. The controversy over Germany's aims in the First World War* (New York: W. W. Norton, 1974).

Frye, B. *Erzberger and German politics, 1914–1921* (Ann Arbor, 1954).

Gatzke, Hans W. *Germany's drive to the west: a study of Germany's war aims during the First World War* (Baltimore, MD, 1950).

Goerlitz, Walter. *Hindenburg: ein Lebensbild* (Bonn, 1953).

Goerlitz, Walter. *History of the German General Staff, 1657–1945* (New York, 1953).

Goerlitz, Walter (ed.). *The Kaiser and his court: the diaries, note books and letters of Admiral Georg Alexander von Müller, Chief of the Naval Cabinet, 1914–1918* (New York, 1964).

Goodspeed, D. J. *Ludendorff: genius of World War I* (Boston, 1966).

Gudmundsson, Bruce I. *Stormtroop tactics. Innovation in the German Army, 1914–1918* (Westport, CT, 1995).

Herwig, Holger H. *The German Naval Officer Corps: a social and political history, 1890–1918* (Oxford, 1973).

Herwig, Holger H. *"Luxury" fleet: The Imperial Germany Navy, 1888–1918* (London, 1980).

Hindenburg, Paul von. *Aus meinem Leben* (Leipzig, 1927).

Hoffmann, Max. *War diaries and other papers* [2 vols], edited by Karl Novak. Translated by Eric Sutton (London, 1929).

Horn, Daniel. *The German naval mutinies of World War I* (New Brunswick, NJ, 1969).

Hubatsch, Walther. *Der Admiralstab und die obersten Marinebehörden in Deutschland, 1848–1945* (Frankfurt, 1958).

Hubatsch, Walter. *Die Ära Tirpitz. Studien zur deutschen Marinepolitik, 1890–1918* (Göttingen, 1955).

Janssen, Karl-Heinz. *Der Kanzler und der General: Die Führungskrise um Bethmann Hollweg und Falkenhayn, 1914–1916* (Göttingen, 1966).

Jarausch, Konrad H. *The enigmatic Chancellor: Bethmann Hollweg and the hubris of Imperial Germany* (New Haven, CT, 1973).

Kessler, Harry Graf von. *Walther Rathenau: his life and work* (New York, 1930).

Kitchen, Martin. *The silent dictatorship: the politics of the German High Command under Hindenburg and Ludendorff, 1916–1918* (New York, 1976).

Kluck, Alexander von. *Der Marsch auf Paris und die Marneschlacht, 1914* (Berlin, 1920).

Krack, Otto. *Generalfeldmarschall von Bülow* (Berlin, 1916).

Ludenodorff, Erich. *My war memories 1914–1918* [2 vols] (London, no date).

Ludenodorff, Erich. *The General Staff and its problems* [2 vols]. Translated by F. A. Holt (London, 1920).

Ludwig, Emil. *Kaiser Wilhelm II* (London, 1926).

Morrow, John H. *German air power in World War I* (Lincoln, NE, 1982).

Palmer, Alan. *The Kaiser: warlord of the Second Reich* (New York, 1978).

Reuter, Ludwig von. *Scapa Flow: Das Grab der deutschen Flotte* (Leipzig, 1921).

Ritter, Gerhard A. & Miller, Susanne (eds). *Die deutsche Revolution 1918–1919* (Frankfurt, 1968).

Rosinski, Herbert. *The German army* (New York, 1966).

Scheer, Reinhard. *Germany's high seas fleet in the World War* (London, 1920).

Scheidemann, Philip. *The making of a new Germany* [2 vols]. Translated by J. E. Mitchell (New York, 1929).

Schorske, Carl E. *German social democracy, 1905–1917: the development of the great schism* (London, 1955).

Tirpitz, Alfred von. *My memoirs* [2 vols] (New York, 1919).

Waldeyer-Hartz, Hugo von. *Admiral von Hipper: Das Lebensbild eines deutschen Flottenführers* (Leipzig, 1930).

Wheeler-Bennett, John W. *Wooden titan: Hindenburg* (London, 1936).

Wilhelm, Crown Prince. *Meine Erinnerungen an Deutschlands Heldenkampf* (Stuttgart, 1922).

Wilhelm II. *My memoirs* (London, 1922).

Zmarzlik, Hans-Günther. *Bethmann Hollweg als Reichskanzler, 1909–1914* (Düsseldorf, 1957).

Zwehl, H. von. *Erich von Falkenhayn, General der Infanterie: ein biographische Studie* (Dresden, 1926).

Great Britain

Barnes, John (ed.). *The Beatty papers: I (1908–1919)* (London, 1970).
Blake, Robert (ed.). *The private papers of Douglas Haig, 1914–1919* (London, 1952).
Blake, Robert (ed.). *Unrepentant Tory: the life and times of Andrew Bonar Law, 1858–1923, Prime Minister of the United Kingdom* (New York, 1956).
Bonham-Carter, Victor. *Soldier true: the life and times of Field Marshal Sir William Robertson* (London, 1963).
Bourne, J. M. *Britain and the Great War* (London, 1989).
Callwell, Charles E. *Field-Marshal Sir Henry Wilson: his life and diaries* [2 vols] (London, 1927).
Callwell, Charles E. *Life of Sir Stanley Maude* (London, 1920).
Cassar, George H. *Asquith as war leader* (London, 1994).
Cassar, George H. *Kitchener: architect of victory* (London, 1977).
Clark, Alan. *The donkeys* (New York, 1962).
Collier, Basil. *Brasshat: a biography of Field-Marshal Sir Henry Wilson* (London, 1961).
Edmonds, Sir. J. E. *Military operations of the British Army in the Western theatre of war (official history)* (London, 1933).
Fisher, John A. *Memories* (London, 1919).
Fisher, John A. *Records* (London, 1919).
French, David. *British strategy and war aims, 1914–1916* (London, 1986).
French, David. *The strategy of the Lloyd George coalition, 1916–1918* (London, 1995).
Gough, Hubert. *The Fifth Army* (London, 1931).
Guinn, Paul. *British strategy and politics 1914 to 1918* (Oxford, 1965).
Haig, Douglas. *The private papers of Douglas Haig, 1914 1919*, edited by Robert Blake (London, 1952).
Harington, Charles. *Plumer of Messines* (London, 1935).
Holmes, Richard. *The little Field-Marshal, Sir John French* (London, 1981).
Jellicoe, Admiral of the Fleet, Earl. *The Grand Fleet, 1914–1916: its creation, development and work* (London, 1919).
Jenkins, Roy. *Asquith* (London, 1964).
Kennedy, Paul M. *The rise and fall of British naval mastery* (New York, 1976).
Lloyd George, David. *War memoirs of David Lloyd George* [2 vols] (London, 1933).
Marder, Arthur J. *From the dreadnought to Scapa Flow: the Royal Navy in the Fisher era, 1904–1919* [5 vols] (Oxford, 1961–1970).
Marshall-Cornwall, Sir James. *Haig as military commander* (New York, 1973).
Marwick, Arthur. *The deluge. British society and the First World War* (Boston, 1966).
Maurice, Sir F. *The life of Lord Rawlinson of Trent* (Cassell, 1928).
Patterson, A. Temple. *Jellicoe: a biography* (London, 1969).
Simkins, Peter. *Kitchener's army. The raising of the new armies, 1914–16* (Manchester, 1988).
Sumida, Jon. *In defense of naval supremacy: finance, technology, and British naval policy* (New York, 1992).
Terraine, John. *Douglas Haig: the educated soldier* (London, 1963).
Turner, John. *British politics and the Great War* (London, 1992).

Vaughan, Edwin Campion. *Some desperate glory. The World War I diary of a British officer, 1917* (New York, 1988).

Wilson, Trevor. *The myriad faces of war: Britain and the Great War, 1914–1918* (Cambridge, 1986).

Winter, Denis. *Haig's command: a reassessment* (New York, 1991).

Winter, J. M. *The Great War and the British people* (London, 1985).

Young, Kenneth. *Arthur James Balfour* (London, 1963).

Greece

Alastos, Doros. *Venizelos: patriot, statesman, revolutionary* (London, 1942).

Leon, George B. *Greece and the Great Powers, 1914–1917* (Thessaloniki, 1974).

Leontaritis, George B. *Greece and the First World War: from neutrality to intervention, 1917–1918* (New York, 1990).

Theodoulou, Christos. *Greece and the Entente, August 1, 1914–September 15, 1916* (Thessaloniki, 1971).

Woodhouse, C. M. *A short history of modern Greece* (New York and Washington, 1968).

Italy

Alatri, Paolo. *Nitti, D'Annunzio e la questione adriatica (1919–1920)* (Milan, 1959).

Bertoldi, Silvio. *Vittorio Emanuele III* (Turin, 1970).

Burgwyn, H. James. *The legend of the mutilated victory. Italy, the Great War, and the Paris Peace Conference, 1915–1919* (Westport, CT, 1993).

Capello, Luigi. *Caporetto, perché?* (Turin, 1967).

Giolitti, Giovanni. *Memoirs of my life* (New York, 1973).

Lowe, C. J., & Marzari, F. *Italian foreign policy 1870–1940* (Boston, 1975).

Mack Smith, Denis. *Italy: a modern history* (Ann Arbor, MI, 1969).

Salandra, Antonio. *Italy and the Great War. From neutrality to intervention.* Translated by Zoe K. Pyne (London, 1932).

Thayer, John A. *Italy and the Great War: politics and culture, 1870–1915* (Madison, WI, 1964).

Whittam, John. *The politics of the Italian army, 1861–1918* (London, 1977).

Poland

Gerson, Louis L. *Woodrow Wilson and the rebirth of Poland, 1919–1920* (New Haven, CT, 1953).

Komarnicki, Titus. *Rebirth of the Polish Republic: a study in the diplomatic history of Europe, 1914–1920* (London, 1957).

Landau, Rom. *Pilsudski and Poland* (New York, 1929).

Romania

Kiritescu, Constantin. *La Roumanie dans la guerre mondiale (1916–1919)* (Paris, 1934).

Seton-Watson, Robert W. *A history of the Roumanians from the Roman times to the completion of unity* (Cambridge, 1934).

Spector, Sherman David. *Romania at the Paris Peace Conference: a study of the diplomacy of Ioan Brătianu* (New York, 1962).

Vinogradov, V. N. *Romania in the period of the First World War* (Moscow, 1969).

Russia

Brusilov, General A. A. *A soldier's note-book* (London, 1930).

Chamberlin, William Henry. *The Russian Revolution, 1917–1921* [2 vols] (New York, 1965).

Danilov, Youri N. *La Russie dans la Guerre Mondiale (1914–1917)* (Paris, 1927).

Debo, Richard K. *Revolution and survival: the foreign policy of Soviet Russia, 1917–18* (Toronto, 1979).

Deutscher, Isaac. *The prophet armed: Trotsky, 1879–1921* (New York, 1954).

Fankland, Noble. *Imperial tragedy: Nicholas II, last of the tsars* (New York, 1961).

Golovin, N. N. *The Russian army in the World War* (New Haven, CT, 1931).

Gurko, Vasilii Iosifovich. *War and revolution in Russia 1914–1917* (New York, 1919).

Pavlovich, N. B. (ed.). *The Fleet in the First World War*, vol. I (Moscow, 1964).

Rostunov, I. I. *General Brusilov* (Moscow, 1964).

Rutherford, Ward. *The Russian army in World War I* (London, 1975).

Saul, Norman E. *Sailors in revolt: The Russian Baltic Fleet in 1917* (Lawrence, KS, 1978).

Sazonov, Serge. *Fateful years, 1909–1916* (New York, 1928).

Smith, C. Jay, Jr. *The Russian struggle for power, 1914–1917: a study of Russian foreign policy during the First World War* (New York, 1956).

Solzhenitsyn, Alexander. *August 1914*. Trans. Michael Glenny (New York, 1971).

Stavrou, Theofanis George (ed.). *Russia under the last tsar* (Minneapolis, MN, 1969).

Wade, Rex A. *The Russian search for peace, February–October 1917* (Stanford, CA, 1969).

Warth, Robert D. *The Allies and the Russian Revolution: from the fall of the monarchy to the Peace of Brest-Litovsk* (Durham, NC, 1954).

Wildman, Allan K. *The end of the Russian Imperial Army* [2 vols] (Princeton, NJ, 1987).

Zeman, Z. A. B. (ed.). *Germany and the Revolution in the Russia, 1915–1918: documents from the archives of the German Foreign Ministry* (London, 1958).

Turkey

Ahmad, Feroz. *The Young Turks: The Committee of Union and Progress in Turkish politics, 1908–1914* (Oxford, 1969).

Djemal Pasha. *Memories of a Turkish statesman 1913–1919* (London, 1922).

Fromkin, David. *A peace to end all peace: the fall of the Ottoman Empire and the creation of the modern Middle East* (New York, 1990).

Kinross, Lord [Patrick Balfour]. *Atatürk: A biography of Mustafa Kemal, father of modern Turkey* (New York, 1965).

Liman von Sanders, Otto. *Five years in Turkey* (Annapolis, MD, 1927).

Shaw, Stanford J. & Shaw, Ezel Kural. *History of the Ottoman Empire and modern Turkey*, vol. II (Cambridge, 1977).

Trumpener, Ulrich. *Germany and the Ottoman Empire, 1914–1918* (Princeton, NJ, 1968).

Weber, Frank G. *Eagles on the crescent: Germany, Austria, and the diplomacy of the Turkish alliance, 1914–1918* (Ithaca, NY, 1970).

United States

Baker, Newton D. *Why we went to war* (New York, 1936).

Baker, R. S. *Woodrow Wilson: life and letters*, vols. VII, VIII (New York, 1939).

Beaver, Daniel. *Newton D. Baker and the American war effort, 1917–1919* (Lincoln, NE, 1966).

Coffman, Edward M. *The hilt of the sword: the career of Peyton C. March* (Madison, WI, 1966).

Coffman, Edward M. *The war to end all wars: the American military experience in World War I* (New York, 1968).

Cronon, E. David (ed.). *The cabinet diaries of Josephus Daniels, 1913–1921* (Lincoln, NE, 1963).

Daniels, J. *The Wilson era: years of war and after, 1917–1923* (Chapel Hill, NC, 1946).

DeWeerd, H. A. *President Wilson fights his war: World War I and the American intervention* (New York, 1968).

Ferrell, Robert H. *Woodrow Wilson & World War I, 1917–1921* (New York, 1985).

Freidel, F. *Franklin D. Roosevelt: the apprenticeship* (Boston, 1952).

Harbord, J. G. *The American army in France, 1917–1919* (Boston, 1936).

Liggett, H. *A.E.F.: ten years ago in France* (New York, 1928).

Link Arthur S. *Woodrow Wilson and the progressive era, 1910–1917* (New York, 1954).

Pershing, J. J. *My experiences in the World War* [2 vols] (New York, 1931).

Stallings, L. *The doughboys: the story of the A.E.F. 1917–1918* (New York, 1963).

Trask, David F. *Captains & cabinets: Anglo-American naval relations, 1917–1918* (Columbia, MO, 1972).

Trask, David F. *General Tasker Howard Bliss and the "Sessions of the Word", 1919* (Philadephia, PA, 1966).

Trask, David F. *The United States in the Supreme War Council: American war aims and inter-Allied strategy, 1917–1918* (Middletown, CT, 1961).

Tuchman, Barbara W. *The Zimmermann telegram* (New York, 1958).

Vandiver, Frank E. *Black Jack: The life and times of John J. Pershing* [2 vols] (College Station, TX, 1977).

Yugoslavia

Dragnich, Alex N. *Serbia, Nikola Pašić and Yugoslavia* (New Brunswick, NJ, 1974).

Eterovich, Francis H. & Christopher Spalatin (eds). *Croatia: land, people, culture*, vol. II (Toronto, 1970).

Jelavich, Charles & Barbara. *The establishment of the Balkan national states, 1804–1920* (London, 1977).

Petrovich, Michael Boro. *A history of modern Serbia, 1804–1918* [2 vols] (London, 1976).

Stavrianos, L. S. *The Balkans since 1453* (New York, 1958).

The Western Front

Asprey, Robert B. *The first battle of the Marne* (Philadelphia: Lippincott, 1962).

Blond, Georges. *Verdun* (London, 1976).

SELECT BIBLIOGRAPHY

Edmonds, Sir James E. *History of the Great War. Military operations: France and Belgium 1914–1918* [13 vols] (London, 1922–1948).

French, Field Marshal Sir John. *1914* (London, 1919).

Griffith, Paddy. *Battle tactics of the Western Front. The British Army's art of attack, 1916–18* (New Haven, CT, 1994).

Hallas, James H. *Squandered victory. The American First Army at St. Mihiel* (Westport, CT, 1995).

Hermanns, William. *The holocaust. From a survivor of Verdun* (New York, 1972).

Horne, Alistair. *The price of glory. Verdun, 1916* (New York, 1962).

Isselin, Henri. *The battle of the Marne* (Garden City, NY, 1966).

Keegan, John. *Opening moves: August 1914* (New York, 1971).

Macdonald, Lyn. *1914: the first months of fighting* (New York, 1988).

Macdonald, Lyn. *1915: the death of innocence* (New York, 1995).

Macdonald, Lyn. *Somme* (London, 1983).

Macdonald, Lyn. *They called it Passchendaele* (New York, 1989).

Middlebrook, Martin. *First day on the Somme* (New York, 1972).

Middlebrook, Martin. *The Kaiser's battle, 21 March 1918: the first day of the German Spring Offensive* (London, 1978).

Prior, Robin Prior & Trevor Wilson. *Command on the Western Front. The military career of Sir Henry Rawlinson, 1914–18* (Oxford, 1992).

Prior, Robin Prior & Trevor Wilson. *Passchendaele, the untold story* (New Haven, CT, 1996).

Rawling, Bill. *Surviving trench warfare: technology and the Canadian Corps* (Toronto, 1992).

Samuels, Martin. *Doctrine and dogma: German and British infantry tactics in the First World War* (Westport, CT, 1992).

Simkins, Peter. *World War I. The Western Front* (New York, 1991).

Terraine, John. *Mons: The retreat to victory* (London, 1960).

Terraine, John. *The Western Front* (Hutchinson, 1964).

Travers, Tim. *How the war was won* (London, 1992).

Travers, Tim. *The killing ground* (London, 1987).

von Kuhl Hermann, *Genesis. execution amd collapse of the German offensive in 1918*. Trans. Army War College [2 vols] (Washington, DC, 1933).

Warner, Philip. *Passchendaele. The tragic victory of 1917* (London, 1987).

The Eastern Front

Brusilov, General A. A. *A soldier's note-book 1914–1918* (London, 1930).

Churchill, Winston S. *The unknown war: the Eastern Front* (London, 1931).

Golovine, Lieut.-Gen, Nicholas N. *The Russian Army in the World War* (New Haven, 1931).

Gourko, Gen. Basil. *Memories & impressions of war and revolution 1914–1917* (London, 1918).

Jukes, Geoffrey. *Carpathian disaster: death of an army* (London, 1971).

Kearsey, A. *A study of the strategy and tactics of the East Prussian campaign, 1914* (London, 1932).

Kettle, Michael. *Russia and the Allies 1917–1920, Vol I: The Allies and the Russian collapse March 1917–March 1918* (London, 1981).

Knox, Maj.-Gen. Sir Alfred. *With the Russian Army 1914–1917* [2 vols] (London, 1921).

Littawer, Vladimir S. *Russian hussar* (London, 1965).

Perrett, Bryan & Anthony Lord. *The Czar's British squadron* (London, 1981).
Reed, John. *The war in Eastern Europe* (London, 1916).
Showalter, Dennis E. *Tannenberg, clash of empires* (Hamden, CT, 1991).
Stone, Norman. *The Eastern Front 1914–1917* (New York, 1975).
Wildman, A. *The end of the Russian Imperial Army* [2 vols] (Princeton, NJ, 1980).
Wrangel, Alexis. *The end of chivalry: the last great cavalry battles 1914–1918* (New York, 1982).

South Europe

Allen, W. E. D. and Paul Muratoff. *Caucasian battlefields: a history of the wars on the Turco-Caucasian border, 1828–1921* (Cambrige, 1953).
Edmonds, Sir James E. & H. R. Davies. *History of the Great War. Military operations: Italy, 1915–1919* (London, 1949).
Falls, Cyril. *The battle of Caporetto* (Philadelphia, 1966).
Falls, Cyril. *History of the Great War. Military operations, Macedonia* [2 vols] (London, 1933–1935).
Palmer, Alan. *The gardeners of Salonika: The Macedonian campaign 1915–1918* (New York, 1965).
Seth, Ronald. *Caporetto: the scapegoat battle* (New York, 1965).

Dardanelles/Gallipoli

Aspinall-Oglander, Cecil F. *History of the Great War. Military operations: Gallipoli* [2 vols] (London, 1929).
Cassar, George H. *The French and the Dardanelles: a study of failure in the conduct of war* (London, 1971).
Dardanelles Commission. *Final report* (London, 1919).
Guépratte, Paul Émile. *L'Expédition des Dardanelles, 1914–1915* (Paris, 1935).
Hamilton, General Sir Ian. *Gallipoli diary* [2 vols] (London, 1920).
Hickey, Michael. *Gallipoli* (London, 1995).
James, Robert Rhodes. *Gallipoli, the history of a noble blunder* (New York, 1965).
Moorehead, Alan. *Gallipoli* (New York, 1956).
Wemyss, Lord Wester. *The navy in the Dardanelles Campaign* (London, 1924).

Middle East

Barker, A. J. *The bastard war. The Mesopotamian campaign of 1914–1918* (New York, 1967).
Falls, Cyril. *Armageddon: 1918* (New York, 1964).
Gardner, Brian. *Allenby of Arabia: Lawrence's general* (New York, 1966).
Mack, John E. *A prince of our disorder: the life of T. E. Lawrence* (Boston, 1976).
Moberly, F. J. *The campaign in Mesopotamia, 1914–1917* [4 vols] (London, 1923–7).
Townshend, C. V. F. *My campaign in Mesopotamia* (London, 1920).
Wavell, Archibald P. *The Palestine campaigns* (London, 1931).
Zeine, Zeine N. *The emergence of Arab nationalism: with a background study of Arab–Turkish relations in the Near East* (New York, 1975).

SELECT BIBLIOGRAPHY

Other Fronts

Burdick, Charles B. *The Japanese siege of Tsingtau: World War I in Asia* (Hamden, CT, 1976).
Chi, Madeleine. *China diplomacy, 1914–1918* (Cambridge, MA, 1970).
Farwell, Byron. *The Great War in Africa, 1914–1918* (New york, 1986).
Louis, William Roger. *Great Britain and Germany's lost colonies 1914–1919* (Oxford, 1967).

Aviation

Bruce, John M. *British aeroplanes, 1914–1918* (New York, 1969).
Fredette, Raymond H. *The sky on fire. The first Battle of Britain 1917–1918 and the birth of the Royal Air Force* (New York, 1976).
Grey, Peter L. and Owen Thetford. *German aircraft of the First World War* (London, 1962).
Hallion, Richard P. *Rise of the fighter aircraft, 1914–1918* (Annapolis, MD, 1984).
Higham, Robin. *Air power: a concise history* (New York, 1973).
Lamberton, W. M. *Fighter aircraft of the 1914–1918 War* (Fallbrook, 1964).
Layman, R. D. *Naval aviation in the First World War. Its impact and influence* (Annapolis, MD, 1996).
Kennett, Lee B. *The first air war, 1914–1918* (New York, 1991).
Levine, I. D. *Mitchell: pioneer of air power* (New York, 1943).
Munson, Kenneth. *Bombers, patrol and reconnaissance aircraft, 1914–19* (New York, 1968).
Munson, Kenneth. *Fighters, attack, and training aircraft, 1914–1919* (New York, 1968).
Norman, Aaron. *The great air war* (New York, 1968).
Weyl, A. R. *Fokker: the creative years* (London, 1965).
Winter, Denis. *The first of the few: fighter pilots of the First World War* (London, 1982).

War at Sea

Bell, A. C. *The blockade of the Central Powers 1914–1918* (London, 1937).
Bennett, Geoffrey M. *The battle of Jutland* (Philadelphia, 1964).
Bennett, Geoffrey M. *Coronel and the Falklands* (London, 1967).
Carson, Edward Henry. *The war on German submarines* (London, 1917).
Corbett, Julian S. & Newbolt, Henry. *History of the Great War: naval operations* [5 vols] (London, 1920–31).
Frost, Holloway H. *The battle of Jutland* (Annapolis, MD, 1964).
Frothingham, T. G. *The naval history of the World War* [3 vols] (Cambridge, MA, 1924–6).
Goldrick, James. *The King's ships were at sea: the war in the North Sea, August 1914–February 1915* (Annapolis, MD, 1984).
Halpern, Paul G. *A naval history of World War I* (Annapolis, MD, 1994).
Halpern, Paul G. *The naval war in the Mediterranean, 1914–1918* (Annapolis, MD, 1987).
Hoehling, A. A. *The Great War at sea* (New York, 1965).
Hough, Richard. *The Great War at sea, 1914–1918* (New York, 1983).
Hough, Richard. *The pursuit of Admiral von Spee* (London, 1969).
Irving, Commander John. *The smoke screen of Jutland* (New York, 1967).
Macintyre, Donald. *Jutland* (New York, 1958).

SELECT BIBLIOGRAPHY

Simpson, Colin. *The Lusitania* (Boston, 1973).
Van Der Vat, Dan. *The ship that changed the world. The escape of the Goeben to the Dardanelles in 1914* (New York, 1986).

Tanks

Cooper, Bryan. *Tank battles of World War I* (London, 1973).
Harris, J. P. *Men, machines and tanks* (Manchester, 1995).
Liddell Hart, Capt, B. H. *The tanks: the history of the Royal Tank Regiment and its predecessors . . . 1914–1945* (London, 1959).
Smithers, A. J. *Cambrai. The first great tank battle 1917* (London, 1992).

Miscellaneous

Beesly, Patrick. *Room 40. British Naval Intelligence 1914–18* (New York, 1982).
Barrie, Alexander. *War underground. The tunnellers of the Great War* (London, 1988).
Brook-Shepherd, Gordon. *November 1918* (Boston, 1981).
Cecil, Hugh & Peter H. Liddle (eds). *Facing Armageddon. The First World War experienced* (London, 1996).
Ellis, John. *Eye-deep in hell* (New York, 1977).
Fussell, Paul. *The Great War and modern memory* (New York, 1985).
Haber, L. F. *The poisonous cloud: chemical warfare in the First World War* (Oxford, 1986).
Hartcup, Guy. *The war of invention. Scientific developments, 1914–18* (London, 1987).
Hogg, Ian V. *The guns 1914–18* (London, 1973).
Hovannisian, Richard G. *Armenia on the road to independence 1918* (Berkeley, CA, 1967).
Johnson, Hubert C. *Breakthrough! tactics, technology, and the search for victory on the Western Front in World War I* (Novato, CA, 1994).
Kahn, David. *The codebreakers: the story of secret writing* (New York, 1973).
Liddell Hart, Basil H. *Reputations: ten years after* (Boston, 1928).
Liddle, Peter. *The soldier's war, 1914–18* (London: Blandford Press, 1988).
Moore, William. *Gas attack: chemical warfare, 1915 to the present day* (London, 1987).
Paret, Peter, ed. *Makers of modern strategy from Machiavelli to the nuclear age* (Princeton, NJ, 1986).
Rommel Erwin. *Infantry attacks*. Trans. G. E. Kidde (Washington, 1944).
Van Creveld, Martin. *Supplying war: logistics from Wallenstein to Patton* (London, 1977).
Williams, John. *The other battleground. The home fronts: Britain, France and Germany, 1914–1918* (New York, 1972).

Wartime Diplomacy

Stevenson, David. *The First World War and international politics* (Oxford, 1988).
Wheeler-Bennett, John W. *Brest-Litovsk: the forgotten peace, March 1918* (London, 1938).
Zeeman, Z. A. B. *The gentleman negotiators: a diplomatic history of World War I* (New York, 1971).

Armistice, 1918 and Paris Peace Conference, 1919

Albrecht Carrié, René. *Italy at the Paris Peace Conference* (New York, 1938).

Baruch, Bernard. *The making of the reparation and economic sections of the treaty* (New York, 1920).

Czernin, Ferdinand. *Versailles, 1919* (New York, 1965).

Deák, Francis. *Hungary at the Paris Peace Conference. The diplomatic history of the Treaty of Trianon* (New York, 1942).

Fromkin, David. *A peace to end all peace. The fall of the Ottoman Empire and the creation of the modern Middle East* (New York, 1989).

Genov, G. P. *Bulgaria and the Treaty of Neuilly* (Sofia, 1935).

Goldstein, Erik. *Winning the peace* (Oxford, 1991).

Helmreich, Paul C. *From Paris to Sèvres: the partition of the Ottoman Empire at the Peace Conference of 1919–1920* (Columbus, OH, 1974).

Keynes, John Maynard. *The economic consequences of the peace* (London, 1919).

Lederer, Ivo J. *Yugoslavia at the Peace Conference: a study in frontiermaking* (New Haven, CT, 1963).

Lentin, A. *Lloyd George, Woodrow Wilson, and the guilt of Germany* (Bath, 1984).

Lévy, Raphael-Georges. *La juste paix: La vérité sur la Traité de Versailles* (Paris, 1920).

Lowry, Bullitt. *Armistice 1918* (Kent State, OH, 1996).

Luckau, Alma. *The German delegation at the Paris Peace Conference* (New York, 1941).

Mayer, Arno J. *Politics and diplomacy of peacemaking: containment and counterrevolution at Versailles, 1918–1919* (New York, 1967).

Mee, Charles L., Jr. *The end of order: Versailles, 1919* (New York, 1980).

Nicolson, Harold. *Peacemaking 1919* (New York, 1937).

Rudin, Harry R. *Armistice, 1918* (New Haven, CT, 1944).

Tardieu, André. *The truth about the treaty* (Indianapolis, 1921).

Temperley, H. W. G. (ed.). *A history of the Peace Conference of Paris* [6 vols] (London, 1920–24).

Weintraub, Stanley. *A stillness heard round the world. The end of the Great War: November 1918* (New York, 1985).

Wolfers, Arnold. *Britain and France between two wars: conflicting strategies of peace since Versailles* (Hamden, CT: Archon Books, 1963).

Historical Atlases and References

Gilbert, Martin. *Atlas of World War I*, 2nd edn (New York, 1994).

Gray, Randal with Christopher Argyle. *Chronicle of the First World War* [2 vols] (Oxford and New York, 1991).

Herwig, Holger & Neil M. Heyman. *Biographical dictionary of World War I* (Westport, CT, 1982).

Livesay, Anthony. *The historical atlas of World War I* (New York, 1994).

Tucker, Spencer C. (ed.). *The Great Powers in the First World War: an encyclopedia* (NY, 1996).

Index